Making Successful Presentations

Making Successful Presentations

GEORGE T. VARDAMAN

amacom

American Management Associations

This book is available at a special
discount when ordered in bulk quantities.
For information, contact Special Sales Department,
American Management Associations, Publications Group,
135 West 50th Street, New York, NY 10020.

Library of Congress Cataloging in Publication Data

Vardaman, George T.
  Making successful presentations.

  Includes index.
  1. Communication in management.   2. Oral communication.
I. Title.
HF5718.V38   658.4'5   81-66225
ISBN 0-8144-5694-4   AACR2
ISBN 0-8144-7617-3 pbk

Printing Number

10 9 8 7 6 5 4 3 2 1

Contents

1

Introduction
TRIM: A Design for
Effective Communication

All experienced managers and professional people know very well that their day-to-day work is carried out largely through communication. Almost all their activities involve some kind of information processing, whether as senders (speaking or writing) or as receivers (listening or reading), whether intrapersonal ("talking" to themselves) or interpersonal (communicating with others). And most of these experienced people will also quickly assent to another proposition: effective communication is by no means easily accomplished. It requires patience, planning, and skill in execution. You can only be admonished on the need for patience; however, planning and skill of execution are faculties that you can definitely learn and apply if you are willing to read and use the ideas discussed in this book. Therefore, let's go directly to our purpose of learning about our subject, starting with a working definition of effective communication.

WHAT EFFECTIVE COMMUNICATION IS

Definitions of communication are countless. To be candid, however, most are of little practical value, so we need not bother ourselves with them. Let's look at a definition which at first may appear a little esoteric, but which, when clarified, will make sense: *Effective com-*

1

munication is purposive symbolic interchange resulting in workable under-standing and agreement between the sender and receiver. So that we can consider its implications for you—the manager or professional—let's go into the definition a little more, taking it part by part.

First, effective communication is *purposive.* And by this is meant that it is *deliberately designed* to achieve a conscious end or objective. In other words, the communicator knows what he is after and plans his approach accordingly. This means that although there are obviously many communications which are not deliberately purposive (such as purely social or fortuitous occasions), these are outside our con-sideration in this book.

Second, according to our definition, communication is the *inter-change of symbols* between people. And what are symbols? Fundamen-tally, they are the verbal (words, mathematical expressions, vocal intonations) and graphic (pictures, diagrams, charts, facial expres-sions) representations of the communicator's ideas. In other words, they are your ways of "coding" and signaling your thoughts and feelings to others.

Third, *effective communication* results in *workable understanding and agreement* between the sender and receiver. This is a most important element. What is meant is that effective communication produces a *sufficient* degree of meaning between the speaker and listener (or writer and reader), together with enough acceptance by both parties, to get the desired results. This does not mean that all communication must always produce "sweetness and light" among all parties. Indeed, this is rare and not necessarily desirable. It does mean, however, that both the communicator and receiver have enough common under-standing about and willingness to accept the ideas presented to use them to get the company's work done at the requisite level. And this is all that is needed for you as an organizational manager or profes-sional.

IMPLICATIONS OF THE DEFINITION

What does all this mean to you? For one thing, it means that in this book you will be studying only that managerial and professional communication which is planned, executed, and evaluated against a *defined objective.* Further, it means that we shall consider only communication *between people.* Important as they are, we shall not be concerned with man-to-machine or machine-to-machine interactions. Moreover, the definition implies that our central focus is *sender-originated* communication. In other words, the communication is *for* the receiver, but it is *from* the sender. Unquestionably communication from reader or listener perspectives is most important, but our basic approach in this book is from that of the *originator* of the presentation.

FURTHER IMPLICATIONS AND LIMITATIONS

Other implications and limitations need clarification. For one thing, we concentrate on ways to handle *important* sender-originated communications, those that are vital for the manager or professional person in getting the job done efficiently and effectively. To be sure, what we discuss is applicable to any kind of communication, whether commonplace or exotic, but the right handling of vital oral presentations determines in large measure whether the modern manager or professional person survives and progresses.

Furthermore, we shall concern ourselves primarily with *person-to-group oral communication,* together with *writing and graphics as supplements* to the spoken means. It goes without saying that in administered organizations, oral communication is the basic vehicle for attaining managerial and professional goals. But of course the oral must often be complemented by appropriate written and visual communications, and it is in this light that we shall consider the combination.

Finally, we are going to work within another restriction: we shall concern ourselves with only the *most important and practical procedures and methods* to get communication across. Much material presented in many traditional speech and writing books is trivial—if not worthless—to the modern manager or professional. We shall deliberately exclude the "junk," focusing directly on those communication principles, procedures, and methods that have genuine relevance for people who must work and produce results in today's firms, agencies, and institutions.

Let's now turn to our task.

PROCEDURE FOR COMMUNICATION DESIGN

How can you, the manager or professional, design your communication to get predictably effective results? The pattern suggested here results from many years of administrative experience, of teaching communication, and of working with executives in business, government, and professional organizations. Properly applied, it will help you in planning and carrying out your job-related presentations.

Let's look at the basic ingredients of the procedure: (1) presentation targets; (2) receiver roles; (3) desired impacts; and (4) presentation methods. To help remember these, let's put them in acronym form: **TRIM.** And now let's see what each means. (We shall explore these in depth in later chapters.)

T: the *target* at which you are aiming—in other words, the mission or purpose of the communication.

R: the *receiver* to whom the communication is addressed—in other words, the willingness and capacity of the listener or reader to understand and accept your message.

I: the *impact* which is needed—in other words, how the communication must affect the receiver if you are to hit the target and influence him or her as needed.

M: the *methods* which must be employed—in other words, the operational procedures which can be used to get (1) the desired impact with (2) the determined receiver role in light of (3) the communication target you are trying to hit.

Proper exploitation of TRIM can give you very effective presentation control. And, although not overly simple (for communication is not a simple subject), it is a practical, useful approach to the planning and carrying out of your presentations. Once learned, TRIM becomes almost automatic in application so that your time and efforts can be rapidly and productively channeled in sizing up the situation and in executing your communication to get the results you want.

THE BOOK'S PRESENTATION

The rest of this book spells out how to go about getting effective communication. Part I, "Background for Effective Communication," presents important working principles. Chapter 2, "Knowing When to Communicate," tells how to know when communication is needed or called for. Chapter 3, "Putting Ideas Together," gives ways to organize and build out the communication. Chapter 4, "Using Communication Media," presents the proper uses of the various vehicles—audiovisual, written, and personal—for communicating your ideas. Part I, then, prepares you to exploit the procedures enumerated in Part II.

Part II, "TRIM: How to Communicate Effectively," presents specific ways to plan and carry out your presentations to get the right results. In addition to detailing practical principles and procedures, each chapter will also refer to numerous examples of how these have been used in presentations by modern managers and professional people. These examples draw heavily from Part III, "Communication Specimens," which is a collection of representative presentations (or excerpts from more lengthy ones). Chapter 5, "Hitting the Target," explains the vital communication missions or purposes. Chapter 6, "Communicating with Receivers," presents the important listener and reader roles which communicators must be prepared to handle if their ideas are to get into the nervous systems of those for whom they are intended. Chapter 7, "Getting the Right Impact," spells out the kinds of receiver effects, with requisite techniques and devices to get your ideas accepted. Chapter 8, "Using the Right Methods," specifies the practical procedures for successful planning and presentation of the ideas you wish to communicate.

Part III, "Communication Specimens," is a collection of communications—both classic and contemporary—by business, government, and professional people. These specimens are used to clarify and exemplify the principles discussed in Parts II and III. For ease of reference, each has been internally numbered—either by paragraph or by other appropriate segment—so that the reader can go quickly to the specific referenced section. A simple reference method is employed throughout the book. For example, (Specimen 20:2) after the item discussed means "Specimen 20, Section 2." This allows quick reader examination of the example in context, as well as in isolation.

The position given for each author is the one held at the time the sample reprinted was originally written.

SUMMARY

Effective communication is purposive symbolic interchange resulting in workable understanding and agreement between the sender and receiver. The purpose of this book is to present the means by which you (the sender) can achieve such effective communication with your receivers in important job-related presentations. The approach involves four elements: (1) communication *targets;* (2) *receiver* roles; (3) desired *impacts;* and (4) communication *methods.* In acronym form, these have been designated TRIM. We shall be exploring each in depth in subsequent chapters.

I

BACKGROUND FOR EFFECTIVE COMMUNICATION

2

Knowing
When to Communicate

Now that we've taken a general look at how we'll be studying our subject, let's get down to the business of learning what must be done to achieve effective communication. The first item—knowing when to communicate—is very important, but unfortunately is seldom given the serious consideration it deserves.

When should you, as a manager or professional, make a purposive presentation? Of course this question cannot be answered simply and absolutely. But it certainly should be raised constantly and given the best possible response. Why? Because the kind of communication we're talking about is in the aggregate a very expensive and time-consuming activity in organizations. If you add up the costs of labor-hours, materials, and other monetary outlays given to presentations in your organizations, you may be shocked at the sum. After a systematic analysis, one aerospace company came up with a minimum annual estimate of over $1,500,000! Its top managers admitted they had no idea of the real dollar costs. Needless to say, some serious studies were then started to determine which presentations were needed and which of them were not. The results? A cut in annual costs of more than $300,000.

To be sure, most companies will not incur costs (or be able to effect savings) of this magnitude. But there is probably no company, agency, or institution with 100 or more people which could not make significant reductions in its presentation costs if it took a hard-nosed look to distinguish vital from unnecessary communications, and to insist that the latter be cut out.

9

Let's now move to a practical but systematic way by which the manager-professional can readily size up whether communication is needed. Steps in the procedure are (1) know the symptoms of need; (2) know the type of need; (3) know whether benefits outweigh costs; (4) know feasibility; and (5) know whether to use an oral or written form. The procedure is illustrated in Figure 2-1.

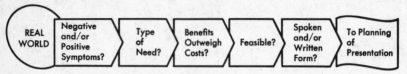

Figure 2-1. Determining when to communicate.

STEP 1: KNOWING SYMPTOMS OF NEED

What observable symptoms (indicators) point to a need for communication? Symptoms may be either *negative* or *positive.* Negative symptoms are exemplified in questions like these: Are some departments exceeding their budgets? Is there an excessive personnel turnover? Is there evidence that employees do not understand the latest policy on overtime work? Or do symptoms indicate that the policy is understood, but is being ignored? Do laboratory specialists actually read and abide by the company's directives on acquisition and disposal of equipment? Do company people show a lack of understanding of what goes on in units other than their own? Is there evidence that outside publics have the wrong image of the organization? If negative symptoms like these exist, either singly or in combination, the manager-professional should carefully note them as pointers to possibly needed communication.

But there are also "positive" symptoms which demand communication. Are people doing good (or superior) jobs? If so, it may be highly important to them (and to the company) that they be commended for their performance. Have some people made unique contributions to the organization (new ideas, new products, new services)? If so, it may be vital to communicate this to other company people, as well as to selected outside publics. Are new developments to be implemented (new policies, new departments, new products, new markets, realignment or reorganization, putting people in new jobs)? If so, there is a strong probability that some communication is in order. Are people doing a "good" job when in fact with even better understandings and attitudes they could be doing superior work? This situation almost always calls for the right kind of communication, because it can result in a maximum payoff for the firm. Is there evidence that the image of the company can be significantly enhanced by a presentation or a program of communications?

Symptoms, then, both negative and positive, should be observed and noted (making sure, of course, that they are in fact reliable and valid); these should then be classified or typed, which is what we'll study next.

STEP 2: KNOWING TYPE OF NEED

The manager-professional can assess the type of communication need by determining which of the following the symptoms point to: (1) information-centered; (2) belief-changing; (3) belief-strengthening; or (4) action-centered. Let's look at each.

Informational Needs

Are there important informational needs? For example, are some new organizational or professional policies or procedures being put into effect? Are new production data needed by certain departments or people in order to insure adequate job performance? Have some new research findings come to light which should be made known to professional peers and colleagues? Is there a need to bring together several pieces of separate data so that they can be more fully understood? Do researchers need to inform administrators about important laboratory procedures and operations? Is there a need to make highly technical information more meaningful to selected nonprofessional persons through, for example, nontechnical communication? These are but a few possible specimens of *informational* needs which could properly call for managerial or professional communication.

Belief-Changing Needs

Are there important attitudes and beliefs which need to be changed? For example, assuming that key people know about the new policy cutting back on overtime work, do they also believe in it? Do

they accept it as right? And even though operators read and understand the reports showing production lags, do they view them as
accurate relative to their own department, as well as other company
units? Even though research findings are clearly conveyed, do other
researchers accept the conclusions as accurate? And in the report
bringing together discrete data, do receivers perceive gaps in sources,
reasoning, or statistical manipulation, any of which could cause them
to doubt the validity of the study? Does the communication about
laboratory processes present information so that administrative
people can constructively appreciate the problems confronting research specialists? And in the attempt to make technical information
more understandable to nontechnical people, are language and format used so as to avoid affronting receivers' intelligence, thereby
avoiding alienation?

It can be seen that changing beliefs goes beyond informational
presentation; it is an important area of need in organizations.

Belief-Strengthening Needs

Are there important attitudes and beliefs which need to be
strengthened? Changing beliefs means communicating against initial
neutrality or opposition. But strengthening outlooks means deepening or heightening preexisting perceptions. This is a very common,
real need in business, government, and professional organizations—
one which is too frequently neglected or poorly done.

We can use the same kinds of hypothetical examples to illustrate
communications addressed to belief-strengthening needs. Assuming
that most people accept the new policy on reduced overtime, is there a
need for management to make employees believe in it even more in
order to get better performance within the limited operational time?
Even though operators place credence in the company's production
reports, is there a need to laud receivers for work well done so that
they are more likely to increase production, as well as to be receptive
to suggestions for improvement where it is indicated? And although
researchers fundamentally accept conclusions presented to them, is
there a need to make them more fully appreciate the time, effort, and
skills that went into the study? Even though administrative personnel
believe in the basic ideas presented about lab procedures, is there a
need to deepen and heighten their awareness and appreciation of the
problems which are part of every functioning laboratory designed to

do important research? Finally, in the attempt to bridge the knowledge gap between the professional and layman, is there a need to dramatize ideas so that the receiver can more fully believe in the importance of the professional's work?

This, then, points up the significance of handling belief-strengthening needs. Let's now turn to another important one, that of action.

Action Needs

Are there important actions which need to be taken? The preceding needs are directed to understandings, attitudes, or beliefs (all of which are mental or psychological states), not to overt behavioral response. But the action-oriented is addressed to the need for performance. Let's again use the general examples to illustrate. Receivers may well understand (be informed about) and accept (believe in) the new overtime policy, but this does not guarantee their abiding by it. They must be moved to act (or perform) as the policy dictates (that is, actually working less overtime). Likewise with the examples (production reports, research findings, laboratory procedures, and nontechnical communication), the receivers must understand and believe sufficiently, but the needed outcome is some desired action.

Review: Types of Communication Needs

You've studied four general needs which may call for communication: (1) presenting information; (2) changing attitudes and beliefs; (3) strengthening attitudes and beliefs; and (4) getting action. Using the negative-positive symptom inputs, you can readily determine which is applicable in a given situation. You should then decide whether or not the need appears sufficiently important to call for further analysis. If it does not, you can stop your presentation activity at this point; if it does, you should proceed to the next step, benefits versus costs.

STEP 3: KNOWING WHETHER
BENEFITS OUTWEIGH COSTS

We've already seen that purposive presentations are often expensive. Therefore, it is only common sense that you should always have some fairly good idea of how much a given presentation (or series of presentations) will cost the company and yourself before going ahead.

At the same time, you must also reckon the immediate and long-range benefits likely to accrue from the communication. And in some instances, although the presentation is certain to cost dearly, the resulting beneficial returns may make even these very high costs a worthwhile investment. In still other situations, irrespective of costs, certain communications may be necessary if the company is to survive and prosper in the long run.

How can you realistically weigh costs against benefits of presentations? Let's start by looking first at costs, after which we'll relate them to benefits.

Costs

These can be determined by examining three types: (1) monetary costs; (2) job costs; and (3) psychological costs.

Monetary costs. These are the directly calculable dollar expenses going into the preparation and carrying out of your presentation. In making this computation, you should include all costs of labor-hours invested (both presenter and receiver time), materials, use of physical plant, and use of equipment.

Labor-hour costs are easily calculated. This is just adding up the time involved by the presenter in his preparation and execution and the time taken by all the receivers of the communication, then multiplying by a realistic dollars-per-hour figure. For example, assuming a simple situation of one person communicating to a group of 20 people, the cost could be computed as shown in Figure 2–2.

Materials costs are easily reckoned by adding visual and written supplement costs. For example, the same 1-to-20 group's materials costs could be something like this:

Duplication of handouts—paper and reprography	$ 25
Visual transparencies—preparation and materials	$ 50
Brochures—cost to company	$ 40
Total Materials Costs	$115

Physical-plant costs are a little more difficult to reckon. But with the aid of the company's accounting unit, you should be able to come up

Figure 2.2. Computing labor-hour costs.

PRESENTER TIME (assuming 1 speaker)

Preparation	Presentation	Rate (per hour)	
(Gathering ideas, composition, pretesting, follow-up)	(Execution, answering questions, follow-up)		
30 labor-hours	2 labor-hours	$20	
	Total Presenter Labor-hour Costs		$640

LISTENER TIME (assuming 20 listeners)

Preparation	Message Reception	Rate (per hour)	
(Reading agenda, anticipating needs, preparing for reception)	(Receiving message, raising questions, follow-up)		
20 labor-hours	60 labor-hours	$10	
	Total Listener Labor-hour Costs		$800
	Total Labor-Hour Costs		**$1,440**

with a square footage or other space cost factor (including the amortized cost of the building, furniture, utilities, and maintenance), which you can use in computation. Once this factor is determined, it can be applied as follows:

> 600 sq ft @ .10 (for 2 hours use) $60
>
> Total Physical-Plant Costs $60

Equipment-cost computation will probably also require consultation with the accounting unit. Here it is a matter of getting a realistic write-off figure (including items such as original cost, depreciation, cost of investment, and maintenance). Using the same situation, let's look at the following hypothetical illustration:

Transparency projector	@ 2.50 per hour factor	$ 5
Film projector	@ 2.50 per hour factor	$ 5
Computer console	@ 15.00 per hour factor	$30
	Total Equipment Costs	$40

Now let's compute total monetary costs from our above examples:

Labor-hour costs	$1,440
Materials costs	$ 115
Physical-plant costs	$ 60
Equipment costs	$ 40
Total Monetary Costs	$1,655

Thus our relatively simple situation (one presenter to 20 listeners) with minimal use of materials, physical plant, and equipment is still going to cost more in direct money expenditures than we may have at first thought. Let's keep this $1,655 figure in mind as we look at the other kinds of costs, the next of which is job costs.

Job costs. These are losses—potential or actual—in work performance resulting from communication. Of course, a proper purposive presentation should result in better job output. But there is always a risk that performance will not be improved, even that it could be worse as a result of communication. And this is a gamble that you must realistically assess in calculating the real costs of a presentation.

Calculating job costs is obviously more subjective than calculating direct money costs. But some fairly valid qualitative estimates can be made by considering the two following questions:

1. *What constructive performance outputs are blocked or delayed?* That is, in addition to the direct money loss in salary paid, what task products are cut off or deferred as a result of key people giving or receiving communication? Assuming that people occupy positions to get certain things done, any delays will cost the company in potential job outputs. And in certain situations (such as emergencies, stepped-up production schedules, and pivotal points in negotiations) the absence of people from their jobs may be costing the company a disproportionate amount.

2. *What job costs may be incurred if performance-related communication*

fails? At first glance this may seem a ridiculous question. It is not. You should always consider the possibility of poor communication impact—even with the best of preparation and skill in execution. Just as the most competent medical doctor using the best knowledge and skill he can command cannot guarantee curing a sick patient (who may die), neither can you, the competent communicator, predict success in every case. And in performance-related presentations, if you do fail, negative job results are almost always built in.

Should failure appear to be likely (in spite of your best efforts), this should give you pause before proceeding. It may be better to forgo the presentation altogether or to await a better time and place. You may have to live with a bad situation rather than risk creating an intolerable one.

You can assess these two questions using the simple form in Figure 2–3.

Psychological costs. These costs are even more subjective, but often have an even more important impact, than either monetary or job costs. It is obviously not easy to make rigorous, precise estimates of the feeling states of people, but it certainly is important to do the best we can. Both immediate and long-range consequences—good or bad—ensue from the ways the receivers feel about the presenter, his ideas, and the situation itself. Several "costs" can be examined to determine this dimension.

What are the costs of required reception? Purposive presentations of

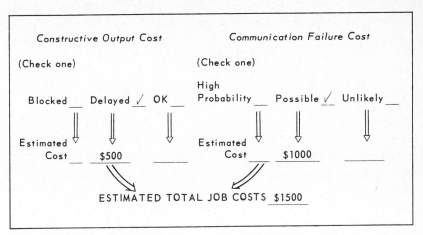

Figure 2-3.   Computing job costs.

the kind we're studying require the attendance (either the immediate or remote presence) of some receiver or receivers. And any time a person is "commanded" to listen to or read a communication, an almost automatic psychological barrier is erected. You should certainly weigh this cost against the estimated need for making the presentation.

What are the costs of inundative communications? All of us are already deluged by all types of communications—conferences, meetings, telephone calls, letters, directives, brochures, forms . . . ad infinitum—and, unless there is a really good reason, to add to the flood is only to create greater stress in the organization. "Is this communication really necessary?" is a vital question to help avoid undue psychological costs at this point.

What are the costs of competitive communications? From the great number and mass of communications to which we are subjected, all of us must select those that seem most important. You should recognize that the psychological cost of requiring a receiver to divert his attention from ongoing "important" communications to yours may be considerable. And you as a presenter should also recognize that a psychological cost is exacted from you in that you must exert that much more effort and skill to get the receiver's attention and interest on your communication, and away from the competition.

What are the costs of looseness versus rigor? In this book we are taking the perspective of purposive oral presentations, and written communications are supplementary. This fix entails a psychological cost which the communicator must certainly consider if he is to know his chances for optimal outcomes.

Looseness is an attribute of oral presentations: that is, spoken communication is fundamentally fluid, of the moment, and inexact. And although these qualities can be advantageous in creating warmth, an interactive atmosphere, and relative lack of receiver defensiveness, they also present hazards in that ideas may be only roughly defined, remembered for only a short time, and subject to rapid erosion. These "costs" are obvious dangers in some important communications.

On the other hand, written communication is essentially more *rigorous.* Since it is recorded, writing is more straightforward, has more continuity, and is more precise than spoken communications.

While potentially assets, these are also "costs" on the other end of the communications continuum.

You must determine which of the costs—looseness or rigor—is least expensive for your situation. For example, if you want a "dialogic" (two-way) atmosphere, then looseness through oral communication is the cost you must be willing to pay; if, on the other hand, you want your receivers to remember ideas exactly, then you must be prepared to pay the price of rigor through written communication.

What are the costs of personalization versus impersonalization? Oral communication is more personal, more warm, more feeling-oriented than writing. And for many situations (such as interviewing a job applicant, getting at the real problems causing production lags, and commending people for achievements), this humanizing quality is desired. But in situations demanding the nonpersonal, the rational, the intellectual (for example, communicating policy changes, reporting production data, communicating how a new procedure is to be followed), writing is the better way.

Both personalization and impersonalization exact psychological costs. Personalization costs in more time and stress by both presenter and receiver; impersonalization costs in creating remoteness, isolation, and anomie among all those communicating. Again, the question is, "Which cost shall I pay?" or, more precisely, "Which is the optimal cost?" The communicator's answer obviously must be given in relation to the communication situation he confronts and in light of what he wants to do.

In summary, psychological costs can be classed as required reception, competitive communications, looseness versus rigor, and personalization versus impersonalization. All are important potential expenditures in your communication, and, therefore, all should be considered as carefully as possible.

Although these costs are admittedly subjective in calculation, you can get some realistic idea of psychological costs by determining their *conservative impacts* on the two preceding costs: monetary and job. You may use the form in Figure 2–4 as a guide to appraise psychological costs.

Total costs are computed by adding the three major costs: monetary, job, and psychological, as illustrated here:

Monetary costs	$1,655
Job costs	1,500
Psychological costs	450
Total Costs	**$3,605**

Benefits

Having considered costs, we will now see how to calculate the constructive and productive outcomes from your communications. For, after all, these constitute your real reasons for communicating in the first place. Benefits can be reckoned by relating them to the same three cost categories: monetary, job, and psychological.

Monetary benefits are those directly calculable potential dollar incomes or savings resulting from presentations. For example, will the presentation (or series of presentations) probably produce increased

Figure 2-4. Computing psychological costs.

Cost Barrier	Monetary Impact[a]	Job Impact[b]	Total
Required reception	$	(in additional $100 graphic aids)	$100
Competitive communications	$	(in additional $100 preparation)	$100
Looseness/rigor	(in additional handouts $250 and visual equipment)	$	$250
Personalization/ impersonalization	$	$	$
		Total Psychological Costs	**$450**

[a]Estimate the added conservative dollar amount which will probably be required (in terms of labor-hours, materials, physical plant, and equipment) to overcome this barrier. For example, in order to overcome the "looseness" dimension, it may be necessary to produce written supplementary materials as handouts, as well as to increase oral communication effectiveness through use of visual aid equipment and to allocate many more labor-hours to follow up in order to assure the right response from receivers.

[b]Estimate the added conservative dollar amount which will probably be required (in terms of potential blocked or delayed performance outputs and possible communication failures) to overcome the barrier. For example, how much more money in, say, labor-hours and materials must be invested in a presentation on a new policy in order to assure optimal attention and response within the context of ten other weekly meetings and 30 major written documents going over the receivers' desks? Or how much more preparation time (labor-hours) and materials (charts, graphs, schematics) will be needed to get optimal reception and impact concerning vital production data which listeners initially view as dry and sterile?

sales revenues of $500,000 annually? Or will the presentation result in operational economies (such as by cutting down work materials consumption or cutting costs of written documents) in the company? Does the award of a contract of, say, $1 million hinge on the prospective client's reaction to the presentation? All these exemplify possible monetary benefits to the firm.

Job benefits are potential increases in task performances that result from presentations. For example, to what extent will the communication cause operators to produce more and better outputs in a given time? Will the presentation probably produce a greater percentage of punctual workers? If so, how much of an increase? Or will the communication result in managers' exercising more control of their supervisors' handling of exit interviews, so that underlying reasons for the high rate of employee turnover can be pinpointed and corrected? If so, what annual dollar savings can be reliably predicted? These are examples of potential job benefits to the organization.

Psychological benefits are those possible constructive increments of receiver feeling states resulting from purposive presentations. For example, will the communication generate more dedication to their jobs on the part of middle managers? Will supervisors believe more deeply in the importance of their units' contributions to the company's growth and development? Will workers be more receptive to needed changes in production systems and procedures? Will customers view the company in a new and better light? Will community leaders be more sympathetic with the firms's aims and objectives? These are but a few of the many situations in which psychological benefits may be paramount.

Clearly, psychological benefits are probably the most common and important outcomes to be sought in many presentations. Admittedly difficult to quantify, they are nevertheless calculable in the context of monetary and job benefits. Let's now look at an example of calculating all three.

Computing total benefits. The form illustrated in Figure 2-5 can be used to calculate presentation benefits, both immediate and long-range. The data used are, of course, hypothetical.

Weighing Costs Against Benefits (Cost-Benefit Computation)

Having computed both potential costs and benefits step by step and independently from one another, let's now put the totals into an

Figure 2-5. Computing total benefits.

Predicted Benefit	Increment	Basis
immediate or One-Time Benefits		
Monetary	$75,000*	New contract award
Job	$10,000	Reduction in project overtime pay
Psychological	*Contract award	As a result of presentation
Total Immediate Benefits	$85,000 +	Psychological benefit of contract award
Long-Range or Continuing Benefits		
Monetary	$125,000**	$25,000 annual continuing work for five years
Job	0	
Psychological	**Continuing work	As a result of initial contract award
Total Long-Range Benefits	$125,000 +	Psychological benefit of five years' work with definite possibility of more.

integrated form so that direct comparisons can be made, leading to your decision concerning the presentation. We'll use the same hypothetical data from the part-by-part calculations. (See Figure 2-6.) The costs-benefits categories (monetary, job, and psychological) are those previously explained and need no further elaboration. However, two items—prediction reliability and decision on presentation—need clarification.

Prediction reliability. This is concerned with the most dependable judgments about each cost and benefit. The simple quadrant pattern suggested has proved very useful. Admittedly these judgments will be based on incomplete data (as finally any judgment must be), but you can learn to use this approach (or some modification of it) to make some surprisingly valid estimates. Any of several methods can be used:

1. *The presenter can rely solely on his own judgment.* Experienced and perceptive communicators can generally make very valid predictions using this approach. And although it is direct, inexpensive, and simple, the disadvantage is obvious: this method is at best subjective, depending as it does on the judgment of one person.

Costs

	Costs	Prediction Reliability		Basis
Monetary	$1655	0–25% ___ 25–50% ___	50–75% ___ 75–100% ✓	Direct calculation of time lost, materials, equipment, physical plant usage
Job	1500	0–25% ___ 25–50% ✓	50–75% ___ 75–100% ___	Consensus of six key department managers
Psychological	450	0–25% ___ 25–50% ___	50–75% ✓ 75–100% ___	Consensus of department managers and sample of representative receivers
TOTAL	$3605			

Benefits

Benefits Immediate/ One-time	Increment	Prediction Reliability		Basis
Monetary	$75,000*	0–25% ___ 25–50% ___	50–75% ✓ 75–100% ___	New contract award
Job	10,000	0–25% ___ 25–50% ___	50–75% ✓ 75–100% ___	Reduction in overtime pay
Psychological	*Contract award	0–25% ___ 25–50% ___	50–75% ___ 75–100% ✓	As a result of presentation
TOTAL IMMEDIATE	$85,000 (plus Psychological Benefit of contract award)			

Long Range or Continuing		Prediction Reliability		
Monetary	$125,000**	0–25% ___ 25–50% ___	50–75% ___ 75–100% ✓	$25,000 per year for 5 years
Job	0	0–25% ___ 25–50% ✓	50–75% ___ 75–100% ___	
Psychological	**Continuing work	0–25% ___ 25–50% ___	50–75% ___ 75–100% ✓	
TOTAL LONG RANGE	$125,000 (plus Psychological Benefit of continuing work from initial contract award)			

Decision on Presentation

✓ Plan and execute with these constraints: Cost maximum of $5000 _____

___ Get more data on: _____

___ Postpone presentation until (time, place, circumstance): _____

___ Cancel presentation unless: _____

___ Other decisions or stipulations: _____

Figure 2-6. Cost-benefit computation

2. *The presenter can informally consult other communicators.* Here he supplements his personal judgment by that of other experienced communicators. This overcomes to some extent the subjective element in the first method. It is, however, more time-consuming, costly, and cumbersome.

3. *The presenter can use a formal presentation screening committee to make cost-benefit evaluations.* Here specific operational criteria and procedures are set up and requisite personnel are assigned to carry out given tasks (such as statistical handling, record keeping, and cost accounting) so that final estimates reflect optimal reliability and validity. This is most applicable to large organizations where many important presentations are carried out. While obviously the most costly and complex, this method, when used appropriately, will pay real returns to the company seeking to balance presentation costs against benefits.

Decision on presentation. This is the judgment made concerning presentation disposition. Using the data in the cost-benefit computation, the presenter or manager (using one of the three above methods) determines what is to be done: whether to go ahead, solicit more information, or put off or eliminate the communication. This approach gives a sound basis for decision making as contrasted to the typical "navel contemplation" or capricious judgment so commonly used in many organizations.

Summary: Determining Whether Benefits Outweigh Costs

We've examined an approach which you can use to know whether constructive outcomes (monetary, job, and psychological) override real costs of presentations. Using the foregoing procedures and forms (or their modifications), you can make more realistic and accurate judgments as to whether the presentation should be given, reconsidered, delayed, or canceled.

You may well ask, "Is all this computation always necessary to determine whether I should communicate?" In simple exposition or certain cases, the answer is obviously no. But in more complex and important situations, neither the communicator nor his organization can afford to proceed impulsively without knowing whether predictable benefits will outweigh costs. To go ahead with a serious purposive presentation without this background is folly of the worst sort, leading to possibly disastrous consequences.

STEP 4: KNOWING COMMUNICATION FEASIBILITY

Steps 1, 2, and 3 were concerned with knowing need symptoms, need type, and cost-benefit relationships. With this background (and assuming that you have decided that it is a good investment), you are now ready to determine the feasibility of the presentation. By feasibility is meant the practicability of carrying out the communication. Obviously, although we may know our symptoms and the type of need, and that benefits outweigh costs, if conditions still dictate infeasibility, then it is senseless to proceed to the presentation—at least under the circumstances predicted.

How can you size up communication feasibility? The following items can serve as useful checkpoints: (1) situational conditions; (2) resource availability; (3) data adequacy; and (4) programming with other communications.

Situational Conditions

These refer to the important circumstances surrounding the presentation, including timing, significance, credibility, and realism.

Situational *timing* greatly affects listeners' attitudes and determines how they will receive the presentation. For example, if hit "cold" on a new procedure, people may not be prepared to give it proper thought. Or if some conflict or upheaval in the firm has just taken place, it may be wise to wait until the situation has settled down before presenting a proposal which you want to be carefully thought over by the group before action is taken. You should therefore make sure that timing is optimal to get the reception you want.

Situational *significance* is certainly a determinant of listener reaction. If they see the communication occasion as vital and meaningful, your receivers are likely to respond favorably; if not, you are up against a real barrier. For example, if listeners can glimpse some tangible personal benefits or some specific gains or some provocative challenges to themselves, you have a real advantage; if not, you should realistically recognize this adverse situational factor.

Situational *credibility* also makes a real difference. Do listeners see the communication setting as something of mutual benefit? Do they feel that you and your organization are trustworthy? Do they deem you and the occasion as worthy of respect? If your listeners believe in you, your ideas, and the organization, you have one of the strongest advantages; if not, you are faced with a serious communication hazard.

Situational *realism* includes the practicality and usefulness of the situation as seen by your listeners. You may see the occasion as one of genuine merit or vital significance, but if your audience views the matter differently, then you had best set your sails accordingly. Do your listeners generally view your ideas as practical? Do they see them as worthwhile? Or in this situation, do they view your ideas as mere "verbal garbage," words to be heard but not heeded? Clearly you should take account of this important element in your assessment of feasibility.

Resource Availability

Resource availability refers to the actual accessibility of necessary money, manpower, and physical facilities to carry out the presentation. Although you have already determined costs, this by no means guarantees that you can actually get all the needed resources to carry out your communication successfully. You must, then, confirm or get approval of needed money, workers, and physical facilities.

Are the needed *dollars* available? And do you have formal approval of your superiors and pertinent company managers (including the budget officer)? For example, if moneys are to be transferred from several different unit budgets (a common practice), have all managers of affected departments been informed about—and have they agreed to—the decision? Is part of the needed money firmly committed, but part only tentative (another common occurrence)? If so, this means either holding off on the presentation until sufficient funds are guaranteed, or planning your communication for the contingency that you may not receive all the expected dollars. It may even be necessary to plan two different communications—one based on the guaranteed money and one based on the total needed dollars.

Obvious as it is, one of the most frequent, grievous errors made by many communicators is not making sure of their money resources before reaching a point of no return in their presentations.

Are all necessary people—presenters, support personnel, and prospective receivers—available? By available is meant *willing and able to devote the necessary time and skill to the project.*

First, this means that you (or other communicators) must be able to give adequate time and talent to the preparation and execution of the presentation. For any busy manager or professional person this involves setting aside a sufficient number of hours out of an already crowded schedule. It means sacrificing some other important task performances in favor of the communication. It means deliberately establishing priorities and acting accordingly. You should realistically assess your "availability" in this light, because only when so considered can you do the effective communication job required in a purposive presentation.

Second, are needed supporting people (graphics specialists, technical editors, clerical personnel, audiovisual technicians) ready and able to give the required hours and expertise to the project? Even "simple" presentations require organizational support of some sort. And in complex presentations, the planning and supervision of support facilities can be a major logistical and management problem. You should check carefully to assure that sufficient supporting personnel are available to do the job at hand.

Third, are receivers available? That is, are all people who should assimilate the message (or messages) able to be present at the desired time and place? For example, can key managers be spared (at a given time) from their jobs? Can out-of-the-city people arrange their schedules so as not to severely disrupt their own important operations? Can proper substitute or backup people be present if first-choice receivers cannot attend? What vital organizational outputs will be adversely affected (delayed, reduced, or cut off) because people are diverted from their primary jobs to attend to the presentation? Will it be necessary to exploit both oral and written communications— even electronic connections—in order to assure optimal receiver exposure?

Finally, are all needed physical resources available? Although you may know requirements and costs, this again is no assurance that needed items are obtainable. Do you know that the printing department can supply the quality of paper you need for your handouts? And even if it is procurable, can the paper be delivered in time to be run to meet your schedule? Can you get the visual transparencies you need to show your charts? And can you get them processed in time to use them when they are needed? Are required equipment and building facilities available? Don't take this as a trivial admonition; in far too many instances, failure to reserve a room or some visual aid equipment has resulted in a failure in the presentation. All the money and time expended in preparation is futile if presentation payoff is blocked because essential building or equipment facilities are unavailable when needed. In sum, you should never underestimate the importance of planning your complete physical-resource needs and following through to assure that all of them will be met.

Data Adequacy

Let's use the term *data* in its broadest sense—that is, any information, ideas, concepts, or principles. Data adequacy is, then, concerned with the availability and quality of any information, ideas, concepts, or principles needed to achieve the presentation's mission. Let's look at data adequacy related to communication feasibility in terms of two elements: availability and quality.

Data *availability* refers to whether you have access to a sufficient range and quantity of information. By *range* of data is meant the coverage or extent of available information. Of course, there will always be some informational gaps, both absolutely and because data acquisition may cost too much beyond a certain point. The real question, then, is "Are *optimal* data available?" Do you have sufficient types to get your message across? Do you have the full extent of needed facts? Or are glaring informational gaps apparent? Can you feasibly (in terms of money and time) gather and put together the data to fill the gaps? You should realistically answer these questions. If you have no data gaps, then a "go" on the presentation is indicated; but if you have voids, then you should determine whether it is possible to get the needed data within your resource and time limitations. If not, you may want to either recast or delay the presentation until a more propitious time. If pertinent data are largely or totally unavailable, you should think of canceling the presentation altogether—at least in terms of the original communication mission and form.

Data *quality* refers to the worth and value of information. Even if there is an apparently sufficient range, do the data meet necessary tests of accuracy, reliability, and validity? Are sources of information trustworthy? Are differing data inputs consistent? Or do some indicate a need for further checking? Do written (reports) and oral (discussions with managers) communications say the same things? Or are there some obvious discrepancies? Do "historical" facts (past sales, production figures) cohere with present data inputs?

Data quality, of course, is relative to the presentation mission and to the receivers of it. In general informational missions to a perceptive group, broad conceptual data may be sufficient. But for very basic presentations to a relatively unsophisticated audience, clearly detailed specific data may be required. You should always judge quality accordingly.

Programming with Other Communications

Here you are concerned that the presentation blends optimally with your and the organization's other ongoing communications. For example, if your firm is in the midst of an intensive cost-cutting program involving setting up numerous department meetings and issuing several company policy and procedure directives, you will be wise to consider a time when your presentation will not be buried in this avalanche. Or if the company has budgeted a certain amount for purposive communications, what will be your presentation's financial impact? That is, how important is it relative to the many others necessary for the firm's survival?

Granted that ego involvement dictates our perceiving our own communications as "vital," the question should be: "What objective contribution will this presentation make to the company's operations in the context of all other important communications?" Moreover, is it possible to capitalize on some already scheduled or ongoing communications? For example, if monthly departmental staff meetings are held, is it feasible to make your presentation at one of these (assuming, of course, that it can fit in)? Or if branch managers are being brought in for briefing about a new company product, can your communication be included in the program (assuming, of course, that it can be made relevant to the branch personnel)?

What we are talking about, of course, is *planning* in terms of the company's total communications. When this is done properly, many apparently infeasible single presentations become feasible, because this approach optimizes the company's resources—money, people, and physical. It is a constructive, coordinated communication pattern, in contrast with the typical cutthroat, competitive one prevalent in too many organizations.

Summary: Communication Feasibility

By looking at situational conditions, resource availability, data adequacy, and programming with other communications, you can realistically determine the feasibility of your proposed presentation. Let's look at the steps summarized in Figure 2-7.

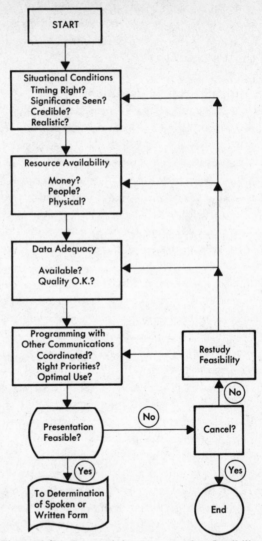

Figure 2-7. Determining presentation feasibility.

STEP 5: KNOWING WHETHER TO USE
SPOKEN OR WRITTEN FORM

Having determined that you want to proceed with the presentation, and that it is feasible to do so, you will now be ready to assess the way in which you should communicate ideas—that is, whether orally or in writing, or a combination of both.

To help you make the right decision, let's list some guides to the proper uses of speaking and writing.

When to Use Speaking

Speaking should generally be used when you face the following conditions:

1. *When confidential matters are to be discussed.* People are more likely to respond positively to confidential or "privileged" oral communication than to the same kind in writing. Moreover, it may be unwise to put some confidential matters in written form.

2. *When warmth and personal qualities are called for.* Speaking is more personal, more "human" than writing. Furthermore, since most oral communication involves face-to-face confrontation, both the speaker and his listeners can get direct feedback and cues which can sensitively guide both parties. Writing lacks this very important quality.

3. *When an atmosphere of openness is desired.* An atmosphere of openness is one of candor and exploration, a situation in which ideas are subject to review and study. Oral communication permits this environment more readily than writing.

4. *When strengthening of feeling states is needed.* This especially applies to the reinforcing of attitudes and beliefs. Oral communication is a powerful medium by which to accomplish this end.

5. *When exactitude and precision are not required.* Speaking is by nature more fluid, momentary, and inexact than writing. Therefore where exactitude and precision are not needed, it is probably better to use the more easily prepared and executed oral means.

6. *When decisions must be communicated quickly.* Oral communication is the primary medium when time is short, when important deadlines must be met, when decisions must be sent rapidly to meet changing conditions.

7. *When crucial situations dictate maximum understanding.* What is meant is that in cases where it is necessary for all parties—both presenter and receivers—to be sure that genuine comprehension will take place, oral communication is the prime means. Its characteristics of face-to-face confrontation, interaction, fluidity, and personalization permit the needed interchange of ideas to get the kind of understanding required in critical circumstances.

8. *When added impact is needed to get the receiver's attention.* Its intrinsic qualities of personalization, warmth, fluidity, informality, and directness make speaking more attention-getting and interest-sustaining

than writing. Oral communication can thus be used to get better receiver attention and interest on written or visual presentations, for example. Used in this supplementary role, it can make one of its most important organizational contributions.

9. *When personal authentication is needed.* Here we refer to a specific individual's authoritativeness or credibility (in the eyes of receivers). For example, the boss is not viewed as merely occupying a position, but is seen as a trustworthy and respected human being. Personal authentication is a powerful means of influence, and oral communication is the primary tool by which it is achieved.

10. *When social or gregarious needs must be met.* When group needs (for example, creating collective cohesiveness or belongingness) must be satisfied, oral communication is generally the best vehicle. Its potential qualities of humaneness, warmth, and informality help create a communication environment conducive to meeting group needs.

These, then, are some of the more important conditions calling for oral communication. Let's now look at those situations where written communication is needed.

When to Use Writing

Writing is generally in order under these circumstances:

1. *When impersonalization is in order.* In contrast to the "human" qualities of oral communication, writing is more impersonal and dispassionate. When the nonpersonal is needed (such as in issuing organizational directives, contracts, or specifications), written communication is the best mode.

2. *When the communicator needs to extend himself in time and space.* Writing permits the presenter to be vicariously represented by symbols on the printed page, permitting communication across temporal and spatial boundaries. Although also possible under certain oral communication conditions (such as video hookups), writing is the basic means for communicating in other than face-to-face situations.

3. *When ideas need to be stored and retrieved.* Writing is recorded. As such, it permits storage and retrieval for short-run or long-run problem solving or decision making. When ideas are to be used for important future reference, writing is the preferred mode of communication.

4. *When idea reliability and validity are important.* Since it is by

definition more precise and of record, writing induces greater reliability and validity than oral communication. Whereas oral communication is subject to erosion and distortion, writing has permanence which builds in greater ideational stability and accuracy.

5. *When idea verification or authentication is important.* As you have already seen, oral communication is better for personal authentication, but *writing* is better for verifying and authenticating ideas. Since it is recorded, writing permits ideas to be used as impersonal guides (for example, company policies, directives, or manuals) in ongoing organizations. Without such written guides, neither managerial control nor the organization is possible.

6. *When objective references are important.* Written documentations allow receivers to refer to the same symbolic stimuli, permitting people to use a common outside source for thought or action. Whereas oral communication is internalized, writing is externalized, thereby allowing greater objectivity.

7. *When written communication is more acceptable.* Some receivers (notably scientific and professional groups) insist on writing as the only acceptable mode for communicating significant ideas. And some critical-minded company managers will not give serious consideration to an idea unless it is written. In such instances, writing is the only way to get a message across and accepted.

8. *When crucial decisions or actions are to be considered.* Since writing permits more dispassionate and objective analysis than speaking, critical proposals should be written up so that the best possible judgments can be made. Oral communication can play an important role in discussion of conflicting views or unclear ideas, highlighting, raising questions, and making further explorations, but the written document should be the essential focus when thinking through crucial decisions or actions in organizations.

9. *When communications are subject to review and reconsideration.* Writing is more susceptible to review than is oral communication. Because they are recorded, written documents are not characterized by the erosion and distortion of the momentarily intelligible spoken form.

10. *When written supplements to oral communications are needed.* In many situations, speaking should be complemented by appropriate written documents. A departmental meeting may be conducted for the most part orally, but minutes and follow-up memoranda will be written. The production manager may telephone a procedural

change to his supervisors, after which he may send a detailed written directive as an authenticating guide. An oral presentation may be made to propound a general proposal, accompanied by a voluminous written document spelling out all items. You should recognize and exploit this important interplay of written and oral communication.

When to Use Combinations of Oral and Written Communication

We have indicated that both speaking and writing should at times complement one another. Let's spell out common conditions where you should consider using the two together. (See Figure 2-8 for ready reference in sizing up presentation media.)

1. *When you want receivers to "carry home" ideas.* Do you want your listeners to take your oral message (or some parts of it) back to their offices for specific thought or action? Do you want them to have a memento of the presentation, even for purely psychological reasons? Do you want them to have notes for future reference? These are just a few "take-home" possibilities. Written handouts, graphic aids, and presentation summaries are useful devices in this respect.

2. *When follow-up activities are in order.* When, after an oral presentation, you want to follow up some action or plan subsequent meetings, written materials, either during or after your speech, are often very helpful. On the other hand, oral communication can valuably supplement written communications to get the desired follow-up. A written directive may be sent out, after which large or small group meetings may be held to assure understanding and compliance. A proposed departmental policy change may be circulated, after which the boss may confer with his key managers to determine their reactions and the need for possible modifications.

3. *When optimal understanding is needed.* Optimal understanding means the highest comprehension of ideas commensurate with economics. As an example, it may be ideal to get a 100 percent understanding of concepts by all parties, but the costs required may be prohibitive. Therefore, some optimal level of comprehension (say, 85 percent) is set to balance costs against a minimum necessary to get a job done. Both oral and written communications may be required for optimization of this sort. Written communication can give an objective and permanent basis for understanding; oral communication can clarify, reinforce, or modify ideas.

Figure 2-8. Summary of conditions for communication form.

Oral	Written	Combined
(1) Confidential matters	(1) Impersonalization desired	(1) "Carry home" ideas desired
(2) Warmth, personal qualities needed	(2) Extension in time and space proper	(2) Follow-up needed
(3) Open atmosphere desired	(3) Storage and retrieval needed	(3) Optimal understanding needed
(4) Stronger feelings needed	(4) Reliability/validity important	(4) Clarity and impact needed
(5) Exactitude/precision not required	(5) Idea verification/authentication needed	(5) Exploratory communication
(6) Immediacy required	(6) Objective references	(6) Audience participation needed
(7) Crucial situations	(7) Writing more acceptable	(7) Abstract/remote ideas
(8) Added receiver impact needed	(8) Crucial decisions/actions	
(9) Personal authentication needed	(9) Review/reconsideration needed	
(10) Meeting social needs	(10) Supplement to speaking	

4. *When both clarity and impact are needed.* While related to the three foregoing conditions, this one differs in that your objective is to get proper receiver understanding *and* reaction. You want listeners to comprehend at a certain level, but you also want them to believe deeply in your message. Although somewhat simplified, writing is the vehicle of clarity and intellectual comprehension; speaking is the medium of sentiments and emotional impacts. Therefore you should think of combining the two media when a clarity-impact mission prevails.

5. *When the presentation is exploratory.* In this "open" situation, you are not giving final answers but seeking ways and means to find workable solutions. The problem—or problems—may not yet be defined. You may be presenting only symptoms and discrepancies for your listeners' (or readers') thought. Or you may have several alternative answers which you want your receivers to weigh. In such cases, combined spoken and written communications may be desired for the reasons already given.

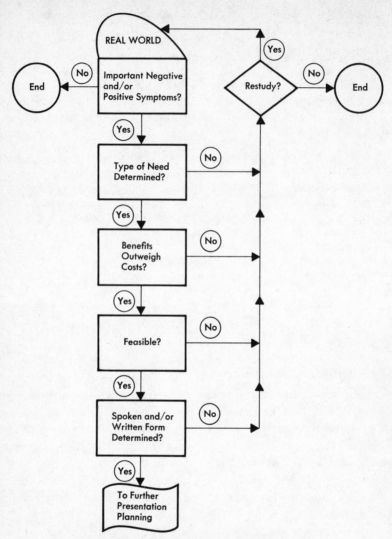

Figure 2-9. Knowing when to communicate.

6. *When audience participation is desired.* This is related to all the foregoing, but here you want your listeners or readers to take an active part in the presentation. Examples of such situations include written case analyses; using group discussion to diagnose problems and determine answers; oral highlighting of a company's financial condition, followed by handing out a detailed written report, about

which audience questions are then entertained; and the circulation of representative letters of complaint, about which a meeting is later held to discuss the problems posed, together with possible means of resolution.

7. *When abstract or "remote" ideas are to be communicated.* Abstract ideas are those of very general nature (to the receivers); remote concepts are those which are initially not directly important (to the receivers). When either condition exists, multiple media, both oral and written (including graphics), are probably required to bring home the message you want to convey. You should always examine your presentation in this light.

These, then, are some of the more important conditions pointing to the need for combined oral and written communications.

SUMMARY: KNOWING WHEN TO COMMUNICATE

We have seen that there are five steps in determining when to communicate: (1) knowing symptoms of need; (2) knowing the type of need; (3) knowing whether benefits outweigh costs; (4) knowing feasibility; and (5) knowing the communication form. The process can be put into an algorithm (sequence of steps), as in Figure 2-9.

Using this approach, you can assess beyond doubt when and what general type of communication is called for. Just as important, you can determine when communication is not needed, thus avoiding unnecessary costs and problems which accompany any purposive presentation.

3

Putting Ideas Together

Having determined that you need to communicate, that cost-benefit ratios are sufficiently favorable, that the presentation is feasible, and that the communication form (oral or written or both) is proper, you are now ready to organize and develop the ideas for your presentation.

You are no doubt aware of the importance of organizing your communication. Since the way you put together your ideas determines largely how well you will give and how well your listeners (or readers) will receive your message, basic understanding of how ideas are put together is vital to presentation success.

At this point we shall examine general methods for putting ideas into communicable form, which in turn will furnish a stockpile from which we will draw in later chapters.

What do you need to know in order to organize and develop (put together) your ideas? The following are basic: (1) structure for receivers; (2) logical sequences; (3) psychological sequences; (4) developing ideas; and (5) introductions and conclusions.

STRUCTURE FOR RECEIVERS

Use of the TRIM design means that you organize ideas for your listeners or readers—not yourself. Of course, you must use patterns of organization with which you feel competent and comfortable, but the basic question should always be, "What idea pattern will most likely hit the intended communication target with my receivers?"

For our purposes let's divide structure into (1) logical sequences; and (2) psychological sequences.

Logical sequences are essentially rational and message-oriented. That is, your emphasis is on getting ideas into the brains of your receivers without great concern for their feelings. Logical approaches are generally overt, clear, and direct. As we shall see, in certain presentations these have important utility and value.

Psychological sequences are fundamentally nonrational and feeling-oriented. Here your primary focus is on handling the receiver's emotional states so that he is prepared to assimilate your message. Psychological approaches are normally covert, palatable, and indirect.

LOGICAL SEQUENCES

As stated, these are rational and message-centered, with a basic purpose of *conveying ideas.* In this respect, logical structures serve two very useful ends: to inform (through instruction, exposition, and explanation) and to convince through logical demonstration. In informing, the basic quality required is clarity; in convincing through logical demonstration, the essential attribute is propositional truth (through proper uses of chains of reasoning, theories, and causal connections).

Since they are generally straightforward and direct, logical sequences are frequently deductive—that is, from the clearly stated general to the equally clearly drawn specific conclusion. A well-written college textbook commonly uses this deductive pattern. This chapter itself is an example.

What are some useful kinds of logical sequences? You will find those discussed here very helpful in putting ideas together for informative and demonstration-centered presentations.

Time sequence puts ideas in chronological or temporal order. While commonly starting with the earliest event and then moving successively to later ones (the typical historical development), it can start from the most recent and "flash back" to the earlier. Sometimes time sequences start from a midpoint and move successively in both directions from it.

Time sequence is especially useful in imparting background or process information. Background information is by definition historical; and any procedure is carried out in a certain order or sequence. A good example of time sequence is Specimen 7:6–10.

Space sequence places ideas in locational relationships or "where things are." It has a variety of possible uses: orientation to buildings and equipment, descriptions of geographical territories (for example, the marketing divisions of a company), and setting the stage for further explanation of a process.

Important elements sequence is another way of logically ordering your ideas. This is a very frequently used pattern in textbooks and articles in professional journals. (You will recognize that this book uses it.)

In addition to texts and professional communications, some other important applications of the important elements pattern include professional papers, policy manuals, oral or written directives, procedural instructions, proposals, and contracts. See Specimens 1 and 17 as examples of usage.

Problem-analysis-solution sequence progresses from a statement of the situation (problem) to why it exists (analysis) to how to handle it (solution). Among other uses, this format is frequently seen in recommendation reports and technical proposals and in introducing changes in the organization.

Proposition-proof-conclusion sequence moves from (1) the statement of that which is to be demonstrated (hypothesis, thesis, proposal) to (2) supporting generalizations, theories, or causal connections which test or prove it to (3) conclusions or implications which logically follow. Properly used, this is verbal demonstration in its most careful and exact form. It is the essence of rational, scientific, and critical thought. Therefore, some of its important applications lie in presenting professional, scientific, and managerial ideas. Refer to Specimen 19 as an illustration of its use.

These, then, are important, practical, logical sequences which you can employ in informative and demonstrative presentations. Obviously, they are not mutually exclusive; indeed, they are frequently used to complement each other, one being perhaps the primary and one or more of the others the supportive means. You will see from our frequent references to them that logical sequences have important applications in purposive presentations.

PSYCHOLOGICAL SEQUENCES

You will recall that, in contrast to logical sequences, these are person- rather than idea-directed. In other words, the "under-the-skin" impact of your message on the receiver is the primary concern.

Stated another way, psychological sequences are designed to control your receiver's feeling states so that he is willing to listen to and accept your ideas.

Where are they most useful in presentations? They are especially applicable in persuasive communications (deepening existing attitudes and beliefs, changing neutral or opposing viewpoints, or "selling" people on some new idea). While not necessarily "illogical," psychological sequences serve best in nonlogical situations. Stated another way, they deal with the "logic" of human feelings rather than of ideas. Since communications frequently arise out of this context, it is clear that psychological sequences are required in many purposive presentations if you are to succeed.

Whereas logical sequences are commonly deductive, psychological formats are often inductive—that is, moving from particulars and specifics to the more general. In some cases the generalization will not be explicitly expounded, but rather left to the receiver to draw his own implications. Let's now explore some useful types of psychological sequences.

The *familiar to unfamiliar sequence* refers, of course, to starting with the known and moving in necessary steps to the unknown. Remember that we are talking about your *receiver*'s familiarity and unfamiliarity. And this is why it is fundamentally a psychological approach. Here you build understanding by using what the listener already knows (and with which he feels secure) to get him to comprehend the new (information, concepts, procedures, products, or services), about which he may feel apprehension, inadequacy, or sophistication.

This pattern has special utility when you are confronted with actual or potential receiver "sophistication" (the person who thinks he already knows as much as or more than you can tell him). See Specimen 11:1–6 as a typical illustration.

The *common to uncommon sequence* involves moving from that which is initially acceptable to that which (without proper receiver preparation) is unacceptable. Whereas the familiar to unfamiliar refers to receiver knowledge states, this pattern is directed to changing listener beliefs and outlooks. Whereas the former is concerned primarily with imparting information, the latter works with receiver acceptance, or belief in your ideas. It has important applications in situations where receivers are initially neutral or opposed to your ideas. Specimen 11 exemplifies this pattern.

The *belief-to-greater-belief sequence* means strengthening or deepening preexisting receiver tenets. If receivers believe already in the worth of their jobs, they are made to see them as even more important. If they feel that the company is a *good* organization, listeners are led to perceive it as a *great* institution. If departmental employees think people in other units are doing satisfactory work, they are made to see them as performing really valuable services in the company. These are but a few of the many possible examples of where the belief-to-greater-belief sequence has application in your presentations. Specimen 7 well illustrates this format.

The *belief-to-action sequence* involves moving your receivers from mental acceptance to desired performance. Your listeners may know, may believe, and may believe deeply, but if action (when needed) is not taken, then your presentation obviously fails. This approach builds on the three preceding ones, using one or more of them as means. Its basic application is apparent—whenever you want actual performance from receivers who have been brought to the point of belief. Specimen 8 is one of the more powerful examples of this sequence.

In summary, there are four psychological sequences: familiar to unfamiliar; common to uncommon; belief to greater belief; and belief to action. Each has its unique contribution in controlling receiver feeling states. We'll be spelling out more details about each as we move along.

DEVELOPING IDEAS

A good sequence, whether logical or psychological, is a most important ingredient to presentation success. But it is also clear that you must effectively build out or develop your basic format if you are to deliver the right communication package.

Essentially, developing ideas means the ways by which you make meaningful or elaborate or support the more general concepts in the essential sequence. In other words, idea development imparts vitality or clarity or credibility to the more abstract ideas in your fundamental outline. Presentational quality can be no better than the quality of its idea development.

Let's now look at some of the general supportive means you can use in this very important phase of presentation planning. Later we'll study detailed techniques and devices for differing presentation targets, receivers, impacts, and methods.

Facts and Statistics

Facts are verbal statements of either observed or generalized data. ' Statistics are quantified data, both observed and generalized. Facts and statistics are widely useful, but have special application to logical sequences.

Comparisons and Contrasts

Although often based on facts and statistics, these develop ideas in unique ways. Comparisons are concerned with similarities and analogies; contrasts refer to dissimilarities. Specimen 10:6 is a good example of the use of comparisons. And the same specimen (10:37–39) shows how contrasts can be effectively employed.

Examples

These can be either a case situation (a detailed event or incident) or real (a shorthand account of an actual happening) or hypothetical (putative or fictional). Examples are powerful means to clarify, explain, or dramatize ideas. They are useful in almost any type of presentation. We'll explore even more types and their uses in later chapters.

Literary Devices

This includes a wide range, such as metaphor (figurative analogy), hyperbole (literary exaggeration), understatement (literary "low key"), satire (lampooning or caricature), paradox (that which goes against common opinion), literary description (an "evaluative" reporting using a complex of several literary techniques), slogan (catchy capsule of an idea), or quotations (using the ideas of someone else). These and others will be elaborated as we discuss various presentation targets, receivers, and impacts.

Stories and Anecdotes

Stories may be humorous (jokes), enigmatic (fables), or moralistic (parables). An anecdote is a *narrative* story—that is, a brief discursive account of an amusing or curious event or happening. Stories and anecdotes have wide appeal and application. See Specimens 15 and 13:1 as examples of use.

Audiovisuals

These include all the hardware and software (equipment and methods for use) in this complex but potentially valuable area. We'll discuss audiovisuals in depth in a separate section of the next chapter.

Demonstration

Here you show the thing or the working of the operation. Therefore, it goes beyond any of the preceding developmental means in that demonstration communicates the nonverbal, the real-world item or process. Demonstration has great impact when properly handled. It is especially valuable in technological and scientific presentations.

Receiver Participation

This means getting your listeners or readers involved in some part of the presentation. You may ask your audience to help solve the problem you are presenting; you may use a question-and-answer follow-up; you may put your listeners into "buzz groups" for further clarification or extension of the ideas you have presented. Receiver participation can be used before, during, and after almost any presentation. Uses, of course, depend on your presentation target, receivers, and intended impact. In Specimen 12, questions and receiver applications are used throughout.

In summary, some general ways to develop your ideas are: facts and statistics; comparisons and contrasts; examples; literary devices; stories and anecdotes; audiovisuals; demonstrations; and receiver participation. As we go along, we'll be looking at all in greater detail in relation to presentation targets, receivers, impacts, and methods.

INTRODUCING AND CONCLUDING PRESENTATIONS

You will note that this topic is discussed last, and for good reason. Only after you have selected your primary and secondary sequences (logical or psychological) of ideas and developed them (using whatever types are proper) will you be able to make wise judgments about starting and ending your communication. Furthermore, some of the preceding items, both sequential and developmental, are directly applicable in introductions and conclusions. Let's consider introductions first.

Introductions

What is an introduction supposed to do? It can be used to accomplish any of these goals: (1) informing receivers about the presentation subject or development; (2) convincing receivers of the importance of the situation or subject; (3) reinforcing receiver attitudes and beliefs toward you, the situation, or your subject; and (4) setting the stage for some specific action or reaction you want from your receivers before, during, or after your presentation. As you can see, it is possible that an introduction using the last (action-centered) could be built on the preceding three. It is also possible that you could use any combination of the four in several different sequences, depending on your presentation objective. The following are different kinds of *informative introductions:*

Pre-summary (Example: Specimen 19:1) is a concise listing of the main points you plan to cover; it is your presentation in outline form. Caution: keep it brief and clear.

Background information (Example: Specimen 7:6–10) is a brief setting forth of pertinent data giving rise to the presentation—the what, why, who, when, and how. Caution: don't put your audience to sleep by overdoing it.

Facts and statistics (Example: Specimen 15:2–5) refer to condensed, substantively relevant information which receivers may need to understand your presentation message. Caution: same as in "Background information."

Examples (Example: Specimen 7:1–3), including striking cases or real situations or hypothetical happenings, are often helpful in making your receivers better understand what is to follow. Caution: use only readily understood and relevant ones.

Types of convincing introductions—striking examples (Example: Specimen 2:1–3), that is, those that get attention, that have impact for receivers, often produce quick conviction. Caution: avoid "marginal" or offensive illustrations.

Quotations from respected sources (Example: Specimen 6:1–2), either documents or people, frequently make for ready receiver credence. Caution: be sure your sources are in fact respected.

Reasoned facts and statistics (Example: Specimen 16:2–8), that is, those that appear valid and reliable to your receivers, can often induce ready reception. Caution: package these carefully and concisely in an introduction.

Demonstration, if well done, is a powerful method to get immediate conviction. If bobbled, however, it can boomerang. Caution: take all steps to assure that your demonstration will work exactly as you want it to.

Audiovisuals (Example: Specimen 19:9, 20) also convince receivers for most of the reasons given for examples, quotations, facts, and demonstration. Beyond these, well-done A/Vs are potent devices for getting and holding receiver attention, as well as directing it to your message. Furthermore, receivers are frequently convinced by good A/Vs by the mere fact that, having taken the time and trouble to prepare them, you evidence your own concern and conviction. Caution: use A/Vs as means of communication, not as ends in themselves.

You can readily see that the items listed under "convincing" are also applicable under *reinforcing introductions.* In addition, these offer very useful possibilities:

Stories (Example: Specimen 15:1), especially human-interest stories, are appealing as possible presentation starts. Caution: make them succinct and pertinent to your message.

Literary devices (Example: Specimen 20:1) are very good introductory means in reinforcement. Metaphors, slogans, unique language and phraseology, literary description, and hyperbole are all possible ways to get the needed early dramatic impact. Caution: don't over-dramatize or appear affected.

Achievements and traditions (Example: Specimen 10:1–5) are good "historical" starters. These refer respectively to accomplishments made by receivers (or others whom they respect) and customs or practices to which they subscribe. Caution: avoid flattery. You should praise people, but you must appear sincere.

Great ideals and goals mean the basic values and aspirations of your receivers or others whom they admire or respect. Achievements and traditions (discussed above) refer to the past; ideals and goals refer to the present and future. References to existing receiver values or their aspirations are often excellent ways to reinforce attitudes and beliefs. Caution: avoid platitudes and clichés; couch these in refreshing language and phraseology.

If you want an *action introduction,* you could possibly use any of the devices discussed under information, conviction, or reinforcing. Here are some others:

Direct statement means starting your presentation by telling your listeners what performance you want. Caution: avoid this technique with hostile or sophisticated receivers.

Posing the problem (Example: Specimen 1:1–4) refers to a direct or indirect setting forth of the trouble or condition about which you are going to communicate. This can be used when you want to move your listeners to think actively with you as you present subsequent analysis and possible solutions to the problem. Caution: this is best used with critically oriented receivers.

Receiver participation is itself a form of action. Whether asking for a show of hands or silently "answering" your rhetorical questions or engaging in pre-presentation group activities which set the stage for your communication, receiver participation is both a means and an end to action. Caution: don't overdo this or create the impression of a children's TV show.

Creating suspense (Example: Specimen 5:1–14) is another means in action-centered introductions. Here you start your communication by making your receivers uncertain about outcomes or where you are going. In so doing they must actively listen to find out. Caution: don't create apathy or hostility by either overdoing or underdoing this technique.

Conclusions

Let's now turn to devices for ending your communication. Since conclusions can serve the same essential purposes as introductions (informing, convincing, reinforcing, or action), we shall consider them under the same headings: informative, convincing, reinforcing, or action conclusions. We begin with *informative conclusions:*

Post-summary (Example: Specimen 1:48–50) is a final capsuling of your ideas, whether by enumeration ("The first point was . . . The second point was . . .") or by succinct paraphrasing of your message. Caution: don't give the presentation all over again!

Important ideas (Example: Specimen 4:26–28) is a setting forth of only the most important idea or ideas that you want your receivers to remember, leaving out the rest. Caution: don't use with a critical-minded group, for these listeners may well ask, "Why did he communicate all the other ideas just to say this?"

Implications and inferences (Example: Specimen 6:19) can also be drawn in this type of conclusion. Here you point out where your ideas lead, what they mean, what "therefores" follow. This is especially useful for critical receivers. Caution: be sure your "therefores" are both clear and proper.

Clarifying examples (Example: Specimen 7:24–31) are also useful to bring abstract ideas down to earth or to make them more meaningful. Caution: there is a danger that the example will be remembered to the exclusion of the basic ideas it exemplifies.

The following are different types of *convincing conclusions:*

Striking examples (Example: Specimen 11:2–3) are often as applicable as in introductions. In conclusions they induce credibility by driving home, by vivifying, or by making your ideas more real. Caution: be sure that your example strikes the right chord. When either underdone or overdone, this device can make your whole presentation ineffectual.

Quotations (Example: Specimen 4:28) also can be used in ending your presentation. Testimony which restates or supports your thesis or points to some important implication is often a fruitful way to conclude with conviction. Caution: use only clearly relevant and credible quotations, otherwise you may lose everything else you have communicated.

Demonstration is, again, another device equally useful in introductions and conclusions. In conclusions, effective demonstrations can be capstones to credibility, devices to get your ideas into the nervous systems of your receivers. Caution: in addition to a possible boomerang from bobbling (mentioned under *introductions*), be careful to avoid having the demonstration the only thing that your receivers remember.

Audiovisuals (Example: Specimen 19:22) also play dual roles—that is, they are applicable to both introductions and conclusions, and for the same reasons. They are especially effective in graphically portraying important ideas or implications; they can also be used to mass auditory and visual examples of what you have said. Caution: as in *demonstration,* unless carefully controlled, there is a danger that a conclusion of this type may obliterate all else you've said.

All of the devices discussed under *reinforcing introductions* apply equally to *reinforcing conclusions.* Therefore, if you need a reminder, go back to that section. Here are three additional ones:

Dramatic details (Example: Specimen 13:25) refer to a climactic ordering of ideas, examples, or other data—a "piling up" effect—with the purpose of overpowering the listener or creating sufficient psychological momentum to carry him where you want to. Caution: avoid theatrics; sincerity is very important here.

Visionary outcomes (Example: Specimen 10:45–47) are those which predict what can be (for example, creating a community free from crime; or a doubling of employee salaries within the next ten years, if production output is increased 25 percent). "Visionary" here does not mean "utopian" or unrealistic; rather, it refers to practical, foreseeable outcomes, ideas that can become reality. Caution: avoid appearing to exaggerate; this will only increase the audience's incredulity.

"We shall overcome" is the conclusion in which you point the way for your receivers to surmount severe adversities or conditions. It is especially appropriate in times of distress or agony, in situations where your group members need reinforcement in order to rise above their immediate anguish and look with hope to the future. Caution: use only in situations similar to the above.

As for *action conclusions,* you may with slight modifications use those devices listed under the parallel section in "Introductions." Additional types can also be employed.

Challenge is constructively throwing down the gauntlet or daring your receivers to do what is needed. A challenge may be either subtle or direct. Caution: design the presentation so that receivers are ready to accept your challenge.

Plan for action (Example: Specimen 19:12–23) spells out the who, what, when, and how something is to be done. It is especially applicable for operationalizing concepts or for introducing new policies, procedures, or programs. Caution: give highlights in oral form; give details in writing.

Appeal for help is (1) asking your receivers to aid in solving some common difficulty or problem; (2) seeking their suggestions for improvements; or (3) trying to get their cooperation and support in carrying out an existing or a new program. Caution: this is best done by emphasizing where and how your receivers will benefit by helping.

Figure 3-1. Summary of introductions.

Objectives	Devices	Cautions
(1) Informing	Pre-summary	Be brief and clear
	Background information	Avoid audience apathy
	Facts and statistics	Avoid audience apathy
	Examples	Use understandable and relevant ones
(2) Convincing	Striking examples	Avoid possibly offensive ones
	Quotations from respected sources	Be sure of receiver respect
	Reasoned facts and statistics	Package carefully and concisely
	Demonstration	Be sure it will work right
	Audiovisuals	Use as means, not ends
(3) Reinforcing	Stories	Make succinct and relevant
	Literary devices	Avoid overdramatics and affectation
	Achievements and traditions	Avoid appearance of flattery
	Great ideals and goals	Avoid platitudes and clichés
(4) Action	Direct statement	Do not use with hostile or sophisticated receivers
	Posing the problem	Best used with critical receivers
	Receiver participation	Avoid overdoing or "Mickey Mouse"
	Creating suspense	Avoid creating apathy or hostility

Summary: Introductions and Conclusions

We have considered four ends which can be met in both introductions and conclusions: (1) to inform; (2) to convince; (3) to reinforce; and (4) to get action. We have listed important devices which can be used to achieve each of these objectives. In capsule form, these are shown in the Figures 3-1 and 3-2.

SUMMARY: PUTTING IDEAS TOGETHER

The quality of the organization and the development of your ideas is directly related to your presentation's success. We have studied how ideas are put together by examining (1) the structure for receivers; (2) logical sequences; (3) psychological sequences; (4) developing ideas; and (5) introductions and conclusions. These steps can be shown graphically, as in Figure 3-3 (on page 52).

Figure 3-2. Summary of conclusions.

Objectives	Devices	Cautions
(1) Informing	Post-summary	Make it brief and to the point
	Important ideas	Avoid with critical receivers
	Implications and inferences	Make conclusions clear and proper
	Clarifying examples	Emphasize relation to basic ideas
(2) Convincing	Striking examples	Avoid overdoing or underdoing
	Quotations	Use relevant and credible ones
	Demonstration	Be sure it works; emphasize relation to ideas
	Audiovisuals	Avoid obliterating or deemphasizing ideas
(3) Reinforcing	All devices listed in "Introductions" Plus	Same as in "Introductions"
	Dramatic details	Avoid theatrics; be sincere
	Visionary outcomes	Avoid exaggeration
	"We shall overcome"	Use only in adverse or distressing conditions
(4) Action	All devices listed in "Introductions" Plus	Same as in "Introductions"
	Challenge	Be sure of receiver readiness
	Plan for action	Give highlights orally; give details in writing
	Appeal for help	Emphasize receiver benefits

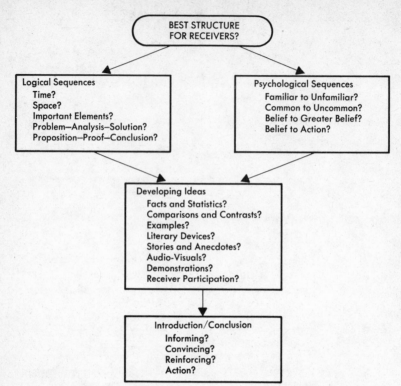

Figure 3-3.   Steps in organizing and developing ideas.

4

Using Communication Media

We've gone over knowing when to communicate (Chapter 2) and basic principles for putting ideas together (Chapter 3). We're now ready to get into the last of the background chapters: using the important types of communication media.

There are three general media: (1) auditory/visual; (2) written; and (3) human. Each has its advantages and uses in supplementing purposive presentations.

AUDITORY/VISUAL MEDIA

What A/Vs Are

We shall use auditory/visual (A/V) to mean the hardware (equipment and materials) and software (methods and techniques) of *extra-human* communication. For example, a transparency projector (equipment) and the transparency slide (material) are hardware; however, using the slide to show a pre-summary of your presentation (method and technique) is software. "Extra-human" refers, of course, to something *beyond* the organism. Therefore, we are talking about most communication media other than people. (As you recall, human media will be discussed in a separate section of this chapter.)

There is one exception: written media (printed handouts, letters, supporting documents), while certainly "visual," are not included here. Because of their unique role, these will also be treated separately in the following section. With this understanding, let's now turn to examining when and how to use A/Vs.

53

When to Use A/Vs

A/Vs should be used when you need to *supplement* your oral (and sometimes written) presentation. This means that A/Vs *support* your communication, but never replace you as the prime means. Up to this point, you have used your judgment as to whether there should be a presentation, and in what form; you have further decided what organization and idea development you need. And now you must determine the *whether* and *what* about A/Vs. This "obvious" truth has been stated as a reminder that you are the *primary* communication medium and that A/Vs are at best important supplementary media.

But properly used, they can be extremely valuable, which means that you should carefully assess when A/Vs should be employed. Let's now examine some conditions which may call for your using them:

1. *When the situation is sufficiently important.* What is meant is that your presentation must be significant enough to warrant your taking the time and trouble, as well as spending the resources (money, men, materials), to prepare and use A/Vs. If you are confronted with a "survival" situation or vital mission, you may decide that you cannot afford to be without them.

2. *When communication control is crucial.* A/Vs are potentially powerful means to influence receivers. When built into a well-designed and professionally executed presentation, these exert an enormous advantageous impact. They may give you just the needed increment to assure communication control.

3. *When professional appearance is important.* The preparation and use of well-done A/Vs can create a professional aura for you and your ideas. This often breeds the respect needed for ready reception by some groups, notably scientific, technical, and critically oriented people.

4. *When time is limited.* What is meant is that when it is vital to get your message across in a minimum period, A/Vs can be very helpful. They permit you to package and marshal your materials so that you can present your ideas with deliberate dispatch, and, at the same time, they help to assure complete coverage so that nothing is left out.

5. *When you want constructive confidence and self-control.* Well-prepared A/Vs can be excellent communication guides to you. In fact, they can be profitably used as a graphic outline in the presentation. Sometimes communicators use visuals as their only "notes"; in

other cases, they may be used in conjunction with other devices. You can see that this kind of guidance can really boost your confidence and self-control.

6. *When distance and time must be bridged.* In situations where receivers are in differing locations, and in cases where you need to make a series of the same (or essentially similar) presentations, A/Vs afford one of your best means to "bind" space and time. For example, electronic hookups can be arranged for people to confer; picture-phone connections permit auditory and visual interaction; and video-tape presentations may be shown anywhere.

7. *When presentation standardization is required.* In cases where the same message must be conveyed to groups in different places or over an extended period, these assure that each presentation will be predictably similar. This condition alone may warrant heavy initial investments in A/Vs for important programmed communications within large firms.

8. *When economics dictate.* Some situations call for A/Vs because solely human media are too costly (when you need to use several very busy—and expensive—professionals to present different facets of the subject, videotaping permits you to bring them to your groups economically). On the other hand, when you cannot risk losing important benefits or payoffs (getting a contract worth $1,000,000 or blocking a vote by employees to unionize, which, if carried, would cost the company $500,000 a year), seemingly expensive A/Vs may in fact be a very cheap investment.

9. *When you need to overcome receiver apathy.* When your listeners are indifferent or are likely to become so, well-done A/Vs can elicit their attention and sustain their interest. However, be warned that when poorly prepared, poorly executed, or irrelevant, these can backfire into even greater audience apathy, if not hostility.

10. *When clarity and emphasis are required.* As support for otherwise well-planned and -presented ideas, A/Vs can further clarify and emphasize your points. The combination of oral and visual stimuli generally make more impact than either does separately.

11. *When receiver conviction is required.* Merely informing your listeners or readers may not be enough; you may need to change their beliefs from either neutral or opposed to favorable. A/Vs, effectively employed, can often lend credence to you, your ideas, and the

situation. Among other reasons, receivers are generally impressed by the very fact that you show enough concern and competence to take the time and trouble to prepare and use them in your presentation.

12. *When dramatic impact is needed.* A/Vs can breathe life into ideas and make them more real and meaningful. A sound film can put across apparently unrelated ideas in ways that no solely personal communication can; a slide projection of a microscopic section of a cell communicates as can no merely verbal description; a videotape playback of a poorly handled conference can tell conferees far more effectively than an oral or written critique what went wrong and why.

13. *When right actions are necessary.* This condition applies to many situations, but especially to instructional or expository communication. For example, if process operators must learn some new procedure (instruction), a well-conceived and well-carried-out videotape presentation may be used to show exactly what must be done and why. The operators could then be taped in roleplaying situations, after which playbacks and verbal critiques could be used to reteach where errors were noted. Or if a new policy has been written up (exposition), a sound slide may be used to highlight important changes and what new responses are required, followed by a question-and-answer session to further clarify, succeeded by a reshowing of the sound slide to reinforce receiver understandings.

14. *When multiple stimulation is needed.* We have already referred to the frequent need for combined oral and visual stimuli. So, in a sense, this condition is a restatement. But the point is important enough to elaborate on it. Undoubtedly communication is enhanced, and therefore success made more sure, when several media (A/V, oral, written) are judiciously unified in a presentation. Of course, you must exercise concern and competence in combining them, and you must also be sure that your cost-benefit ratio is optimum. Therefore, multiple stimuli should be brought to bear when the presentation is important enough, when you want to assure success, or when potential benefits outweigh costs. A prudent use of A/Vs can be very helpful to this end.

Figure 4-1 gives a good summary of when to use A/Vs.

HOW TO USE AUDIOVISUALS: GENERAL PRINCIPLES

The seven general principles of audiovisualization given here are essentially judgmental guidelines. You may not be able to meet all of

Figure 4-1. When to use audiovisuals.

Condition	Remarks
(1) Sufficiently important situation	May be needed to assure success
(2) Communication control crucial	May give needed "push"
(3) Professional appearance vital	Generates respect, especially from scientific, technical, and critical receivers
(4) Limited time	Permit efficient and effective coverage
(5) Presenter confidence and self-control needed	Helpful as outline to both presenter and receiver
(6) Bridging distance and time	Permit vicarious representation; better economies
(7) Standardization required	Assure similar presentations; better economies
(8) Economic dictates	Permit substitution for human media; help assure success in high-payoff cases
(9) Receiver apathy exists	Get attention and sustain interest
(10) Clarity and emphasis required	Combined oral/visual create greater impact
(11) Receiver conviction needed	Can create credence for presenter, ideas, or situation
(12) Dramatic impact needed	Can make ideas vital, real, meaningful
(13) Right actions necessary	Especially applicable to instruction or exposition
(14) Multiple stimuli needed	Use when presentation is sufficiently important, success is necessary, or benefits outweigh costs

them satisfactorily in a given presentation. But you should have determined priorities so that you can decide which are most important. Your A/Vs should then be planned and used accordingly.

Principle 1: *A/Vs must be audible and/or visible to all receivers.* Although "obvious," this is one of the most commonly violated principles. If a listener cannot hear or a viewer cannot see what is being communicated, then the A/V is not only futile, it may actually increase the chances for the failure of the presentation.

Principle 2: *A/Vs must be feasible respecting hardware, software, and utility.* That is, equipment must be feasible relative to cost and potential effectiveness. Methods must be feasible relative to your and your receivers' sophistication, as well as to the level demanded by the equipment. Utilization must be feasible for the situation at hand. For example, its lack of mobility disallows the use of a large computer for visual demonstration to an audience of 500 in an auditorium. For a group of up to 25, however, it may be feasible to use the computer room as the presentation arena.

Principle 3: *A/Vs should reflect optimal simplicity.* Stated another way, this means that you should avoid unnecessary complexity or "overdoing," whether with machinery, techniques, or messages. Why use all the "jazzy" (and costly) visual equipment when a blackboard will do just as well? Why employ all the possible gimmicky devices when straightforward oral exposition is all that is needed? Why confuse your receivers with nonessential ideas? Generally, the more simple the audiovisualization, the better.

Principle 4: *A/Vs should be immediately intelligible.* Frequently good auditory and visual aids speak for themselves. In any event, their point or points should be explicable with minimal additional verbiage. A chart which does not readily and clearly convey its essential point or points is not a good visual. A tape recording of a rambling and incoherent presentation will probably communicate only rambling and incoherent noises, not the intended ideas. A "piling on" of incidental ideas or details will produce psychological obliteration rather than useful perception and retention by receivers.

Principle 5: *A/Vs must be proper in form, style, and consistency.* Here we are talking about the conscious and subconscious impacts on receivers resulting from (1) the type of hardware and software; and (2) the overall compatibility or coherence of equipment and methods to do the job intended. If you use overly exotic equipment to carry out a simple presentation, you are likely to call attention to the hardware, not to your ideas. If you want to set a conversational atmosphere, "canned" or "slick" audiovisuals will probably defeat this purpose. If you jump abruptly back and forth from one type of equipment (say, a blackboard) to another (say, a transparency projector), you will create an appearance of inconsistency and disorder in the receiver's eye.

Principle 6: *A/Vs must be supplemental to and synchronized with your ideas.* We have already discussed A/Vs as supporting (or supplemental) means. And certainly they must also be properly timed and paced to your presentation of ideas. A visual left on the screen after you have finished talking about it will continue to attract receivers' attention, diverting their focus away from you and what you subsequently say. Too fast or too slow pacing of audiovisual exhibition will likely create receiver hostility or apathy, or, in any event, confusion.

Principle 7: *A/Vs must work in the presentation.* This is another "obvious" principle, but it is another one that is violated very frequently. Even though you may have measured up on the preceding six guidelines, if this one is not met, all else is futile. You must do everything humanly possible to be sure that your machinery will work (including, for example, making sure that you have an electrical outlet or an extension cord!), that people will be able to see and hear with ease (including testing the mike and checking reception from the most distant part of the room before the presentation), and that your aids are in proper sequence and are easily handled (including placing them in some convenient spot and putting them in final order before the presentation).

Unfortunately, even with the most careful planning and checking, your equipment may fail or your anticipated methods may not do the job. The answer? Prepare for contingencies; have some useful backup means, if only some always workable "software," such as good cases, stories, and relevant jokes!

The seven basic principles of using audiovisuals are summarized here. A/Vs must be:

1. Audible and visible.
2. Feasible.
3. Optimally simple.
4. Immediately intelligible.
5. Proper in form, style, consistency.
6. Supplemental to and synchronized with ideas.
7. Workable in presentation.

TYPES OF EQUIPMENT: METHODS AND APPLICATIONS

We'll skip all the how-to-do-it detailed step-by-step handling of audiovisual machinery—there are many excellent volumes and brochures spelling these out. And there is a constant stream of new equipment from manufacturers, along with specific techniques for operation, so that any presentation dealing with brand names, models, or specific types is quickly outdated. Here we shall be concerned wtih the more general types of equipment, methods, and applications. Let's now turn to these, discussing also how they are used and for what presentation situations. We'll start with relatively simple and easy types and from there move to the more complex and technical.

Blackboard

Whether stationary or mobile, a blackboard is a versatile visual device. And because of its ubiquity, you will generally have access to one. Following a few simple suggestions can make the blackboard an effective communication medium.

1. Stand to the side of (rather than in front of) what you are writing. This allows people to see your ideas—not just you. Furthermore, this permits you to keep eye contact with your listeners rather than giving a monolog to the board.

2. Make heavy lines and, for more complex schematics, use contrasting chalk colors and symbols. Again your audience can more easily and readily get your ideas.

3. Put ideas into an orderly pattern. Indiscriminate scribbling and scratching all over the board may be very clear to you, but not to your listeners.

4. Thoroughly know how best to present your basic ideas. That is, if you judge enumerated captions or simple paradigms or even stick-figure schematics to be your best approach, prepare accordingly, even to the extent of putting them on notes so that you can reproduce them quickly and accurately on the board. Nothing ruins a blackboard presentation quicker than slovenliness and disorder.

5. Erase ideas when you have finished your discussion of them. (An exception is when you are merely writing a topical outline of your presentation.) This synchronizes the receivers' attention with each idea.

When is the blackboard to be used? It is a good medium for (1) spontaneous or developmental presentations—that is, where you want ideas to evolve on the spot; (2) audience-participation presentations, that is, where you want any interchange with listeners before, during, or after the presentation; (3) informal exposition, that is, where you want to create a climate of openness and warmth, avoiding the appearance of a "canned" presentation; and (4) presentational economy, that is, where you want the probably least costly (in dollars) of all media. While not necessarily inexpensive in psychological costs, the blackboard is economical monetarily.

Manual and Flip Charts

These, too, are widely used. "Manual" here refers to unmounted charts (handled by the presenter); "flip" charts are mounted, either on a table-size easel (which frequently sits on the lectern) or a standard easel (which stands by itself). The table easel is often about the size of a loose-leaf binder, and is useful for very small group presentations; the standard easel (considerably larger) can be used with groups of up to 50.

Here are some suggestions for effective preparation and use of charts.

1. Make the charts easily and clearly visible. This goes back to one of our general principles. Specifically, use heavy (rather than fine) lines; use appropriate contrasting colors and symbols. And make the chart large enough for *all* receivers to see.

2. Simplify as much as possible (another basic principle). In charts, leave out every unnecessary detail; include only the essential.

3. Each chart should clearly communicate one central idea. Put other ideas on separate charts; then, if needed, use one (or more) to summarize.

4. Keep audience contact. Talk to your listeners, not the chart. If you stand to the side of a mounted chart and use a pointer, this is easily done. With unmounted charts, hold each one in the center of your body and point to ideas from above. If you thoroughly know your message, this is also easy.

5. Synchronize chart display with ideas. If you have prepared well and placed your charts in a ready location, it is just a matter of exhibiting each as needed. Show the chart neither prematurely nor after you have finished with an idea. Keep it under cover, remove it from sight, or eradicate it as appropriate.

What are appropriate uses of manual and flip charts? Charts can be either prepared or developmental. In the latter case, they have all the utility of a blackboard. They are even better in potential handiness and neatness.

Prepared charts have most advantages of the blackboard, as well as these:

1. The professional appearance of well-designed and well-manipulated charts creates respect for you and gives added impact to your presentation. (A suggestion: professional help in preparing these is often a good investment; most of us have neither the time nor the aptitude to create effective charts.)

2. The flexibility of handling is another advantage. You can shift the order, go back or ahead, emphasize or reemphasize as needed.

3. Your presentation control can be enhanced. Well-prepared charts give you direct guidance in communicating ideas. They help assure audience attention and retention.

Magnetic and Flannel Boards

Magnetic boards are thin metallic visuals with magnets on the back. As you present an idea, you place the magnetized visual on the board. Flannel boards are used in the same way; the board, however, is covered with flannel (or substitute), and the visual is backed with an adhesive.

Since suggestions and uses are essentially the same as those given for blackboards and charts, we'll not repeat them. Applications are also similar, with this exception: magnetic and flannel boards often give the appearance of a "canned" presentation. Furthermore, costs are considerably higher than for either of the preceding media. However, when well-prepared and well-handled, both magnetic and flannel boards can be very effective to give a series of the same presentation.

Opaque Projectors

Opaque projectors project from original materials (pages of a book, a drawing, and so forth)—they show form, but not color. Because preparation and cost are minimal, they can be used when these suggestions are remembered.

1. Make sure the materials can be feasibly projected. Some books, some paper, and some plastics are either very awkward or unusable (for example, too-thick books or too-flimsy pages). Check these out before you decide on this medium.

2. Make sure that sharpness and resolution are sufficient to get your intended impact. If these are of sufficient quality, this medium is OK; if not, you should consider an alternative means, perhaps a transparency.

3. Make sure the projector does not block audience view and hearing. You may find that in order to get sharp focus, you must place the machine so that some listeners cannot see. Furthermore, some machines are quite noisy (from heat-reducing fans), disrupting audibility. In either case, you should consider another medium.

4. Make sure the projector offers sufficient ease of use. In using opaque projectors, it is often difficult, time-consuming, and frustrating to put in and take out certain kinds of materials; furthermore, the

placement and keeping track of several books, pamphlets, and pages can produce unforeseen problems. Again, check this out before making your decision.

When is it profitable to use the opaque projector? (1) When you have limited time to prepare aids; (2) When you have limited access to materials (one of a kind, the only copy, no permission to reproduce); (3) When sharpness and color are not important to communicate the idea.

Transparency Projectors

These are clear acetate sheets ("slides"), either framed or unframed. In contrast with opaque projectors, they show color. Furthermore, sharpness and vividness are much better, along with far more flexibility in handling. Equipment is portable, easy to use, and inexpensive to maintain.

When using transparency projectors, these suggestions are helpful:

1. Make lettering and drawings clearly visible (back to one of our original principles). Although standard typewritten materials can be used to make transparencies, a special large type is available which makes much more perceivable copy. If you hand letter or draw, be sure that your product can be easily seen by your prospective group.

2. Use contrasting colors and symbols. Special pens are available for coloring, and templates can be procured for symbolizing. Check with your visual aid representative or supply house.

3. Make sure (as with opaque projectors) that projection machinery will not block audience view, that slides give sharp focus, and that projector and slides can be readily and easily used.

4. Make sure that benefits outweigh costs. This is especially applicable in considering preparation of numerous, detailed slides. Costs of equipment and raw materials may be nominal, but expenditures for professionally prepared visuals can be high. But in many instances, results can also be very fruitful.

When is it proper to use transparency projectors? They are especially applicable in: (1) Training or instructional courses, when they offer a preset, but at the same time very flexible, teaching approach. (2) A series of similar (but not exactly the same) presentations. Transparencies permit message persistence, while allowing for needed changes to meet different conditions. (3) Developmental or spontaneous presentations. In this sense they offer all the advantages of blackboards or flip charts, but, since you face your group, they permit better audience control than either.

Slide Projectors

These show the regular 2″ × 2″ slide. The less expensive models are quite simple and are manually operated. However, better projectors have trays (holding up to 100 slides), as well as automatic interval timers (5 or 8 or 15 seconds). Push-button controls allowing several remote operations (sequential slide changing, forwarding-reversing, focusing, and random access) are also features of the best equipment. In addition to the traditional "silent" type, sound slide projectors (with a subsonic "beep") can also be obtained. These, however, are not as flexible as silent projectors. Whichever type you select, suggestions for use are as follows:

1. Use expertly prepared slides for best results. Here you are moving into the world of professional presentations. Make yours harmonize with that universe.

2. Use for essential, continuing presentations where appearance and standardization are important and where you can afford a sizable initial investment.

3. Use in conjunction with a well-prepared (and probably well-referenced) manuscript or topical outline. Although slides may be topical, many will be graphic. Therefore your accompanying verbal presentation must be just as professional as the slides you show.

Where are slide projectors most useful? (1) Where mobility is needed. The silent projector is relatively small and light, and is therefore easily carried from place to place. This gives it wide utility, especially for "traveling circuses." (2) Where room size is limited. The projector's smallness makes it easy for people to get an unobstructed view from almost any angle. (3) Where simplicity of use and quality of product are demanded. It is easy for almost anyone to learn to use a slide projector, and in so doing you go a long way to guaranteeing a good presentation—provided, of course, the verbal ideas and the slides are well designed.

Moving Picture Projectors

These are both "sound and sight" media most commonly showing 16 mm film. They are so familiar that we won't spend any more time on them. The more important question is, "When should movies be used?"

1. When there are continuing, very important messages to be communicated. But be warned that costs of film production, purchase, or rental make imperative a critical examination of this first item.

2. When the impact of combined sound and sight are required. There is no question about the dynamism of a good sound film—it can get and hold attention, dramatize ideas, and appeal to people as few media can.

Tape Recorders

Familiar, conventional sound recorders (which vary widely in cost and complexity) can be used for taping selected audible portions of talks, which can then be played back. Here are some tips for use.

1. Use a recorder with acceptable fidelity. "Acceptable" is of course relative, but certainly quality of tone, volume, and discrimination are important. Some cheaper recorders may pick up all the "noises" made, but their playback may be totally useless for your purposes.

2. Use a recorder with sufficient portability. Again this is relative. If your company has an audiovisual room or studio, then heavy, stationary equipment will be satisfactory. But if (as is often the case) you must move equipment from room to room or from plant to plant, you should have a recorder which can be easily carried and set up.

3. Check your equipment carefully before recording. This most obvious tip is the one most frequently causing grief. If a mike is not working or is not properly connected, the "recording" won't take place. Or if speakers are too far away from the mike or use it wrongly, either a garbled message or no pickup will result. Or if a tape is not completely erased before recording again, results are equally disastrous.

4. Place equipment in the most unobtrusive locations. Recorders can be distracting to both speakers and listeners. Some speakers dislike, even fear, them; and listeners' attention can be diverted from the speaker by machinery that is too conspicuous. Locate recorders where they can be used without being unduly noted.

When can tape recorders be useful? (1) They can be especially valuable in the preparation of your presentation. You can record, listen, refine, and re-record until you have the product you want. (2) They are excellent also for "postmortems" on the actual talk. You can listen to the recording (including stopping or going back as needed), make notes for improvement, and, if desirable, record and review your "new" speech. (3) Tape recorders can also give excellent feedback to other company people, from their group or from face-to-face oral communications. (4) They also have utility in your presentation itself. For example, if you wish to quote what the boss said in the latest department meeting, the tape recorder can speak very effectively. Or if you wish to communicate how poorly incoming telephone calls are being handled, representative conversations can be picked up and played back to your listeners. This could be followed by recorded roleplaying for correction of errors and then played back for further audience analysis.

Videotape Equipment

Recently videotape machines have become widely used by business, government, and professional organizations. In one sense, they are a "poor man's" movies or television. Combining sight and sound, these are applicable in a broad variety of circumstances, especially in preparing presentations and training company communicators.

But "poor man" is another relative term. Complete videotape equipment costs range from about $2,500 to over $10,000, and prices are generally proportional to the quality of resolution. Therefore, you should examine your own needs and get equipment to meet them optimally. Any reputable A/V dealer will give you all the information you want, and most will permit your company to try out the equipment before purchase. Some will also lease or offer lease/purchase options.

Rather than get into all the technical details of operation (which the manufacturer or dealer will supply in abundance), let's look at the more important uses of videotape equipment.

1. Training company communicators is one of the most valuable applications. The qualities of immediate playback, as well as being able to reverse or go forward as necessary, make this a versatile and powerful medium for speakers to see themselves in action, to identify needs for improvement, and to make corrections.

2. Use for rehearsing individual presentations is also very worthwhile. In this, videotape has all the flexibility of a sound recorder, as

well as all the dynamic impact of the communicator's seeing and hearing himself in action.

3. Continuing, standardized presentations can be given by means of videotape. Training courses, sales presentations, and orientation lectures are just a few of the many possible examples.

4. Supplementing your presentation is another videotape application. Among many other features, you can use it to give audiovisual demonstrations, show closeups, and present montages. Indeed, it has most of the advantages of sound movies, along with frequently lower costs.

Learning how to operate the less expensive videotape equipment is fairly easy: nonprofessional people can master most details quickly. However, the more sophisticated and expensive models generally require professionals. Again differences in resolution between the "nonprofessional" and "professional" types are pronounced. You should determine the quality you need and act accordingly.

Electronic Equipment

Although most of the foregoing are technically "electronic," here we'll briefly look at uses for a miscellany, including microphones, telephones, radios, television, and display consoles.

Microphones are, of course, amplifying media for oral presentations. Unless you have a voice which carries far, you will probably need a mike for addressing a group of more than 40 people in an average-size room. To really know, it is wise to actually test the room (from the most distant part) before speaking. Have someone listen to you speaking in your normal voice; if you can't be easily heard, get a microphone.

And if you need one, be sure to check the mike for proper volume, placement, and workability before the speech. Mike trouble can be very bothersome for both listeners and yourself.

Telephones have some limited applications in oral presentations. Sometimes national or regional hookups are arranged so that a prominent person can address a group. The more recent picture-phone brings together sight and sound, making it a miniature "television" presentation. Also, telephone conferences can be conducted either between people or for a gathering. When properly carried out, both telephone presentations and conferences can be most effective in communicating ideas.

Radios are also effective media in particular cases. "In-plant" communications are sometimes conducted by radio (for example, if the president addresses employees at work on some notable occasion or about some important happening; or if important announcements are made to company people).

Commercial or educational radio stations also sometimes ask managers or professionals to give talks or to be interviewed. In this instance, all principles of purposive presentations apply.

Television presentations can be made through closed-circuit (generally "in-house"), commercial, or educational stations. Television's applications and uses are the same as those for radio, both of which are very effective in maximizing presentational exposure to mass groups.

Display consoles include CRT terminals, transcribers, and other media for electronically sending and receiving written and graphic communications. In large organizations, consoles are often located at key positions so that important people and departments can quickly communicate with one another (as used in management information centers). Uses for purposive presentations are largely as visual support (for example, showing a group the latest production figures by using a report transmitted from the manufacturing department).

Figure 4-2 summarizes the uses of the various kinds of audiovisual equipment and gives you a ready reference in evaluating them.

WRITTEN MEDIA TYPES*

In purposive presentations, written media may be viewed as "printed hardware." Bear in mind that although we are emphasizing oral communication, writing also plays an important role in many managerial and professional presentations. For example, papers are read aloud word for word to peers at professional conventions. In this case, the written is primary, and the oral merely verbal reinforcement. Or in order to help employees remember accurately what he said at the weekly staff meeting, the boss may send a written summary follow-up.

*For a thorough treatment of organizational written media, see George T. Vardaman and Patricia B. Vardaman, *Communication in Modern Organizations*. New York: John Wiley & Sons, 1973.

Figure 4-2. Types and applications of audiovisual equipment.

Equipment	When Applicable
Blackboard	Developmental, spontaneous presentations
	Audience participation
	Informal exposition
	If presentational economies are vital
Flip charts	Same as blackboard
	If professional appearance is important
	If flexibility of handling is needed
	If presentation control is important
Magnetic/flannel boards	Same as blackboard
	Series of same presentations
Opaque projectors	If preparation time is limited
	If access to materials is limited
	If sharpness or color is not vital
Slide projectors	If mobility is needed
	Limited room size
	If simplicity and quality art required
Motion picture projectors	Continuing, important presentations
	Combined sight/sound impact needed
	Supplement to presentation ideas
	If vicarious demonstration is important
Tape recorders	Preparation of presentation
	"Postmortems" of presentations
	Informational feedback to other people
	Demonstration/testimony in presentation
Videotape equipment	Training organization's communicators
	Preparation or rehearsing of important presentations
	Making continuing, standardized presentations
	Supplementing oral presentations
Electronic equipment	
Microphones	If amplification is needed
Telephones	Telephone presentations
	Telephone conferences
Radios	In-plant communications
	Announcements
	Station talks/interviews
Television	Same as radio
Display consoles	Rapid interdepartmental communication
	Visual support

What are common organizational written media? Let's highlight some of the more important ones, together with their gainful purposes in presentations.

Letters and Memorandums

Letters and memorandums are useful to (1) arrange for a presentation (notifying of time, place, agenda); (2) follow up on the presentation (summary, "for the record" communication, request for action, notification of further presentations); (3) use as testimonial communication (specimen letters of complaint, examples of poor company letters to customers); and (4) vitalize the oral presentation (communicating importance, pointing out potential benefits).

Reports

Reports can be used (1) to document or support ideas in the oral presentation; (2) to focus discussion on some specific aspect (such as sales decreases or production discrepancies); (3) to act as an outline or guide for the oral presentation (discussing a production report item by item, or pointing out where improvements are needed in accuracy and validity of certain data reported); (4) to present important conclusions from meetings, conferences, or exploratory communications; and (5) as the essential presentation itself, whether extemporized or read aloud verbatim.

Directives

As guides for action, these can be used to (1) authenticate oral presentation on policy or procedural interpretation (such as to clarify what an existing policy means and why or to sanction a new procedure); (2) help introduce a policy or procedural change (for example, a different basis for hiring minority applicants or a new way to process paperwork); (3) help reinforce interpretations and actions called for (such as to remind people of a policy's existence or to renew understandings of how things are to be done); and (4) be the central focus for a presentation (where item-by-item oral analysis and interpretation of the directive is needed).

Proposals

These put forth ideas for consideration, generally for the purpose of decision or action (for example, plans for redesign of the company's production plant or a bid for the sale of some product or service). They are frequently employed (1) as the essential basis of the presentation (for example, aerospace engineers spelling out the what, when, where, and how of a bid to representatives of the Department of Defense); (2) as a result of prior oral presentation or discussion (such as when the boss asks certain individuals to come up with a plan to overcome departmental difficulties discussed in a staff meeting); (3) as the definitive spelling out of more general orally presented ideas (for example, oral highlighting of the company's proposed departmental shifts, followed by a detailed step-by-step written scheme).

Agreements and Commitments

Agreements are written "dialogs" between two or more parties—that is, they are bi- or multilateral. Commitments, on the other hand, are essentially unilateral. Agreements may be intracompany (such as write-ups of different departmental responsibilities in carrying out a cost-cutting program) or intercompany (such as understandings between the company and various suppliers about delivery schedules and payment procedures).

Commitments "bind" the originator to the service or use of the receiver (such as a contract to build a facility at a given price, within a certain time, following explicit specifications).

Both agreements and commitments tend to technical rigor, specificity, and detail, all necessary so that all parties know exactly to what they agree or are committed.

Where are written agreements and commitments useful in presentations? (1) As bases for clarification and interpretation (for example, of the exact meaning of contractual details); (2) as supporting documents in more broadly based presentations; (3) as written follow-ups to prior oral agreements or commitments.

Manuals

These are "directives" or guides to actions for specific groups (such as machine operators, clerical workers, or first-line supervisors). Generally they are published in loose or bound form for continuing guidance. Manuals are often the most important job-related documents in an organization. As such, they can be used in presentations to: (1) renew understandings of small or large segments of task-oriented information; (2) introduce new ways of doing things; (3) get feedback on operators' understandings of existing instructions; and (4) get suggestions for improvements in methods and procedures.

Forms

Many and varied, these provide the organization's basic means of shaping its routine information efficiently and effectively. Forms permit users to give or get informational responses in light of explicit instructions and formats. They are, therefore, key written communication media.

How can forms be helpful in presentations? (1) As bases for clarification, interpretation, and completion (what each segment calls for and how it is to be filled out); (2) as specimens of discrepancies (for example, incomplete sales data as a result of incorrect forms reporting or the sales problems indicated by information received on periodic forms); (3) as means to point up the importance of certain information (the kinds of decisions or actions taken off data supplied by key forms); (4) as means for analysis and interpretation of information (for example, getting listener evaluations of reported data); and (5) as bases for needed actions (correcting the job discrepancies indicated from forms data).

House Organs

Including "in-house" communications such as informal company newsletters, periodic newspapers, and "slick" magazines, these are often used as basic presentational media. In fact, management often employs the house organ as its principal means of communication with employees.

How can they be used to supplement a purposive oral presentation? (1) As announcements for meetings, conferences, and the like; (2) as means for communicating the importance of forthcoming presentations; (3) as ways to solicit ideas, suggestions, gripes, and so on, which could lead to needed presentations; (4) as testimonials in presentations (such as quoting the president's remarks on the importance of community activities or a "letter to the editor" from an employee complaining about working conditions); and (5) as follow-ups to presentations (reinforcement of key ideas, requests for specific related actions or decisions).

Brochures

These are formal written "packages" for specific receiver groups (such as stockholders, customers, or employees). Be they annual reports, write-ups of some new product, or booklets on the company's retirement plan, they carry specific messages to selected target readers.

How can brochures be effectively employed as supplements in oral presentations? (1) As principal bases for the communication, whether sent before, or given out during, the presentation; (2) as "teasers" to get attention and interest, either before or during the presentation; (3) as detailed explanations of ideas highlighted in oral presentations; (4) as audience control devices during the presentation (for example, directing listeners to specific segments at intervals or using to help answer questions raised during or after the presentation); and (5) as follow-ups for the listeners or for dissemination to an even broader target group (for example, sending the president's annual address to company managers in other firms).

Professional Papers

Common in managerial, professional, and scientific circles, these are critically oriented written communications concerning important problems, theories, concepts, methodologies, and research findings. With this kind of communication medium, the written document is actually primary, the oral reading of the paper serving only to highlight or emphasize ideas. The paper is also the focus in subsequent interrogations and critiques.

Functions of the professional paper include the following: (1) They are the basic presentation for situations where serious managerial, professional, or scientific ideas are to be communicated. (2) They can be published for wider distribution (such as in professional journals). (3) They can be sent to colleagues for technical critique or review, either before or after the presentation. (4) They can be sent to a larger body of potentially interested professionals for their information (which can add to the stature of both the communicator and his company). (5) And finally, they can be "popularized" for mass distribution to nonprofessionals (in newspapers or trade journals, for instance).

Figure 4-3 summarizes the uses of the various media.

Figure 4-3. Types and uses of written media.

Written Medium	Presentation Uses
Letters/memorandums	Arrange for presentation
	Follow-up
	Testimonial communication
	Vitalize oral presentation
Reports	Documentation of oral presentation
	Focus discussion
	Outline or idea guide
	Present conclusions
	As the basic presentation
Directives	Authenticate oral presentation
	Introduce change
	Reinforce interpretations or actions
	Central focus for presentation
Proposals	Essential basis for presentation
	Result of prior oral communications
	Elaboration of more general oral presentation
Agreements/commitments	Bases for clarification or interpretation
	Supporting documents
	Follow-up to prior oral agreements or commitments
Manuals	Renew understandings
	Introduce new procedures
	Get feedback on understandings
	Get suggestions for procedural improvement
Forms	Bases for clarification, interpretation, and completion
	Specimens of discrepancies
	Emphasizing informational importance
	Analysis or interpretation of data
	Bases for needed actions
House organs	Announcements of presentations
	Communicating presentational importance
	Solicitation of useful ideas
	Testimonial communication
	Follow-up communication
Brochures	Bases for principal presentation
	Attention-getting
	Detailed explanation of general oral presentation
	Audience control
	Follow-up communication
Professional papers	As the basic presentation
	Publication for distribution
	Critique by professional colleagues
	Information to interested professionals
	Popularized for wider distribution

WRITTEN MEDIA PRESENTATION

Now that we've seen the types and presentational uses of important organizational documents, let's highlight communication principles for each. We will not go into voluminous detail here. (For example, basic grammar, diction, and written composition will not be covered; it is assumed that you know these. And if you need review, refer to some of the better books on writing.)

Our discussion is confined to the essential dimensions for achieving presentational success, things seldom considered in most books on speaking or writing. Let's now turn to our subject, taking the same documents in the same order.

Letters and Memoranda

The purposes of letters are many and varied, ranging from simple and direct to very complex and subtle. The essential emphasis, however, is *personalization*—that is, they are addressed to specific people in specific situations. Letters are generally addressed to people outside the organization, while memoranda are most often "in-house."

To obtain the desired personal impact, keep these principles in mind:

1. Know your reader (who, what, when, why).

2. Make the reader feel you are communicating *with* him (not *to* him).

3. Use the reader's language level (which is not necessarily yours).

4. Communicate in terms of the reader's understanding of the subject (whether little or much).

5. Communicate the right *company* image (not yours alone).

6. Be as formal or informal as the situation dictates (keeping in mind your purpose).

7. Use to set the stage, follow up, or support the oral presentation (as the situation dictates).

Reports

A report is written in response to some specific request, whether routine or special. Therefore, the purpose of a given report is spelled out in its requirements and attendant instructions. Like letters and memoranda, reports also originate from some identified person and are addressed to some named person or people.

To make reports communicative and helpful in your presentation, you should remember these guidelines:

1. Know exactly what the report calls for (from its instructions).

2. Be sure that you cover all the information called for (as best you can).

3. If certain information cannot be supplied, state the reasons (and when you'll supply the missing data).

4. Follow exactly the format and style called for (and if these are not explicated, create appropriate ones).

5. In oral presentations, visual devices (such as transparencies or $2'' \times 2''$ slides) can be used to supplement the conventional report (in keeping listener attention and permitting better emphasis).

Directives

As with letters and reports, directives also originate from specific people and go to specific people. As guides to operational activities, however, they have a more impersonal appearance. Clarity and explicitness are necessary for directives. To make them communicate accordingly, bear in mind these guides in using directives with presentations.

1. Know the people you are addressing (their intelligence, education, and positions).

2. Know exactly what must be said to assure the right operational outcomes (and say nothing else).

3. Authenticate the directive (that is, your aim and the company's authoritative basis for issuing).

4. Supplement as needed with other communications (both written and oral).

5. In oral presentations, written handouts (complete or extracts), together with proper A/Vs, are helpful (again, in keeping attention and permitting emphasis).

6. Send out directives before or after, or give them out during the oral presentation (as appropriate to achieve your purpose with your receivers in the given situation).

Proposals

Since these focus on getting a favorable decision or action about some idea, plan, or scheme, and since proposals are frequently the presentation proper, you should keep the following in mind:

1. Know exactly the proposal's mission (whether it is a decision or an action, and specifically what decision or action).

2. Select and include only those data to meet the mission (including both descriptive and evaluative data).

3. Build your (or other proposer's) competence and credibility to carry out the proposal's objectives.

4. Clearly and cogently state your way of implementing your plan or scheme (what, when, where, and how).

5. Address the proposal to a person or position with sanction to approve (that is, a real organizational leverage point).

6. In presentations, highlight orally; spell out details in writing.

7. Use as preparatory and summary materials (sending out prior to presentation), backup (during presentation), or follow-up (after presentation).

8. Use A/Vs to get better understanding and to help induce conviction (in other words, as multiple stimuli to receivers).

Agreements and Commitments

Essentially "contractual," they must be explicit and clear as to what is expected of all parties involved. These are guides to presentational effectiveness:

1. Set forth the exact requirements to be met (tasks, times, costs, and manpower).

2. Set forth the specific parties involved (names, positions, and organizations represented).

3. Set forth "penalties" or other means of satisfaction if any party fails in his assigned role (or if no penalties, say so).

4. Get oral agreement first, followed by detailed written documents (which should also be thoroughly discussed to assure complete understanding by all parties).

5. Use prior to, during, or after the presentation proper (depending on indicated need).

Manuals

As broad guides to action, these are addressed to as wide a reader spectrum as possible, commensurate with assuring proper job performance. (For example, in most organizations, a manual can be written for all secretaries regardless of their department or unit, and an employees' handbook can be composed for the majority of company personnel.) However, care must be taken to get proper understanding and acceptance of the document. Therefore, manual differentiation within the firm is frequently necessary (for instance, between sales manuals and machine operator manuals).

With these things in mind, here are some guides to make manuals communicative in presentations.

1. Use language and graphics which can be understood by all in the target group (secretaries, machine operators, sales personnel).

2. Use "persuasive instruction" where possible (to assure acceptance by readers).

3. Make the manual attractive in appearance, format, and style (so that it has appeal to the reader).

4. Make the manual flexible so that it can be updated (for instance, use looseleaf binding).

5. Get continuing user feedback on manual utility (so that needed improvements can be made and, through participation, users are brought to greater acceptance of manual information).

6. In oral presentations, use before, during, or after as needed (whether as the central focus or as backup).

7. Use A/Vs to reinforce ideas and help induce desired conviction and action (through multiple stimulation).

8. Always provide an opportunity for receivers to give reactions, raise questions, or seek interpretations during or after the presentation (so that optimal understanding can be gained from the interchange of ideas).

Forms

These are tightly structured and styled media for gathering, reporting, computing, and storing information. As such, they must both suit the organization's informational purpose and get user acceptance. Here are some suggestions for construction and use in presentations.

1. Make the form both complete and attractive (including needed instructions for use).

2. Know the form and address it to a specific target purpose (one that is clearly identified and feasible to achieve).

3. Optimize costs (monetary, job, and psychological) in the numbers and types of forms used (eliminating, combining, or adding as appropriate).

4. Make the form communicate clearly and cogently with users (in content, format, language, style, and ease of handling).

5. Set out clearly and cogently the processing and flow of the form (origin, intermediate handling, destination, and storage).

6. In presentations, use for clarification, analysis, backup, emphasis, or action (either singly or in combination with other means).

7. If it is the presentational focus, use A/Vs and specimens of forms to reinforce ideas and induce conviction (again, multiple stimulation).

8. In presentations (and on other occasions), solicit user feedback (to get improvement in design and handling).

House Organs

Since these are in-house, broad-spectrum written media, they should communicate effectively with almost all members of the organization. Generally mass distributed, house organs are directed to both organizational and individual receiver needs. Here are some general suggestions for communicability and presentational utility:

1. Use appropriate format and style (for the majority of receivers).

2. Make the house organ appear to serve readers' social (or individual) needs, with organizational needs secondary.

3. Use plenty of pictures, charts, condensations, and personal "tidbits" (adapting them as appropriate).

4. Make appearance optimally attractive (neither too "slick" nor too amateurish).

5. With presentations, use for announcing and follow-up (when and where, what was said, what it means, and so on).

6. Use as testimonials or backup in presentations (for example, indicating problem areas, needs to be met, and so forth).

Brochures

As carriers of information to particular target groups (both inside and outside the company), brochures should be composed and used in these ways:

1. Know the specific target group or groups for which they are intended (for instance, customers, stockholders, suppliers, community at large).

2. Know the exact message which is to be communicated (services offered, profits made or losses incurred, specifications to be met, economic impact on region).

3. Communicate to hit the target group with maximal message impact.

4. Optimize costs (combining, eliminating, or adding brochures to communicate with all major target groups).

5. In presentations, use as handouts (prior to, during, or after).

6. Use in conjunction with the presentation to reinforce, elaborate, induce conviction, or get action (planning and executing your communication accordingly).

7. Use to follow up the presentation (mailing, displaying, distributing through departmental channels).

Professional Papers

As we have seen, these carry critical-based messages about significant ideas, issues, problems, or actions in managerial, professional, and scientific circles. And, as noted, the professional paper is often the primary presentation vehicle for such occasions. It serves as a common, objective reference for analysis, review, critique, and (if needed) modification.

In addition to the basic, conventional requirements for technical validity, proper reasoning, and substantively appropriate format, you should bear in mind these suggestions in presentations of professional papers.

1. Pretest your paper on several representative, competent, candid colleagues, and rewrite if their feedback indicates the need (otherwise you invite failure).

2. Send out copies of your final draft to your prospective listeners before the presentation (assuming, of course, circumstantial feasibility).

3. Invite *written* reactions and critiques before you are to give the presentation (so that you can make any necessary final revisions and also to allow your preparation of anticipatory answers).

4. Present your paper aloud in an objective, but communicative manner (that is, keep the critical view, but remember you are addressing human beings whose attention and interest must be sustained).

5. Always allow plenty of time for questions, reactions, comments (and diatribes), which is the real crucible for testing your ideas.

6. Invite follow-up reactions from your auditors (that is, ask them

to call or talk with you—or, even better, to write up their thoughts after thinking through your ideas).

7. *If you see the need,* rewrite the paper after inputs of the kind described in 5 and 6—and from your own rethinking of your presentation.

8. Distribute or publish the paper as appropriate (assuming, of course, that this is desirable and feasible).

9. In the oral presentation, A/Vs are often helpful to clarify ideas and focus attention, but be careful not to create antagonism by appearing to "put on a show" to a critically oriented group.

Some general guidelines for using written media in presentations have been outlined here. Of course, they must be viewed and employed with care and good judgment. But when so handled, what has been discussed in this section can serve as practical and worthwhile principles for planning and carrying out successful presentations.

HUMAN MEDIA

What Human Media Are

These include all the personal media for conveying ideas. And the most obvious personal medium is yourself. It is also clear that human media are the most important of the three discussed in this chapter, because this is the fundamental perspective of this book.

Beyond you, the presenter, there are other important forms of human media (such as audience participation, meetings, and conferences) which can be valuable supplements in your presentation. We'll be exploring all of these at length, but we'll start with you, the oral communicator.

You as a Communication Medium

In a technical sense, you are "hardware"—that is, a *communication carrier* with certain characteristics (auditory perception, vocal capacity, reasoning ability). Your "software" then is your "programming" (how you've learned to hear and listen, how you use your voice, and the ways you think).

If you are willing to take this view of yourself, it can be quite helpful in developing the perspective needed to maximize your communication capability. Again, from this book's viewpoint, you are the most important of all media; therefore, we need to do whatever we can to make you an effective communication carrier.

What should you know and be able to do in order to develop personal presentation capability? The two items discussed here are fundamental.

1. *Develop proper attitudes and outlooks.* Without being overly exhortatory, and much of the literature is little else, you need to recognize some basic things which can make or break you as an oral communicator.

First, communication *objectivity* is necessary. This is an ability to view yourself and your presentation with proper detachment, and to see both in proper perspective. This is necessary if you are to know yourself, the communication situation, and what needs to be done if you are to succeed. It is essential also if you are to strengthen your communication assets and to eliminate or ameliorate liabilities. While there is no easy way to attain this objectivity (unless you were fortunate enough to have been born and reared in the right environment), you can (1) constantly remind yourself of the need for objectivity; (2) solicit information and feedback from critically constructive people with whom you communicate; and, using the backgrounds in this book, (3) chart a deliberate plan to develop the objectivity described here.

Second, a *sense of idea and receiver commitment* is essential to a good presentation. Do you feel that your ideas are really important? And do they have real importance for your group? Will it make a significant difference if your listeners properly understand and react to your message? Or if they misunderstand with attendant wrong reactions? Answers to questions like these are reliable indicators of your sense of presentation and listener commitment. If you do not have it, you may well fail, because the degree of constructive commitment is tied directly to the degree of success in oral communication. Obviously, what we've said goes right back to the assessment of need for communication. If there is a real need to be met, your commitment should follow; if there is no need, your commitment will be absent.

Third, *constructive confidence* is a must in successful oral communication. This does not mean a seductive "Pollyanna" outlook—that superficial "sweetness and light" view of yourself and the world.

What is meant is confidence that springs from objectivity and commitment, together with a view of yourself as a worthy and competent communicator. Do you feel that you have something important to say? Do you know what you're talking about? Have you thoroughly prepared yourself? Have you marshaled all the necessary ideas for your receivers in the situation? Have you assured the necessary resources to carry out your mission? Have you planned for contingencies?

If you can unequivocally answer "yes" to questions like these, you should have the constructive confidence needed to successfully carry out your presentation. To the extent that you cannot give affirmative answers, confidence will be lacking.

2. *Develop personal communication competence.* You've already seen that your confidence is in large part based on your communication competence. Several elements are included in communication competence, some of which we have discussed in previous chapters and sections.

Communication planning (about which much of this book is written) refers to the ability to size up the situation, to know the need for communication, to select media, to specify your mission and message, and to give general shape to your message. These have been discussed in depth in Chapter 2, "Knowing When to Communicate."

Communication composition means the refined organization and development of your ideas. Included are your selecting and stating basic ideas, your determination of backup and supportive means, and your casting of an appropriate introduction and conclusion. These elements have been presented in detail in Chapter 3, "Putting Ideas Together."

Communication media usage concerns all that we've mentioned in this chapter. We've already gone through A/Vs and written media, and we're now dealing with human media. It is sufficient here to say that presentation success is closely related to the communicator's competence to exploit the different media (including his own "hardware and software") optimally in achieving the presentation's ends.

Verbal, vocal, and physical communication refers to your ability to use language, the voice, and the body in presenting ideas. All these are output factors—that is, all are involved in the oral presentation proper. It is clear that even the best planning, composition, and media usage may be for naught if you fail at this stage.

Do you use symbols correctly (appropriate grammar, diction, and terminology)? Do you pronounce words correctly (that is, within situationally acceptable limits)? Do you speak distinctly (acceptable articulation and enunciation)? Do you use directness in phrasing ideas (rather than garbled and rambling syntax)? Is your speaking characterized by clarity and simplicity (rather than fogginess and unnecessary jargon)? Do you use a sufficient variety of words, phrases, and terms (rather than the deadly repeating of the same "noises" over and over again)? Do you observe propriety of speech (or do you offend people by unnecessarily "vulgar" or "out-of-place" communication)? Do you effectively use eye contact, facial expression, posture, gestures, and proper appearance?

These are questions you should carefully ponder. And you may not be able to answer them accurately right away. As a suggestion, try this: (1) Record your next presentation (or even informal conversation) and play it back. This can be very revealing (if not sometimes shocking). (2) Ask a group of constructively critical people with whom you communicate often to fill out the critique sheet given in Chapter 8. Then compare their analysis with your own. You may be surprised at the consensus of outsiders' (and at the deviations from your own) judgments. You can generally assume that the outsiders' evaluations are valid, and you should be guided accordingly in shaping up your verbal, vocal, and physical communication. You may find that you come across far differently than you think.

If you want professional counseling (and this may be highly desirable), consult with a good teacher of speech or (if it has one) with the company's presentation coach. You may even decide to take academic or nonacademic courses to improve your skills (highly recommended if you can get the right instructor and class). We shall be dealing more with this subject in the last chapter of the book, "Using the Right Methods."

Communication sensitivity means your ability to recognize and handle receiver feelings, roles, and informational needs—in other words, your capacity to communicate to meet important psychological and logical demands of the listener or reader. This is a dimension that pervades all of communication planning, execution, and follow-up. It will be discussed at length in the next four chapters.

Summary: You as a Communication Medium   We've discussed two dimensions affecting you as a presentation medium: (1) your attitudes and outlook; and (2) your personal communication competence. Let's summarize by putting each of these in a separate analysis form (Figures 4-4 and 4-5). These can be used for both self-evaluation and outsiders' critiques. And for an even more detailed evaluation, you may use the "Critique Checklist," Figure 8.4 in Chapter 8.

Using Other Human Communication Media

Beyond yourself there are other important personal communication media—some purely human, others combining human and mechanical means.

Audience participation means getting some directed overt responses from receivers. One of the most common ways is through *question-and-answer sessions* after (and sometimes before or during) the presentation. This is very useful to clarify ideas, get disagreements out in the open, get direct feedback on listener understanding and acceptance. Question-and-answer sessions should generally be planned and used in most purposive presentations.

Another audience participation device is the *buzz session*. Here receivers are divided into work groups (six to ten people) for the purposes of seeking further clarification, giving reactions, making implications, or suggesting courses of action. Each buzz group ad-

Factor	Evaluation (check)					Needed Improvement (Specify)
	Poor	Fair	Good	Excellent	Superior	
Objectivity						
Idea/Receiver Commitment						
Constructive Confidence						

Figure 4-4.   Evaluation of attitudes and outlooks.

Factor	Evaluation (check)					Needed Improvement (Specify)
	Poor	Fair	Good	Excellent	Superior	
Communication Planning						
Communication Composition						
Verbal/Vocal/ Physical Communication						
Communication Sensitivity						

Figure 4-5.   Evaluation of personal communication competence.

dresses its questions or remarks through a chosen spokesman. Buzz groups are especially applicable when you want specific audience responses from a large number of receivers (50 or more), because you can get some participation from everyone.

Conferences are face-to-face, interactive oral communication situations. Generally confined to a few people (5 to 25), they are for problem exploration, decision making, planning, policy formulation, and allied purposes. These usually precede or follow purposive presentations—that is, they are used in planning, pretesting, or reviewing presentations, as well as in discussing the ideas given.

Meetings are frequently presentational in nature. When true, all the principles we've discussed apply. There are some more informal meetings (many of which are really conferences) where freewheeling interaction goes on. In this case, they may supplement your presentation in planning or in follow-up.

Electronic and mechanical interconnections refer to all those hardware items for transmitting and receiving human communication. Included are telephone hookups, amplifying systems, radio, television, and videotape. We've already considered these under A/Vs, so we won't go into further details. As you can see, all can serve as presentational vehicles, as well as supplementary media. Use them as appropriate.

SUMMARY: USING COMMUNICATION MEDIA

We've seen that there are three basic kinds of communication media: (1) auditory and visual, (2) written, and (3) human.

Auditory and visual media are mechanical hardware that can be used in various ways to enhance presentational effectiveness. These have been enumerated and explained.

Written media are the printed documents that can be employed to supplement your oral communication. The most important types of written media have been specified and their uses have been spelled out.

Human media are means of personal communication for conveying ideas. The most important human medium is, of course, you—the presenter. The ways by which you can become a more capable communicator have been discussed, together with a setting out of model critique forms which can help you to achieve this goal. Other human media have also been listed and their uses have been given.

This chapter completes the general backgrounds for effective presentations. You are now ready to go on to the more specific principles, techniques, and methods for presentational use. These are set forth in the next four chapters.

II

TRIM: HOW TO COMMUNICATE EFFECTIVELY

5

Hitting the Target

As you'll remember from Chapter 1, our design for getting presentational effectiveness is TRIM, which is

T   the communication *target* at which you are shooting.
R   the *receiver* to which your communication is addressed.
I   the *impact* needed to influence the receiver as desired.
M   the *methods* which can be used to get the job done.

In this chapter we're going to take the first item, the communication target or mission. Simply defined, the communication target is
the purpose which must be met in order to resolve the need (or
problem) giving rise to your presentation. As you'll recall, in Chapter
2, we discussed how to determine whether there is a need for
presentation—and if so, what kind. The kinds of needs set forth there
are directly related to the four types of presentation targets: (1)
information-centered; (2) conviction-centered; (3) reinforcement-
centered; and (4) action-centered. Let's now explore these in this
relationship.

INFORMATION-CENTERED TARGETS

Here the mission is to communicate descriptively, reportorially, or
factually. In other words, the emphasis is on presenting a picture of
things as they are.

Uses and Examples

What are common presentation situations where information is the emphasis? Giving production reports, making financial reports, clarifying policies or procedures, stipulating specifications, setting forth the provisions of contracts are common examples.

In addition, many presentations made by business, government, and professional people to outside publics focus wholly or in part on the informational mission. Glenn T. Seaborg in "The Environment" (Specimen 16:8) goes into historical natural catastrophes:

> We . . . forget the extent to which nature destroys—and pollutes— segments of itself, sporadically and violently—with man often a major victim. . . . Witness the great earthquakes, volcanic eruptions, tidal waves, floods, and epidemics that have been recorded. Among the greatest of these were the earthquake in Shensi Province of China in 1556, killing an estimated 800,000 people, and the one in Japan in 1923 which took close to 150,000 lives and destroyed more than half a million homes; the volcanic eruption of 1470 B.C. that destroyed much of Minoan civilization; the 1883 explosion of Krakatoa . . . which, in addition to wiping out 163 villages and killing 36,000 people, sent rock and dust falling for ten days as far as 3,000 miles away.

In presentations, giving information may be the primary mission or, more commonly, it is used as the basis from which to build to one of the other purposes: conviction, reinforcement, or action. As examples of the latter, see Specimens 2:1–4 and 7:4–10.

Organization and Development

In what ways can you structure and support ideas in giving information? Here we'll draw in part from what we've said in Chapter 3, "Putting Ideas Together."

Sequence. Both logical and psychological sequences are useful in information-giving. Logical sequences are common in situations where straightforward communication is the mode (scientific and professional presentations and classroom lectures). Here time sequence, space sequence, and important elements are appropriate patterns of communication.

Psychological sequences are also very useful, although not as commonly employed as the more traditional logical patterns. You should remember that receivers are not always ready to listen to or read attentively even the most important information. Often they must be *prepared* to receive, and psychological patterns are designed to do this. Glenn T. Seaborg's presentation (Specimen 16:8) uses a psychological approach (familiar to unfamiliar) to prepare his receivers to assimilate the data he presents.

In selecting sequence, then, determine whether your receivers are ready to receive the information you are to present. If ready, then the logical sequence is probably the right one; if not, then the psychological sequence is probably your best bet.

Development. Some of the more common *supportive means* are facts and statistics, examples (illustrated by Glenn T. Seaborg above), audiovisuals, and demonstration. The last two are especially good in longer or more complex situations.

In *introducing* your informational presentation, the *pre-summary* and *background* are useful ways to set the stage for logical sequences. *Striking examples* or situations are often used to get listener attention in presentations calling for a psychological sequence.

In *concluding*, the *post-summary* is the most obvious means in the logical sequence. *Important ideas* and *implications and inferences* are more applicable to psychological sequences.

CONVICTION-CENTERED TARGETS

Whereas information-centered missions are descriptive, conviction-centered presentations aim at getting belief in or mental assent to ideas. Generally, this means that your receivers are initially neutral or opposed. It can be seen that you may present the most important information but if your ideas are not credible to listeners, your communication fails.

Uses and Examples

What are typical uses of conviction-centered missions? Here are a few among the many: getting employees to believe that a newly introduced procedure is worthwhile; getting union members to believe that the terms offered in a new contract are not a mere facade for management's ulterior motives; getting customers to see that the new product (replacing the discontinued item) is even better than the former one. Additionally, company advertising, recruitment, and communication of employee benefits are common situations where conviction-centered presentations play a major role.

Note how Robert F. Kennedy, in addressing the University of Georgia Law School on Law Day (Specimen 11:5–6), starts building listener belief:

> We meet at this great university, in this old state, the fourth of the original thirteen, to observe Law Day.
>
> In his proclamation urging us to observe this day, the President emphasized two thoughts: he pointed out that to remain free, the people must "cherish their freedoms, understand the responsibilities they entail, and nurture the will to preserve them." He then went on to point out that "law is the strongest link between man and freedom."

As in informational missions, conviction can be a primary or supportive mission. As an example of the primary mission, see Specimen 4; the one above exemplifies the supportive mission.

Organization and Development

What sequential and development patterns lend themselves to conviction-centered missions? Again, let's draw from what we've discussed in Chapter 3.

Sequence. Logical sequences are appropriate for critically oriented groups (such as professional peers or "scientific" managers). The *important elements* sequence is very common. Clark E. Beck (Specimen 1) clearly illustrates this pattern in addressing his professional colleagues. *Problem-analysis-solution* is also frequently employed. Cornelius Gallagher (Specimen 4) uses this general sequence in his presentation. And *proposition-proof-conclusion* is a form of logical demonstration often used when the speaker is already known for his views and he therefore decides to convince the group by fairly open argument. Philip Harris uses this sequence in "Patterns of Racial Exclusion in Top Management" (Specimen 6).

Psychological sequences should be used for other than critical-minded receivers. The *familiar-to-unfamiliar* is often employed to get psychological momentum, starting with the familiar, in order to carry receivers with you when you come to unacceptable ideas—the unfamiliar. John F. Kennedy employs this sequence in "A New Social Order" (Specimen 10).

The *common-to-uncommon* sequence may be employed to build new receiver understandings or insights before moving to an otherwise unacceptable conclusion. Robert F. Kennedy's "Law Day" (Specimen 11) is a classic illustration of this approach.

Therefore, in selecting sequence (logical or psychological), you should again be guided by whether your receiver group is fundamentally critical or noncritical. If critical, it will probably need a logical pattern; if noncritical, then one of the two above psychological sequences is in order.

Development. Facts and statistics (especially compelling data) are effective supportive means in conviction-centered missions.

Striking or massed examples are also supportive means with powerful credibility. Glenn T. Seaborg well illustrates the use of these (Specimen 16:10–15).

Literary devices are especially applicable to noncritical receivers, although they can be used discreetly with critical-minded people. *Metaphor* is exemplified by Cornelius E. Gallagher when he compares modern American technology to a heathen idol (Specimen 4:5–6).

Quotations are, of course, frequently employed to gain conviction. See Specimens 4:19 and 6:2 as examples of this very worthwhile device to induce belief.

Stories and ancedotes also have a definite place in conviction missions.

Audiovisuals and demonstration are also potent means of persuasion. George T. Vardaman uses visual schematics to illustrate and drive home implicative conceptual schemes (Specimen 19:12, 20).

In *introducing* conviction-centered missions, you can use *striking examples* as good possibilities to direct audience attention to your ideas. Note how Lawrence A. Dysart uses an impelling hypothetical example (Specimen 2:1–3). *Quotations* are also very helpful in setting the stage for conviction.

Reasoned facts and statistics are also often very effective for introducing conviction-centered presentations. Seaborg uses this technique very adroitly (Specimen 16:1–8).

In *concluding,* the use of *striking examples* can be as effective as in introductions. James P. Hendrick uses a series of examples in building to a climactic conclusion in his presentation, "Interpol" (Specimen 7:24–30).

Quotations, too, are often used to end on a convincing note. Note how John F. Kennedy quotes Goethe at the conclusion of "A New Social Order" (Specimen 10:47).

Visuals are used by Vardaman to pull together the essential concepts and implications of his presentation, "Controlling Written Communications" (Specimen 19:19–23). Visuals lend themselves especially well to induce conviction where abstract and complex ideas are presented.

REINFORCEMENT-CENTERED TARGETS

Whereas conviction is concerned with changing beliefs (from initial neutrality or opposition), reinforcement aims at strengthening or deepening preexisting beliefs. In other words, rather than "saving the sinner" (the aim of conviction), it is directed to "saving the saved."

Uses and Examples

One of the most important presentation missions in organizations (although too often poorly done), some typical examples of reinforcement missions are annual stockholder meetings; presentations awarding recognition to employees for long and dedicated service; goodwill speeches to community groups (trade or professional organizations, service clubs, schools, churches, government agencies); communications to ameliorate serious crises or tragic situations; and presentations to "set the record straight" in order to enhance the company's image.

An example of communication to meet a tragedy is Lyndon B. Johnson's "Eulogy to John F. Kennedy" (Specimen 8). In such instances the presentation may be very brief; lengthy discourse may not be needed (indeed, may be inappropriate), for frequently the occasion itself communicates beyond anything the speaker can utter. Here is all Johnson said:

> This is a sad time for all people.
> We have suffered a loss that cannot be weighed.
> For me it is a deep personal tragedy.
> I know the world shares the sorrow that Mrs. Kennedy and her family
>   bear.
> I will do my best.
> That is all I can do.
> I ask for your help—and God's.

Another example of the reinforcement-centered presentation is Thomas J. Watson, Jr.'s commencement address to the graduating class at Lafayette College. Note how he appeals to the ideals and aspirations of his audience:

All of you graduating today possess something much more important than your body. I am speaking of your mind, your spirit, your ability to think and speak independently, and your ability ... as college seniors to stand up and be counted with a clear and firm position on nearly any of the issues which affect your life or the life of the nation.*

Reinforcement missions are built into some of the most frequent and important presentations for today's manager or professional person. Like the two preceding missions (information and conviction), reinforcement may be the primary end or the means to accomplish another.

Organization and Development

Sequence. Logical sequences have a limited place in reinforcement, generally serving supportive more than primary roles. For example, Hendrick uses time order in recounting events leading to the development of Interpol (Specimen 7:6–10), and Gerald J. Skibbins uses important elements in setting forth the yardsticks of the conservative (Specimen 17:1–10), but the preceding and following ideas in both presentations point to the more important reinforcement objective of each speaker.

As you have no doubt already inferred, psychological sequences are more basic to reinforcement. All those enumerated in Chapter 3 can be used. An example of *familiar to unfamiliar* sequence is Clifford D. Owsley's "Abraham Lincoln: The Writer" (Specimen 13). Robert F. Kennedy's "Law Day" illustrates the use of the *common to uncommon* pattern (Specimen 11). Skibbins (Specimen 17) epitomizes belief to greater belief; and Lynch (Specimen 12) is a model of belief to action.

To be "too logical" is to "labor the obvious" in situations demanding reinforcement. You should be concerned with deepening or strengthening feelings rather than appealing to listener intellectuality. This is why psychological sequences are generally called for.

Development. In order to strengthen beliefs and attitudes, you should emphasize supportive devices with real emotional appeal. The more powerful ones are literary devices, comparisons and contrasts, striking examples, and receiver participation.

*Presented as the commencement address, Lafayette College, Easton, Pennsylvania, June 1964. Reprinted from *Vital Speeches of the Day*, Vol. 30, No. 4, July 15, 1964, p. 599.

Literary devices are exemplified by almost all reinforcement-centered presentation specimens. To take only a few, John F. Kennedy uses *literary description* throughout "A New Social Order" (Specimen 10; see 7–9). *Quotations* are almost always used in important reinforcement missions (Specimens 4:7–8 and 11:6, 10–11). *Great people, traditions, and ideals* are also frequently involved.

The use of *comparisons and contrasts* is well exemplified by John F. Kennedy in comparing the American Revolution with the German revolution of 1848 (Specimen 10:5) and by Owsley in contrasting Lincoln with Keats (Specimen 13:5).

Striking examples also are often part of the fabric in reinforcement missions. Max Rafferty uses a series of story-examples (Specimen 15:1–9); and Seaborg cites a mass of provocative historical illustrations (Specimen 16:7–16).

Receiver participation is frequently employed to deepen beliefs (religious worship services making use of responsive readings, hymns, and participative prayers).

Introductions to reinforcement-centered presentations can employ all of the devices listed above (literary, comparisons and contrasts, striking examples, and receiver participation). *Stories* are also frequently used (Specimen 13:1); *achievements and traditions* can be recounted (Specimen 4:1); the *importance of the occasion* can be brought to the receivers' attention (Specimen 11:1–6).

Conclusions use all the techniques under introductions, plus these: *Dramatic details* are frequently used. *Visionary outcome* is used by Robert F. Kennedy in "Law Day" (Specimen 11:69–73).

ACTION-CENTERED TARGETS

These are aimed to get some specific desired performance response: for example, employees to follow new procedures or customers to buy or stockholders to vote the way company management wants. And you have probably already surmised the obvious: action missions grow out of one or more of the preceding (information, conviction, reinforcement). Figure 5.1 helps to clarify how this happens.

Two Routes to Action

Figure 5-1 shows that there are two fundamental paths to action: (1) the information → conviction approach, and (2) the information → reinforcement approach.

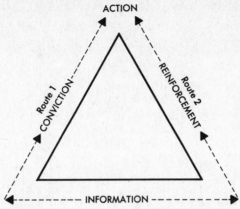

Figure 5-1. Two basic routes to action.

Although both are sometimes used in the same presentation (first getting conviction, followed by reinforcement), one or the other is normally called for in a given communication setting. Route one (information → conviction) should be used when you are faced with changing listeners or readers from neutrality or opposition to beliefs you want. Route two (information → reinforcement) should be used when your listeners already fundamentally believe in your ideas.

Unfortunately, many communicators do not plan their presentations in light of these two different routes to action, thereby leading to failure. To take the information → conviction route with "believers" will often alienate them because the presenter is "laboring the obvious"; on the other hand, taking the information → reinforcement route with "unbelievers" is clearly an invitation to receiver hostility or apathy, and consequent communication disaster.

It is highly important, then, to know which path you need to pursue to get the action you want from your receivers. Since we have already discussed sequences and devices for information, conviction, and reinforcement missions, let's now review some specimens to see how contemporary speakers have used these two routes to action.

Example of Route 1: Information → Conviction → Action

Specimen 11: Robert F. Kennedy, "Law Day." Clearly Kennedy was confronted by opposition to his basic idea that civil rights laws must be obeyed by all (including Southerners) when he addressed a group of University of Georgia law students in 1961. He therefore uses a great array of devices and techniques to convince his listeners (1–4: the

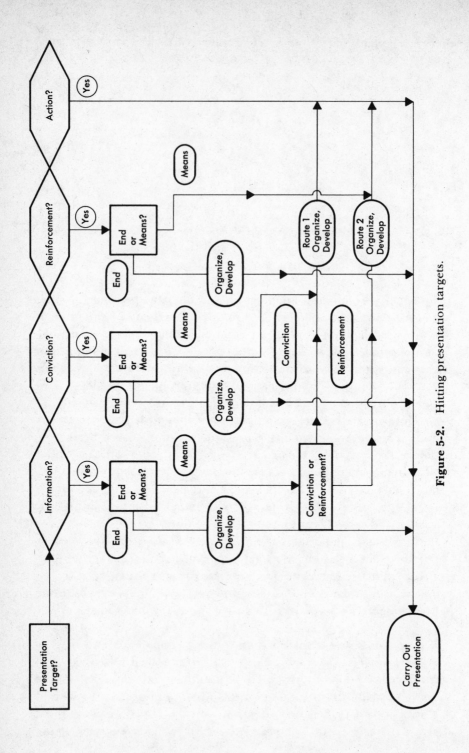

Figure 5-2. Hitting presentation targets.

example of a Georgian who evidenced bravery; 5–9: the *common ground*—especially to law students—that respect for law is essential in a free society; 10–11: *quoting* the opinion of a *respected source*—the Supreme Court of Georgia—to sustain his thesis).

Throughout the presentation, Kennedy keeps coming back to his fundamental tenet: respect for the law (6, 12, 25, 33, 39, 41–42, 54); and he concludes his presentation (59–73) by asking for his listeners' support of his enforcement of civil rights—and all other—statutes.

Example of Route 2: Information → Reinforcement → Action

Specimen 12: Edith M. Lynch, "How Women Can Get Out of Dead-End Jobs." Most women readers are probably receptive to having this subject put into Route 2 structure. Lynch starts by challenging readers to observe for themselves typical exclusions of women from managerial positions. She then cites legal and regulatory decisions granting women back pay because they are not promoted as rapidly as men. Next, she emphasizes that "an enormous number" of women feel stuck in "dull, no-advancement jobs," after which she relates by quotes five different female "lamentations." The remainder of the article focuses on needed actions as ten questions for reader answers .

HITTING THE TARGET: A MODEL

We've now seen that there are four basic presentation missions: (1) information; (2) conviction; (3) reinforcement; and (4) action. We've also noted that the first three may be ends in themselves or means to accomplish an action purpose. Furthermore, we've formulated two basic paths to action: (1) the information → conviction → action route (to overcome neutrality or opposition); and (2) the information → reinforcement → action route (to deepen preexisting belief). And, in order to see how contemporary speakers have used them, we applied the two patterns to specimens.

Let's now turn to a simple model which pulls together what we've said in this chapter, and which you can use as a visual guide to zero in on your presentation target (Figure 5-2).

6

Communicating with Receivers

We are now ready to examine the second factor of the TRIM sequence: the receivers of the presentation. And while your communication can certainly be better from knowing your target (or mission) and how best to hit it, the likelihood of even greater effectiveness lies in hitting that target in conjunction with your listeners' or readers' predominant feeling-thinking roles. It is to these receiver states that we'll address ourselves in this chapter.

What are basic receiver roles? For presentation purposes, there are five: (1) apathetic; (2) sophisticated; (3) hostile; (4) credent; and (5) critical. Let's examine each.

THE APATHETIC ROLE

What It Is

Its Greek root, *apatheia* (meaning "without feeling"), is key. For the apathetic receiver is psychologically dead to your communication. His indifference, his "couldn't care less" attitude, creates a situation in which communication with him is impossible. Needless to say, receiver apathy is an intolerable condition if you are to carry out an effective presentation.

Situations Causing Apathy

What produces apathy? Generally these situations: (1) "command performances"; (2) prior deadly presentations; (3) receiver saturation; and (4) poor physical context.

"Command performances" are where the receiver is (explicitly or implicitly) required to listen to or read the communication. Numerous examples come to mind, among them: the weekly staff meeting; a breakfast meeting of United Fund volunteers; or the typical annual management presentation to point out "challenges and opportunities" to company supervisors and staff.

Prior deadly presentations include poor previous oral or written communications, whether from a person or department or on a specific subject. Such history preconditions the listener to an apathetic response.

Receiver saturation refers to those situations where the listener or reader knows (or thinks he knows) all about the presentation's subject. The receiver sees no point in spending the time or effort to attend to the speaker's messages, thereby frequently inducing deep apathy.

Poor physical context includes such factors as room appearance, temperature, ventilation, seating, lighting, and audibility and visibility of the presenter. Many otherwise good presentations have failed abysmally because of improper physical surroundings. And if your listeners have previously been subjected to poor facilities (e.g., the same poorly ventilated room), chances are good that they will be dormant before they even appear on the scene.

In addition to these four specific conditions, you should recognize also that *apathy is possible in any communication* situation. To pay attention, to concentrate on a presentation, requires real effort, and you should realistically recognize that not everyone is willing to work that hard unless a real reason is seen for doing so.

The Basic Impact to Overcome Apathy

As we've seen, apathy is intolerable if you are to get anywhere in your presentation. Since, as long as apathy exists, your receivers are "dead" to you and your ideas, you must "resurrect" them as quickly as possible.

The basic impact you should seek is to *get your receivers' attention and sustain their interest*—that is, you must in some way get listener focus on you and your message, and away from whatever distracting influences are causing inattention.

We'll look over a general sequence for dynamic analysis of receiver roles at the end of this chapter. And in Chapters 7 and 8, we'll spell out specific techniques and methods for overcoming apathy and moving your receiver to the desired role. Let's now examine some of our specimens to see how modern speakers have handled apathetic receivers.

Examples of Overcoming Apathy

Specimen 2: Lawrence A. Dysart, 'Wanted: Effective Communicators." Speaking to a regional convention of secretaries of petroleum and related firms (The Desk and Derrick Clubs), Dysart takes immediate steps to overcome this traditional apathy-inducing situation (as almost any convention presentation is). He starts by asking his group to "participate" in "fantasy" with him (1), proceeding from this to a very interesting and informative presentation on the development of the English language from the eleventh century to date (1–5). He then moves to the need for linguistic simplicity (6) and communication for the receiver (7). This extract ends with an anecdote of how Dysart's son ignored his father's didactic communication, but "listened" and responded to a girl friend (8).

You can see that, throughout, Dysart is adroitly using devices to achieve the desired basic impact for overcoming apathy: getting attention and sustaining interest.

Specimen 15: Max Rafferty, "Today's Challenge in Education." This is only the first part of a longer presentation, but it exemplifies well Rafferty's skill in gaining and maintaining his audience's interest. Note how he starts with a humorous story on himself (1); then, with a series of stories, he illustrates some of the ordeals of a political candidate (2–9). His entire initial approach is to create a magnetic attention and interest impact.

THE SOPHISTICATED ROLE

What It Is

"Sophisticated" is also derived from Greek (*sophos* meaning "wisdom"). And this helps to understand what the role implies: the "wise-guy" outlook. In other words, a sophisticated receiver assumes that he knows as much as or more than you can tell him. Stated another way, it means that your receiver is unteachable and that he is unwilling to learn from you. Clearly, this is another intolerable condition for effective communication.

Situations Causing Sophistication

Most of the previously mentioned apathy-inducing conditions ("command performances," prior deadly communication) can also produce sophistication. Therefore, these should be borne in mind here.

Additionally, the following circumstances are always potential "wise-guy" producers: (1) "old hat" communications; (2) nonexpert-to-expert situations; (3) subordinate-to-superior cases; (4) peer-to-peer communication; and (5) staff-to-line conditions.

"Old hat" communications, such as recommendations from standing committees, the reading of the minutes of meetings, and routine oral or written reports from department heads, are almost always accompanied by receiver sophistication.

Nonexpert-to-expert situations (and sometimes the reverse) also bring about the "you can't tell me anything" view. After all, the expert "knows" more than the nonexpert, so why should he bother to listen to one who has less knowledge?

Subordinate-to-superior cases certainly make for sophistication. Whether he actually knows, the boss no doubt *thinks* he knows about his employees, their jobs, and what needs to be done in his unit. The sophistication barrier is almost automatic in upward communications.

Peer-to-peer communication, such as a professor presenting ideas to other professors (especially when all are within the same discipline), is a direct invitation to receiver sophistication. Other examples include one department head communicating with other department chiefs or a statistical staff person presenting a proposal to other company statisticians.

Staff-to-line conditions (or the opposite) often create pernicious receiver sophistication. The staff person is frequently viewed as knowing nothing of what really goes on in the firm's operational units, or he may be seen as a "fast-burner" theoretician with little of practical value to offer. It is easy to see that the staff person may also look condescendingly on the line communicator when the situation is reversed.

The Basic Impact to Overcome Sophistication

Since you face another intolerable condition, you must move your receiver out of this role as quickly as possible if you are to get constructive reception for your ideas. Here you must create this basic impact: to *get your receivers to see you and your ideas in a new light.* That is, you must change your listeners' perceptions from "I already know this," to "Gee, that's a different angle!"

We'll explore the means by which you can get this done in Chapters 7 and 8. Let's now turn to some specimens to see how two of our speakers have handled receiver sophistication.

Examples of Overcoming Sophistication

Specimen 1: Clark E. Beck, "Evaluation of Research and Development Proposals." This was a presentation to professional technical writer colleagues at a national convention. Beck is certainly confronting receivers who think they know (and obviously *do* know) something about proposal writing. He therefore takes steps to handle this sophistication by first limiting his presentation to "solicited research and development technical proposals written by Industry and directed to the United States Air Force" (1). This puts "sideboards" on his presentation, and, since it is in Beck's area of expertise, is likely to make for less listener sophistication.

Beck then introduces the notion that a proposal is basically a *persuasive* instrument (undoubtedly a "new angle" to many in his audience), plus the idea that the writer must make his proposal "customer-oriented" rather than writer-centered (2). He then (modestly) suggests that his presentation may be of help in raising the averages of proposal acceptances (3).

Thus, it can be seen that Beck has gently but deftly dealt with receiver sophistication by approaching his subject in a different way, hopefully to induce his listeners to see it in a new light. He is then ready to communicate with them in a more desirable framework (which we'll discuss later in this chapter).

Specimen 13: Clifford D. Owsley, "Abraham Lincoln: The Writer." Addressing the Lincoln Group of the District of Columbia, Owsley was certainly dealing with an initially sophisticated group. And because his listeners undoubtedly already knew much about Lincoln, their sophistication was justified.

After starting with an attention-getting, humorous Lincoln anecdote, Owsley "confirms" what his listeners probably already knew and believed: that studying Lincoln is exciting, should be more scholarly, and should be a required course in college (2–3). He then moves to his thesis: that Lincoln was a genius with words, that he was "first and foremost a writer" (4–6).

Thus, Owsley has set the stage for his basic presentation to this sophisticated group by approaching his subject in a new way, thereby making his listeners ready and willing to receive the rest of his message. A little later we'll see how he communicates with his receivers in their new role.

THE HOSTILE ROLE

What It Is

"Hostile" is derived from the Latin word *hostilis,* meaning "enemy." The hostile receiver opposes either you or your ideas or the presentation situation. Such opposition can range from rampant and open (rioting college students) to the unconscious and covert (e.g., a manager's vague feeling that "something is wrong" with a recommendation from his staff). In any form, open or concealed, conscious or unconscious, the hostile receiver role is destructive to your communication, and is therefore intolerable.

Situations Causing Hostility

Hostility can arise from poor handling of any of the conditions we've listed as causing apathy or sophistication. Therefore, this makes it all the more important that these be effectively controlled. Additional factors are: (1) threatening situations; (2) inimical people, organizations, or sources; (3) hidden agendas; and (4) cross-cultural situations.

Threatening situations are those which your *listeners think* are against their interests. Any change (a new procedure), any ambiguous situation (for example, where workers are not clear on the implications of a new production policy), any case where job pay, status, or security appears to be adversely affected (such as an announcement eliminating overtime for employees) is threatening and therefore hostility-inducing.

Inimical people, organizations, or sources can be exemplified by a badly-thought-of manager, a staff unit which has a poor reputation, and a company policy which has little or no support from the firm's employees. All these invite automatic receiver opposition.

Hidden agendas include anything that your receivers *suspect* about your motives or intentions. What receivers suspect may be false, but their suspicions govern their hostile outlooks. This is one of the most common causes of real and potential receiver opposition, and you must carefully assess whether it exists in the situation before you.

Cross-cultural situations almost always invite open or covert opposition. Examples include management presentations to union officers or members, a staff research specialist talking to a group of line supervisors, the company comptroller communicating with company salespeople, and a member of one ethnic group trying to convince people of another ethnic identity.

The Basic Impact to Overcome Hostility

As with apathy and sophistication, hostility is clearly destructive to your communication. As long as your receivers are in opposition, you can't convince them to adopt your views (even worse there is the ever-present danger of intensifying opposition, which can make your task more difficult, if not impossible).

Therefore, the basic impact must be to *eliminate or abate receiver opposition while moving your listeners to conviction.* That is, you must get rid of or soften the negative outlooks of your audience and at the same time get them to believe in you and your ideas. Chapter 7 will elaborate on how this impact can be achieved.

Examples of Overcoming Hostility

Specimen 11: Robert F. Kennedy, "Law Day." As you recall, Kennedy was addressing law students at the University of Georgia on Law Day, 1961. Without question, his basic thesis that "civil rights laws will be enforced" was hostility-inducing to this group at this time. To attenuate ill feelings and at the same time establish a common ground, Kennedy refers to this Georgia setting as his first formal speech as Attorney General (1), then to the recent award by the President of a medal for bravery to a young Georgian (2), followed by a humorous takeoff on the fact that he has no Georgia kinfolk; but he then stresses that Georgia's giving John F. Kennedy the biggest percentage majority of any state in the 1960 election "was even better than kinfolk" (4).

Having taken steps to soften hostility, Kennedy then launches into the more serious part of his presentation. He refers to the university setting, in the fourth oldest state, and to the occasion, Law Day (5). He has thus set the stage for his basic means of overcoming the hostility and creating conviction on the part of this law student audience. As we have noted in discussing this specimen in Chapter 5, he hammers repeatedly on the theme of Law Day—respect for the law (5, 8, 12, 16, 33, 35, 39, 41, 53, 59). Kennedy ends on a note with which anyone of legal bent must agree: that all laws (including civil rights) will be enforced vigorously, but without bias or political prejudice (67). He caps his presentation by quoting a revered Georgian, Henry W. Grady, to the effect that there must be an end to divisive regional outlooks, that there must be a unified national view in America (69–72).

Careful reading of his presentation shows that throughout, Robert F. Kennedy was using deliberate devices and methods to achieve the basic impact of overcoming opposition, and, at the same time, to build receiver conviction for himself and his ideas.

Specimen 18: Robert Van Riper, "Some Things That Worry Me About Public Relations." Speaking to a group of public relations people (who are constantly concerned about their "professional" image), Van Riper (in this excerpt which is actually the conclusion of a longer speech) uses the time-tested common ground approach. Stating that there are two essentials to successful public relations, his first point of the need for mastery of public relations technique (1) is certainly designed to get a mental "yes" from his auditors. Having gained this psychological momentum, he then moves to the second essential: the ability to see things as others see them (3). And he uses this to get over the idea that if public relations people will develop this basic projective ability, the problem of whether or not public relations is a profession will be inconsequential (4).

This abbreviated version of Van Riper's more lengthy communication exemplifies the direct use of the "common-to-uncommon" sequence to which we referred in Chapter 3. It is a frequently used pattern to handle potentially hostile receivers.

THE CREDENT ROLE

What It Is

"Credent" comes from the Latin *credere,* "to believe." The credent receiver already accepts you and your message. In other words, he is already convinced or "saved." Thus, it differs from the three preceding roles in that credence is a potentially *constructive* (rather than destructive) presentation situation. Generally, therefore, you want to preserve and intensify this feeling state.

Situations Calling for Presentation

Since your receivers are already convinced, your main concern is not with causal factors, but with the conditions that signal the need for credent-centered communications. Some of the more important signals are: (1) performance plateaus or drops; (2) apprehension and ambiguity; (3) new goals; (4) jobs well done; (5) job failures; and (6) job routines.

Performance plateaus or drops, as shown by performance charts, may mean that people need to be restimulated. An effective credent-centered presentation is often one of the best ways to do this.

Apprehension and ambiguity within the company may call for relieving tensions, clearing the air, and getting issues out into the open. Credent-centered presentations (frequently combined with other oral and written communications) are helpful ways to achieve these important objectives.

New goals or tasks can often be communicated effectively through credent communication. And in getting people to understand and affirmatively accept them, their realization is more sure.

Jobs well done deserve a pat on the back. When people perform above the norm or carry out their tasks in better ways or evidence constructive initiative, they should be commended.

Job failures should not automatically call for supervisory censure. Rather, a more constructive managerial approach is to give support, to lend encouragement, and to help those who have failed (or who feel they have failed) to try again.

Job routines constitute the most important ongoing activities of an organization. The company would not survive if its people at all levels did not carry out all their grubby, grimy day-to-day operations. It is, therefore, most important that encouragement and deserved appreciation be communicated. The credent presentation is one of the best vehicles to accomplish this objective.

The Basic Impact to Strengthen Credence

As noted, this is a feeling state you may want to perpetuate. But if so, you want to deepen or intensify the credence and to move your listeners from "mild" to "strong" belief.

The basic impact in this case is to *dramatize to make more meaningful your receivers' beliefs and attitudes*. That is, you must stir your listeners' imaginations, deepen their values, excite their aspirations, and strengthen their tenets so that all become more vital to them. Specific techniques and methods by which this can be done will be given in the next two chapters.

Examples of Strengthening Credence

Specimen 17: Gerald J. Skibbins, "The Ten Marks of the Conservative." In this speech, presented to the Central New Jersey Conference of Conservatives, the situation itself builds in a credent-centered presentation. Skibbins uses a common ground starting point: that conservatism is little understood and that conservatives "have a tremendous educational task" on their hands.

He then traces in some detail the historical roots of conservatism and the basic objectives of the conservative movement, no doubt imparting some new and dramatic data to many of his hearers. He then sets forth his ten marks of the conservative, explaining and exemplifying each in turn (1–10); again he uses dramatic detail, much of which was probably new to his listeners. His summary dramatizes through use of historical figures what a right conception of conservatism means to people and that research studies show people "just don't know" what conservative beliefs are. He ends by pointing out that the conservative's winning of the educational contest "is this nation's sole guarantee of dynamic economic growth, international peace, and personal happiness."

It can be seen throughout that Skibbins has assumed believing receivers, and that his whole approach is designed to strengthen and deepen their beliefs.

Specimen 13: Clifford D. Owsley, "Abraham Lincoln: The Writer." As you recall, we used this earlier as an example of overcoming sophistication (1–6). We saw that Owsley took deliberate steps to handle this first receiver role. But, having overcome sophistication, his listeners are now credent. Stated another way, their *backup role* is credent. We'll be explaining this concept more fully later in this chapter. For the moment, let's look at Owsley's listeners in their new believer state.

Starting at section 7, Owsley traces Lincoln's youthful interest in words, his early attempts at writing (8), his membership in a literary society, and his admiration of Shakespeare and Robert Burns (9). He then traces some of Lincoln's early adult literary efforts, and Lincoln's view of the primacy of writing over speaking (11–12). Up to this point Owsley has used little-known telling detail to dramatize.

Owsley now turns to his own newly discovered facts as to how Lincoln wrote the Gettysburg Address. Using specific names, places, and word counts, he analyzes the presentation part by part (13–18). After giving these unfamiliar dramatic details about this very familiar and revered speech by Lincoln, Owsley then postulates three phases in Lincoln's development as a writer (19–21), again using dramatic details. He moves to a climactic conclusion by stating that Lincoln's writing production of about a million words equaled Shakespeare's (22), that H. G. Wells dubbed him one of the six immortals of history (23), that it is amazing that Lincoln, "with such bare beginnings, ended up an undisputed master of the language" (23). The answer, says Owsley (paraphrasing Yeats), was that Lincoln's thoughts were "not only in his mind; they went deeper, to be part of his bones" (24). Lincoln is then compared to the "Gods and heroes of mythology," is pictured as one who embodied the natural goodness and valor of humanity and as one who revealed the key to sublimity. Owsley ends with a powerful dramatic thrust by stating (25):

> The freedom he loved and defended will endure. As it covers the earth, Abraham Lincoln's name will go with it, to reign in the hearts and minds of people, forever enthroned in the hallowed temples of democracy.

This is a clear-cut specimen of a credent-centered presentation to a believing audience; dramatic devices are used directly to deepen and strengthen listener beliefs about Lincoln.

THE CRITICAL ROLE

What It Is

Also derived from Greek (*krinein*, meaning "to judge" or "to discern"), critical, as used here, refers to a thinking or scientific viewpoint. It does not mean a carping or censorious, negative role (which is included in the "hostile" receiver state) but a willingness to accept ideas based on fact and sound reasoning. In other words, the validity, the reliability, and the truth of your ideas will convince the critical listener. Thus, you can see that this is another potentially desirable (constructive) receiver state.

Situations Calling for Presentation

When is critical communication in order? Here are some important indexes: (1) when people are capable of criticality; (2) when professionals or specialists communicate; (3) when listeners are rationally oriented; (4) when you are considering crucial issues; (5) when you are "educating" for criticality.

When people are capable of criticality means, of course, that both you and your receivers are willing and able to communicate within the rational realm. When communicators possess the necessary intelligence, knowledge, judgment, and reasonableness, the critical presentation may be proper. Without these attributes, it cannot be successful.

When professionals or specialists communicate, there is a likelihood (but no guarantee) that the critical presentation is proper. The rational outlook generally prevails in intra-professional communication.

When listeners are rationally oriented, they tend to the critical perspective. Here we are talking about a general ability to think through ideas (irrespective of discipline), a quality possessed by many top managers and professional people.

When considering crucial issues both you and your receivers are required to assume the critical posture. The reason is obvious: The very survival of the organization may be at stake, with a wrong decision leading to possible disaster, and the right decision resulting in inestimable long-range benefits.

When "educating" for criticality, that is, when developing people to think through ideas, to weigh decisions, or to solve problems, the critical stance is the only legitimate role. Presentations in this context must be planned and executed accordingly.

The Basic Impact in Criticality

When any of the above conditions prevail, the critical receiver state is probably called for. And here you must take a different approach from that in the four preceding roles.

The basic impact in critical presentations is to *get your receivers to accept your ideas as valid in a context of openness and scrutiny.* That is, you attempt to create a "persuasive impact" here through the best available facts and the most logical reasoning. And your presentation is open to criticism (in the critical sense we have discussed here) and review, which may result in modification of your ideas.

Examples of Handling Criticality

Specimen 1: Clark E. Beck, "Evaluation of Research and Development Proposals." As we saw earlier, Beck has taken steps to move his professional colleagues from initial sophistication (1–3). And he was no doubt aiming to get his receivers to the critical roles, as we'll see in his subsequent handling.

He speaks to the difficulties in evaluating R&D proposals (4), the nature of a solicited proposal (5), and some of the realities which must be faced in reading the request for proposal (6–8). He then launches into an item-by-item description of the importance of a proposal's contents (9–16), a description of how the proposal is evaluated (17–24), and a detailed description of criteria for evaluation (25–47). Beck's summary lists salient features of his presentation, together with implications for his listeners.

It can be seen that once he has handled initial sophistication, Beck uses a fundamentally straightforward logical sequence to present his ideas to this professional audience. His is a very good example of a critically oriented presentation.

Specimen 6: Philip Harris, "Patterns of Racial Exclusion in Top Management." Having presented this as a professional paper to a convention of the Academy of Management, Harris is clearly communicating in a critical context.

Note how Harris gets attention (overcomes initial apathy) by citing a newspaper headline about a New York bank charged with discrimination against Negro employees (1). He then moves to the problem of hiring for executive positions in American industry, giving some little-known, startling evidence pointing to discrimination in employing Negroes, Puerto Ricans, and Jews for executive jobs (2–3), devices designed to overcome his receivers' potential sophistication.

After this, Harris proceeds to outline a study he conducted, the results of which led to the above conclusion on discrimination in executive hiring. He defines his specific research categories (7–10), explains the use of job titles (11), and gives a table of basic data gathered (15) with interpretation (16), followed by the explanations offered by company representatives (16), then a listing by interviewees of ways to overcome barriers to executive hiring (17). His "conclusions" go beyond the descriptive to more significant interpretations, ending with an appeal for remedies (18).

It is evident that once he overcomes potential initial apathy and sophistication, Harris's presentation takes on a necessarily critical aura.

RECEIVER ROLE DYNAMICS

Initial, Backup, and Desired Roles

We have looked at each of the five receiver roles (apathetic, sophisticated, hostile, credent, and critical) separately. But clearly these interact with one another, so we now need to consider their interrelationships. In some of the specimen examples, the presenter has overcome some initial role or roles before presenting his ideas within a more desirable receiver context (for example, Beck, Specimen 1; Harris, Specimen 6; and Owsley, Specimen 13). Let's now explicate the process of handling receiver role dynamics.

The *initial* role is the expected beginning receiver state, which could be any one of the foregoing five. The *backup role* is the likely outlook once the initial condition is overcome (if you need to overcome it), which can be any of the remaining four. The *desired role* is either the credent or critical perspective (since these are the two constructive states). Figure 6-1 illustrates the process.

It can be seen from this figure that (1) you determine and handle the initial receiver state, whether destructive or constructive. If the constructive role is the desired one (that is, you may want a critical rather than the expected credent role), then you can proceed to your basic presentation. (2) If, as is more likely, you find that you must move your listeners to a more desired role, you determine whether or not their backup role is what you want. If it is, then you can plan to go on to your fundamental communication. If not, then (3) you must shift your listeners to the desired role, whether credent or critical, before carrying out your intended presentation.

Review of a Specimen Example

Let's quickly look again at a specimen to see how a speaker actually planned for and used this dynamic sequence.

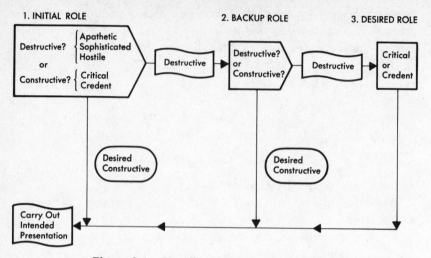

Figure 6-1.   Handling receiver role dynamics.

Specimen 1: Clark E. Beck, "Evaluation of Research and Development Proposals." We've already alluded to this specimen several times, so we'll briefly summarize Beck's handling of receiver role dynamics.

As we've seen, he deals first with a sophisticated receiver role by getting his auditors to see his subject in a new light (1–3). After this, his presentation is a straightforward, logical (essential elements sequence) exposition designed directly for critical receivers. Thus, Beck's presentation moved from handling the initial destructive role (sophistication) to communicating his basic ideas within the desired constructive role (critical).

SEQUENCE FOR CONTROLLING RECEIVER ROLES

Let's now put what we've said in this chapter into a practical framework which you can use to recognize and plan for handling the receiver states that you are likely to encounter in a given presentation. The following is a sequence of questions which you can ask and answer:

1. What receiver roles are most likely in the presentation?
      Initial?
      Backup?
      Desired?

2. From what evidence do I infer the above expected role or roles?

   Hard data?

   Experience with group?

   Reliable reports?

   Casual conversations?

3. What situations probably produced the destructive roles, and what conditions call for the desired constructive role? (Refer to discussions of the respective roles.)

4. Which situations and conditions can be most feasibly used to achieve an effective presentation? (From those identified in 3.)

5. What specific techniques and methods should be used to handle the situations and conditions selected in 4? (This question can be answered from our discussions in the next two chapters, for which we're now ready.)

7
Getting the Right Impact

Having studied the first two TRIM factors (the target and the receivers), we are now ready to examine the third element—impact.

Impact refers to the effect your communication has on your receivers. You may have the most important message, delivered in the most eloquent manner, but if it strikes your listeners in the wrong way (has the wrong impact), your presentation fails.

In our discussion of the five receiver roles (Chapter 6), we briefly alluded to the basic impact to be achieved in handling each. However, we did not go into the specific techniques and devices by which to achieve these effects. This is what this chapter is about.

As you recall, the five impacts are: (1) getting attention and sustaining interest; (2) inducing a new receiver perspective; (3) eliminating or abating opposition; (4) dramatizing to make ideas more meaningful; and (5) getting acceptance through validation and scrutiny.

GETTING ATTENTION AND SUSTAINING INTEREST

Remember that you must achieve this impact to overcome receiver apathy. Importantly, you must both get attention (immediate receiver focus) and sustain interest (continuing receiver focus). In other words, you cannot assume that once you have your listeners' concentration, it is permanent. Quite the contrary, attention is momentary and fleeting; therefore, you must work constantly to keep receiver interest. Let's now look at some techniques and devices to achieve this very important impact.

The Shocking

This means anything which startles, jars, shakes, or sharply surprises receivers. For example, the news account of an eight-year-old East Pakistani boy being swallowed by a python is certainly shocking. And the reports that most Americans have dangerous deposits of DDT in their bodies is clear cause for alarm. Or the charges leveled after a Senate investigation that certain doctors are making between $150,000 and $200,000 a year from Medicare and Medicaid by faking laboratory charges (and engaging in other dishonest practices) is certainly a startling allegation. Philip Harris uses this device in stating that "discrimination in executive hiring extends to Jews who have otherwise been integrated into the nation's workforce for many years" (Specimen 6:3).

Suspense

Here you leave your listeners in doubt as to outcomes (literally "leave them hanging"), or keep them guessing until the right moment. For example:

> Millions of Americans lost sleep; Europeans were either late for work or didn't show up. In India most activity stopped at noon. In Japan all work stopped in late afternoon. Indeed the event stopped most of the world cold. What event? The first footsteps of man on the moon on July 20–21, 1969.

Humor

One of the most frequently used devices to get attention and sustain interest, humor can be an effective way to overcome apathy. Note how Robert F. Kennedy uses it to get attention in his speech to law students at the University of Georgia (Specimen 11:4). See also how Max Rafferty employs one humorous story after another to gain attention and sustain his listeners' interests (Specimen 15:1–9).

When effectively handled, humor can be very helpful in getting attention and keeping interest. But if poorly done, it can create hostility or even greater apathy. It should always be relevant to your ideas and in proper taste for your audience.

The Novel

This refers to the new or the different. Innovative ideas, "way out" schemes, and new company products are examples. The listener's attention perks up when items like these are presented to him.

The Familiar

In contrast with the novel, this device appeals to listener interest through that which is already known. If not overdone, it is a very good way to bring an audience out of apathy. John F. Kennedy effectively uses it in reciting German history and quoting Goethe to a West German audience in Frankfurt (Specimen 10; see sections 3, 6, 10, 47).

The Inside Story

This is "getting the message from the horse's mouth" or "what's really going on." It is one of the most effective devices to awaken sleepy listeners. Hendrick is setting the record straight in describing Interpol (Specimen 7:1–4). And Robert F. Kennedy (as Attorney General) was "giving the word" on enforcement of civil rights laws to his Georgia listeners (Specimen 11).

Directness and Animation

Here we mean the effect of your own physical communication—that is, its impact through establishing rapport and evidencing your interest in your subject and listeners. It goes without saying that if you telegraph apathy on your part to your receivers, this will guarantee their own indifference. Although this is not to suggest your putting on an oafish exhibition, you should open up, use plenty of appropriate gestures, keep continuing eye contact, use change of pace, and get sufficient variety of vocal pitch and volume in presentation situations where apathy exists or is potential.

Other Devices

These include items previously discussed in the section "Developing Ideas," Chapter 3. Since they've already been explained and exemplified, and since their applications to overcoming apathy are obvious, we'll merely list them here: *stories and anecdotes; demonstration; audiovisuals;* and *audience participation.*

General Suggestions: Getting Attention and Sustaining Interest

Here are some things to keep in mind in using the devices listed above.

1. Use the techniques and devices most suitable to the occasion and audience (humor may be inappropriate in a very serious situation).

2. Don't give the impression of merely "putting on a show." After all, yours is a purposive presentation.

3. Use a sufficient variety of devices in a given presentation. Don't get pegged as a "one-device" man.

4. Remember that these techniques and devices are generally supportive. Therefore, use them to supplement—not to supplant—your ideas.

INDUCING A NEW RECEIVER PERSPECTIVE

This impact is, of course, required to overcome sophistication. It is important to remember that this "wise guy" role exists independently of whether receivers know or merely think they know as much as or more than you can tell them. In either case, basic devices are the same.

Building Receiver Respect

This means getting your listeners to have more respect for you, your subject, and your ideas. Sometimes you can use pre-presentation handouts listing your background and competence to speak on the subject. At the time of presentation, the person introducing you can also do much to enhance your stature. And during the presentation, your own well-placed allusions can help ("when we did this research, we found that . . ." or "I spoke with the well-known James Johnson about this . . ."), provided you do not create an impression of name-dropping or braggadocio. Needless to say, the best way to build listener respect for you is to give the best possible presentation. John F. Kennedy was employing this device in part when he started his presentation by citing facts about the German revolution of 1848 to his West German audience (Specimen 10:3–6).

Face Validity

This refers to appearance of validity in the sophisticated receiver's eyes. While your facts and reasoning may indeed be correct, your objective here is to satisfy the values and beliefs of your listeners, not the requirements of impeccable logic. In other words, you use "rhetorical" rather than "textbook" reasoning.

Face validity, then, reasons from the assumptions and values held by your receivers to conclusions you want them to accept. Robert F.

Kennedy is doing this throughout his "Law Day" presentation to University of Georgia law students (Specimen 11). If you'll examine the speech carefully, you'll see that he is constantly reasoning from an assumption his listeners must hold: respect for the law.

"As You Know"

Here you impute to the listener an idea which he knows (or ought to know) so that you can move to ideas he doesn't know. Since he doesn't like to admit cognitive gaps, the sophisticated listener is often vulnerable to this device. "You are no doubt familiar with . . . ," "You've certainly experienced this . . . ," "Everyone knows that . . . ," and "All of us have done this . . ." are synonyms for "as you know." Lynn A. Townsend is using this technique when he says:

> All of us, as communicators, have worked hard for many years, to explain the tried and tested merits of the business system that has served our country and much of the world so well. But what has been clear and evident to us has not always seemed so clear and evident to others. There have been, as you well know, a number of questions about the worth of our competitive system.

In using the "as you know" device, you permit the sophisticated receiver to save face and at the same time you create the likelihood of his being more receptive to new ideas.

Snob Appeal

Sophistication implies a degree of condescension. Therefore, the snob appeal device exploits this perspective. This is a "we know, but they don't," a "pity the poor plebe" technique. It is especially applicable within learned societies, professions, or tight-knit cultural groupings. Clifford D. Owsley uses it in addressing a Lincoln Group (Specimen 13:4):

> While most Americans know that Lincoln was a great man, a great President, and those who have done much reading know that he was a great writer, I say that most Americans have not yet come to realize the true stature of this fantastic man. They will someday, but not yet.

In addition to these techniques, other devices (mentioned in Chapter 3) applicable to getting receivers to see you and your presentation in a new light are *metaphor* and *quotations from respected persons or sources.*

General Suggestions: Inducing A New Receiver Perspective

Keep these points in view when planning for use of the above devices to overcome sophistication:

1. Select techniques appropriate to your audience and situation.

2. Avoid the appearance of "lecturing" listeners. Remember, sophistication implies a rejection of learning, so stay away from pedantry.

3. Use techniques and devices best calculated to move listeners to your desired constructive role, rather than any which could trigger hostility or apathy (even more destructive roles).

4. Above all, don't give an impression of your being "sophisticated" (or condescending) toward your sophisticated listeners. This will automatically trigger hostility.

ELIMINATING OR ABATING OPPOSITION

This impact is, of course, necessary to overcome hostility. Here the receiver does not merely assume he knows as much as or more than you do (as in sophistication); rather he "knows" that he is right and that you are wrong. Therefore you have the difficult job of changing his beliefs.

And you need to recognize that overcoming hostility is one of the toughest tasks you can face in presentations. Realistically you should accept the fact that there are situations where you may never be able to get significant shifts in receiver opposition. Sometimes all you can hope for is to get a fair hearing. In other cases, a series of communications over an extended period may be necessary to get your receivers from opposition to belief. The point is that you should be realistic in assessing your chances for overcoming hostility in given situations, and plan your presentations accordingly.

Let's now examine some techniques and devices for possible hostility elimination or abatement.

Common Ground

This is a general category covering several subordinate devices, *starting with common values and beliefs.* In this approach you begin with assumptions or beliefs with which the listener will agree, and later move to the idea with which he initially disagrees, under the theory that the psychological momentum will carry the receiver to a mental "yes." This is Robert F. Kennedy's pattern early in his "Law Day" presentation (Specimen 11:1–12). *Using respected sources or people* has already been discussed in Chapter 3. Its application in overcoming hostility is obvious. Kennedy also employs this device in quoting the Georgia Supreme Court (10–11) and Henry W. Grady (69–71). *Commendation for achievements or tradition* is lauding your listeners for things done well or for their normal ways of doing things. John F. Kennedy, in praising West Germans for their postwar participation in building a new Europe, is employing this technique (Specimen 10:8–9). *Placing disagreement in a broader context of agreement* is showing where narrow opposing views actually harmonize in a larger sphere.

Case Examples

This refers to the use of compelling illustrations, incidents, and happenings which in and of themselves persuade the hostile listener to your view. Sometimes the communicator may not draw explicit conclusions from the examples cited, but rather, by marshaling his illustrations in a convincing sequence, he depends on his hostile listeners' drawing the "obvious" implication. More frequently, the presenter builds his case sequence so that the audience is likely to accept the conclusion drawn by him.

Candor

Common ground and case example devices are often appropriate when your listeners neither know nor suspect your "hostile" ideas. Candor is more common when listeners already know your "alien" views, or where they suspect you of inimical ideas. Like common ground it takes several forms: *the compromise* is an attempt to get a *modus vivendi* or some working arrangement in spite of disagreement. If you can get your listeners to hear you out, and if they are sufficiently flexible, you may be able to get effective compromises. *Laying it on the line* is, without equivocation, stating your views and why, often accompanied by an appeal to listeners to reconsider their opinions. *Gaining receiver respect* means getting your listeners to think more of you and your viewpoint (even though they may still disagree) as a result of hearing you out. Cornelius E. Gallagher has taken this approach in part in his presentation to a chapter of the Institute of Management Sciences wherein he pleads for individual privacy in the midst of technological intrusion into human affairs (Specimen 4). *Admission of wrong-doing* means to admit your errors openly, accompanied often by a promise for amendment.

General Suggestions: Eliminating or Abating Opposition

Your handling of hostility can be improved if you keep these pointers in mind:

1. Select devices very carefully in light of which ones are most likely to succeed (common ground for listeners unaware of your opposing ideas; candor for those who already "know" you).

2. Don't expect too much change in listener beliefs. One presentation (or several) cannot always be expected to "save sinners."

3. While you can get attention (overcome apathy) by inciting hostility, this approach has obvious dangers. Therefore, you had better have well-laid plans to overcome opposition if you try to awaken sleepy listeners this way.

4. Above all, don't appear "hostile" to receiver hostility, because it can only deepen listener opposition.

DRAMATIZING TO MAKE IDEAS MORE MEANINGFUL

Here, of course, you are aiming to deepen or strengthen the credence of already-believing listeners. To reiterate, this is one of the most important presentation tasks confronting the modern manager or professional person. All too frequently, however, it is poorly done.

And when this is done badly, the resulting bad impact can turn believing listeners into hostile, sophisticated, or apathetic receivers, a regressive rather than progressive effect. On the other hand, when the job is done well, you build more dedication, commitment, and potential for constructive receiver participation.

What is meant by "dramatizing ideas?" As stated in Chapter 6, it means stirring receivers' imaginations, deepening their values, exciting their aspirations, and strengthening their tenets. Let's now look at some devices and techniques through which you may effectively dramatize ideas for credent receivers.

The Heart-Rending Story

This is an incident with a tragic ending. Major Steven Pless, a Vietnam veteran, who had been decorated with the Congressional

Medal of Honor, had flown 780 helicopter combat missions, and was later killed by a motorcycle accident in Florida, is an example of the tragic incident.

The Heart-Interest Story

This is the reverse of the heart-rending story, because it epitomizes a "happy ending." As an example, Robert F. Kennedy cites the award of a medal for bravery to a Georgia youth (Specimen 11:2–3).

Telling Details

These are "tidbits" of nonessential data, incidental information with dramatic appeal. Hendrick uses this device in telling about "Carbine" Williams and his development of the M-1 rifle (Specimen 7:17–18). And Max Rafferty gives one telling detail after another in relating his campaign stories (Specimen 15:3–8).

Appeal to Authority

Here you use influential people (such as the boss), sources (such as the law), or standards (cultural codes) to give influence or weight to your ideas. Robert F. Kennedy is using "respect for the law" in this sense (Specimen 11).

Conflict

Well-narrated conflict is, of course, always dramatic. Hendrick is using the continuing strife between international crime and international law throughout his presentation (Specimen 7).

Dramatic Event

Here is a powerful device to strengthen feelings. Owsley's description of Lincoln's development of the Gettysburg Address (Specimen 13:13–18) exemplifies this technique.

Other Devices

We've already discussed these very useful techniques for dramatization: *literary devices* (including the several to which we've referred), *"We shall overcome," dramatic details,* and *great ideals and goals.* Refer to Chapter 3 for review and exemplification.

General Suggestions:
Dramatizing and Making Ideas More Meaningful

You can assure more successful results in dramatizing ideas by following these tips:

1. Select and use the devices and techniques most appropriate to your group and situation.

2. Don't use too many dramatic devices in a given presentation. Choose and use well the relatively few that will best accomplish the job.

3. Use sufficient physical communication, voice, and directness in your presentation. This is no place for half-hearted gestures, monotonous vocal quality, or poor audience contact. And don't worry about "hamming it"; it's better to overdo than to understate in dramatizing.

4. Above all, in everything you say and do, make your audience know that *you believe* your ideas. With credent listeners, evidence of your own belief is essential to get them to believe deeper.

GETTING ACCEPTANCE THROUGH
VALIDATION AND SCRUTINY

This impact is necessary to persuade the critical receiver. And it is most important to remember that this is a fundamentally different role from the preceding four. Whereas the others are essentially feeling-oriented, the critical is idea- and fact-centered. In other words, persuasion of the listener or reader is done through open, rational, and logical presentation, never through indirection or concealment.

Getting acceptance through validation and scrutiny, then, means convincing your critical listeners and readers to discern your ideas (basic and supportive) as "true and reasonable," as based in fact and rationally sound. In other words, your receivers want to know that your ideas have real-world authenticity and that your inferences and reasoning meet acceptable standards. Any perceived deviations from these expectations will trigger one or more of the destructive roles (apathetic, sophisticated, or hostile), which, in most cases, results in automatic presentation failure.

What are techniques and devices to get critical acceptance? Since this is a fundamentally different form of "persuasion," the techniques and devices discussed will also be basically different from those given in the foregoing noncritical roles. In very tight rigorous presentations, you may need to use all; in less rigorous situations, a few only may be required.

Stating Basic Assumptions and Premises

This means clearly setting forth your important suppositions and presumptions. What do you assume to be axiomatic or given? What are self-evident ideas? What are reasonable mental starting points? Any presentation starts from implicit or explicit basic assumptions and premises. In critical presentations it is often important to make these explicit and precise at the beginning. Gallagher applies this technique early in his presentation: ". . . technology should be morally neutral—it should have no values itself other than the manner in which society chooses to apply it" (Specimen 4:1).

Stating Purpose, Thesis, or Hypothesis

These are your presentation mission, proposition, or idea to be tested. In a given critical presentation, you may include one or all of them. In explicating any one of these you are revealing where you intend to go, what you want to demonstrate, or what you propose to examine. This permits your receivers to follow and evaluate your presentation accordingly. Note Harris's statement of his thesis, "The evidence is clear that the failure of our society to integrate members of minority groups into the workforce is more than matched by their effective exclusion from the executive suite" (Specimen 6:3).

Stating Viewpoint, Scope, Limitations

These refer to setting forth your perspective, your idea range, and your exclusions. All critical presentations include these "sideboards," whether stringently stated or implied. The critical communicator knows that "truth" is always relative to these three elements, and he knows that his critical receivers will judge his ideas accordingly. Beck includes both viewpoint and limitations in his presentation (Specimen 1:1–2). Vardaman states his basic viewpoint: ". . . controlling the firm's communications is no easy task. . . . This means that all of us need a clear understanding of current attempts to solve this very complex and costly organizational problem" (Specimen 19:2).

Stating Procedures, Methods

Here you set forth how you went about gathering and interpreting your ideas, in other words, how you collected your data and reasoned through them. Often sources of data are also stated. Clearly this is another important way to alert your listeners to attend critically to your presentation. Note how Harris explicitly details the methodology of his study before launching into his findings (Specimen 6:5–13).

Stating Findings

Here you give the *descriptive* results of your investigation, study, or search. Facts, statistics, tables, graphs, any appropriate qualitative or quantitative symbols are used to report findings. In critical presentations, findings should be packaged so that you balance simplicity of communication against possible distortion of data. But in most instances you should probably explain your categories and how you manipulated data. See how Harris does this in his presentation (Specimen 6:7–13).

Stating Conclusions, Implications

These refer to "therefores" from your findings. What do your reportorial data mean? What do they add up to? What significance do they have? Which point to almost certain conclusions? And which indicate more tentative implications?

Stating Gaps, Weaknesses

In critical presentations you explicate where your ideas may be only tentative or faulty or where there are omissions in data. And this is done openly and candidly, together with reasons (such as the unavailability of data, the complexity of the problem, inadequate resources, limited time, faulty procedures). Here you should feel no compunction in "confessing your sins"; this is a code of conduct in critical communications. Seaborg is using this device in part when he talks about the enormous complexity of environmental problems (Specimen 16:22–25).

Providing Opportunity for Critique

This is another code of conduct for critical presentations. Opportunities for listener examination and discussion of your ideas before (sending a preliminary paper), during (permitting interrogation as you go along), or after (a post-presentation question-and-answer session) are always allowed, indeed encouraged. In critical presentations you should assume that your listeners are there to help you test your ideas, and, if needed, to suggest modifications of them.

Modifying and Communicating

Growing out of the preceding critique, you may need to reshape, restate, or even discard some or all of your original ideas. Modification may also require your making a follow-up presentation (or presentations); indeed, it may be necessary for you to recycle the entire critical presentation one or several times before the results are satisfactory.

General Suggestions:
Getting Acceptance through Validation and Scrutiny

The above are general devices and techniques for planning and carrying out critical presentations. In choosing and using them, keep in mind these principles:

1. In addition to the general techniques and devices, you must meet the critical standards within your discipline or subject area (principles, concepts, terminology, technology, and methodology).

2. Keep the critical presentation open to criticism and modification. It fact, you should actively solicit criticism from your listeners. Here you are concerned with the best-thought-out product, not a short-circuiting of rational thinking.

3. Bear in mind that the *validity of ideas* is primary; your ego and feelings can be badly bruised if you do not deliberately assume this perspective.

4. Make your presentation a truly cooperative, interactive endeavor between your listeners and yourself. Critical presentations can be very productive, constructive, and stimulating when this stance is taken.

SUMMARY: GETTING THE RIGHT IMPACT

In this chapter we've gone over the five basic receiver impacts: (1) getting attention and sustaining interest; (2) inducing a new receiver perspective; (3) eliminating or abating opposition; (4) dramatizing to make ideas more meaningful; and (5) getting acceptance through

Figure 7-1. Summary of impacts and devices.

Desired Impact	Devices
Attention/interest (apathy)	The shocking or the novel
	Humor
	The familiar
	The inside story
	Directness or animation
	Stories and anecdotes
	Demonstration
	Audiovisuals
	Audience participation
New receiver perspective (sophistication)	Building receiver respect
	Face validity
	"As you know"
	Snob appeal
	Metaphor and hyperbole
	Quotations from respected persons and sources
Eliminating or abating opposition (hostility)	Common ground
	Starting with common values or beliefs
	Using respected sources or people
	Commendations for achievements and tradition
	Placing disagreement in the broader context of agreement
	Case examples
	Candor
	Compromise
	Laying it on the line
	Gaining receiver respect
	Admission of wrongdoing
Dramatizing (credence)	Heart-rending story
	Heart-interest story
	Telling details
	Appeal to authority
	Conflict or dramatic event
	Literary devices
	"We shall overcome"
	Dramatic details
	Great ideals or goals
Validation/scrutiny (critical)	Stating basic assumptions and premises
	Stating purposes, thesis, and hypothesis
	Stating viewpoint, scope, and limitations
	Stating procedures and methods
	Stating conclusions or implications
	Stating gaps or weaknesses
	Providing for critique
	Modifying or communicating

validation and scrutiny. These correspond to the apathetic, sophisticated, hostile, credent, and critical roles discussed in Chapter 6. Using the Specimens, this chapter has enumerated, explained, and exemplified the techniques which can be used to achieve each impact. Figure 7-1 summarizes impacts and related devices. You can use it for ready reference.

With this background, you are now ready to put all the ingredients together in the final TRIM component—*methods* for effective presentation, the subject of Chapter 8.

8

Using the Right Methods

We're now ready to put all the backgrounds from Chapters 1–7 into practical methods which you can use in the real planning and execution of your presentation. These procedures are most important because they are your presentation payoff. Based on all the foregoing materials, they are systematic ways for actually sizing up and carrying out your communication.

These basic methods will be presented for you to follow in your own presentation planning and delivery: (1) planning the presentation; (2) getting yourself ready; (3) testing and revising the presentation; (4) carrying out the presentation; and (5) evaluating the presentation.

PLANNING THE PRESENTATION

Let's assume that you've established the need for presentation, that its benefits outweigh costs, that its feasibility has been determined, and that you have chosen the presentation form—oral or written or combined. (All the foregoing are discussed in Chapter 2, "Knowing When to Communicate.") Therefore, you are now ready to put your presentation into shape. Here is a practical, systematic plan of attack: (1) specify your presentation target; (2) specify your receivers; (3) specify impacts and devices; and (4) outline your ideas.

Specifying Your Presentation Target

Here you identify two things: your general target (information, conviction, reinforcement, action) and your specific message target.

The *general target* is one of the four discussed in Chapter 5. And, of course, you must know both basic and supplemental purposes. Furthermore, if action is your desired end, clearly identify which route is best (Route 1: information → conviction → action; or Route 2: information → reinforcement → action).

Next determine your *specific message target*. Here you relate the general target to the essential message you want to convey. For example, if your general target is "conviction," the specific message target could be "to convince company employees that the new practice of hiring outsiders is not a threat to existing personnel."

You should state your specific message target as simply and as succinctly as possible, because you then have a practical, tangible yardstick by which to judge the content of your whole presentation.

Specifying Your Receivers

Here, of course, you determine which feeling–thinking states most aptly typify your listeners or readers (apathetic, sophisticated, hostile, credent, critical). These have been described in Chapter 6, to which you may want to refer for review.

Judgment is called for at this point: you must infer the most descriptive category for most (or the most influential) listeners. And this then is where you pitch your presentation.

Furthermore, you need to identify the initial, backup, and desired roles of your receivers. As you'll remember, you want to move your receivers from any one of the apathetic, sophisticated, or hostile (destructive) roles to either a credent or critical (constructive) view. Since this step will essentially determine your idea sequence as well as the techniques and devices to control your receivers, extreme care should be exercised to assure accuracy.

Specifying Impacts and Devices

Having determined initial, backup, and desired receiver roles, you select corresponding impacts, which are to get attention and interest (apathetic role); to get a new receiver perspective (sophisticated role); to eliminate or abate opposition (hostile role); to dramatize to make beliefs more meaningful (credent role); and to validate with openness and scrutiny (critical role).

You then choose devices and techniques which seem most likely to gain the succession of predicted impacts. And in so doing, it is

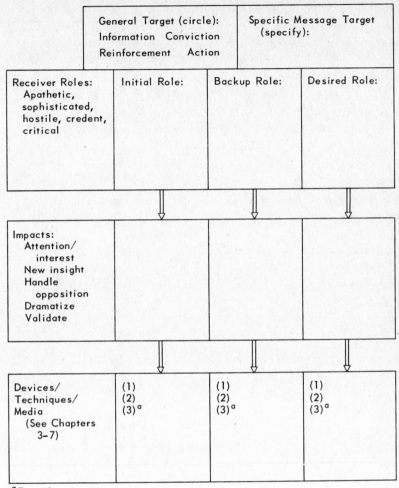

General Target (circle): Information Conviction Reinforcement Action		Specific Message Target (specify):	

Receiver Roles:
  Apathetic,
  sophisticated,
  hostile, credent,
  critical
	Initial Role:	Backup Role:	Desired Role:

Impacts:
  Attention/
    interest
  New insight
  Handle
    opposition
  Dramatize
  Validate			

Devices/
Techniques/
Media
  (See Chapters
    3–7)
	(1)
	(2)
	(3)ª
		(1)
		(2)
		(3)ª
			(1)
			(2)
			(3)ª

ªExtend as necessary.

Figure 8-1.   Size-up for presentation.

generally wise to select a few (rather than many) techniques. It is much better to do a good job with a minimum number of techniques than to risk achieving mediocre results from trying too many of them.

Outlining Your Ideas

You are now ready to put your ideas into a tentative outline. A convenient approach is to first size up your presentation, after which you make your outline. Figure 8-1 is for size-up; Figure 8-2 suggests a

Figure 8-2. Outlining presentation.

Type   Introduction (Summarize content, using chosen devices
                      and media for initial/backup receiver roles)

_____   _____
                      _____
                      _____

                      Basic Ideas: Primary sequence _____
                               Supporting sequences _____
                                                     _____
                                                     _____

Device/Medium   *Content* (Use caption, phrase, or sentence form)
(specify)
_____   (1) _____
   _____   (a) _____
   _____   (b) _____
   _____   (c)*_____
_____   (2) _____
   _____   (a) _____
   _____   (b) _____
   _____   (c)*_____
_____   (3)*_____
   _____   (a) _____
   _____   (b) _____
   _____   (c)*_____

Type   Conclusion (Summarize content, using chosen
                      devices and media for desired receiver role)

_____   _____
                      _____
                      _____

*Extend as necessary.

way to outline your ideas from what your size-up reveals. While both
suggest concise (but complete) ways to organize your presentation,
you can modify them or design your own instruments.

You can see that Figures 8-1 and 8-2 are based on all the TRIM
components, some of which are listed for your quick recall and use. If
you need review, you should refer to relevant chapters and sections.

Now that you've done a preliminary shaping of your ideas, let's turn to the next important variable: your personal preparation.

GETTING YOURSELF READY

If you've done all the preceding, you are well on your way to getting yourself ready. These specific checkpoints and suggestions will further prepare you.

Know Your Message

While obvious, it is so important that a reminder is in order. You should be so imbued with the ideas you want to convey that they are in the "marrow of your bones." If you have studied and applied the principles we've discussed in this book, you ought to know your subject as no one else will. And this is an essential base for personal preparation.

Know Your Group

You have already identified your receivers' psychological states. But here you analyze listener "logic." Questions like these should be asked and answered: What is the basic *intelligence* of the group (high, average, or low)? What are the general *education* (high school, college, advanced degrees), *training* (professional certification, management development program, labor-management relations), and *experience* (long, some, little) of the listeners? What do the receivers *know* about this subject, and what do they *need* to *know*? What *questions* will receivers probably *want answered*? And what do listeners expect you to say (for instance, expecting you to approach your subject from a different angle than you plan or expecting oo much or too little from you)?

Knowing answers to questions like these allows your building the presentation to deal with items of importance.

Prepare Presentation Aids

Specifically this means planning, constructing, or obtaining the audiovisuals (equipment and materials) and written media needed to make an effective presentation. Looking at your tentative outline, where have you indicated the need for visuals to clarify or to reinforce your ideas? Where do you need special equipment? Is professional preparation (artwork or technical editing) needed? In other words, you look over your plans to determine your exact audiovisual and written media requirements; then you take necessary steps to get all in readiness.

Prepare Presentation Notes

These are your personal communication aids, and they are very important in most managerial or professional presentations. Why? Because they are your guides, your means of assuring that you hit your intended presentation target with the right impact.

Notes can be in several forms: *traditional written outline* (in caption, phrase, or sentence style), on either regular pages or cards; *graphic notes* (such as flow charts, schematics, and paradigms). An example of a flow chart outline (which was used to explain a concept) is shown on page 255, Specimen 19; *manuscripts* are verbatim presentations, that is, exact word-for-word "notes." Let's see when and how to use each of the three.

Traditional written notes (usually following the outline pattern shown in Figure 8.2) are very common and useful. Whether your ideas are set out as captions, phrases, or sentences, you should remember these guidelines:

1. Reduce your ideas to essential (but helpful) words. Generally a given idea (basic or subordinate) should not be longer than one typewritten line.

2. Space sufficiently between ideas so that you can follow basic and subordinate ideas and so that you can easily refer to notes without losing your place.

3. Use marginal notes (handwritten, schematics, technical symbols) to cue you when to bring in supporting materials (visuals) or where to emphasize certain ideas.

4. Make sure you can easily and effectively handle your notes in the actual circumstances (using the same or similar lectern, microphone, or room) *before* the real thing. Getting the "feel" of your notes in this way is very important to your self-confidence and ultimately to your idea control.

Graphic notes (such as the flow chart in Specimen 19) are very useful guides when you are communicating abstract concepts, procedures, sequences, and relationships. Whether used as basic or supplemental guides, they can often be one of your best means of getting attention on and retention of your message. They are especially valuable when displayed visually (in written handouts and transparency projection, for example) so that you can direct listeners' attention idea by idea. Here, of course, all the principles of audiovisualization apply (Chapter 4).

Manuscripts should be used when you must assure as nearly complete an understanding as possible of very important ideas. Examples are professional papers, recommendation reports, and technical proposals. Here every word counts, and you can take no chance on impromptu remarks. Furthermore, you want a record of exactly what was said in the event some question is raised or in case of misinterpretation of your message.

When you need to read a manuscript to an audience, these tips will help.

1. Make the "reading" sound like your normal speech. The all-too-common word-for-word, jerky, monotonous reading of a manuscript is one of the surest ways to induce audience apathy.

2. Keep audience contact. You should be so familiar with your manuscript that you can merely glance down to key yourself from idea to idea, thereby permitting yourself to maintain eye contact with your listeners most of the time.

3. Use underlines, typographical devices, or other visual cues to help you emphasize ideas.

4. If your listeners are following from a handout manuscript, you may need to use even more emphasis, greater vocal and rate variety, and more physical communication to keep their interest and focus.

Prepare for Contingencies

Any experienced speaker will tell you that, even with the best planning and execution of a presentation, the unexpected will happen. We are, after all, human beings, not God. So you'll be well advised to "expect the unexpected" (and if nothing untoward happens, great).

But even here you can anticipate some outcomes which are more likely than others. For one thing your analysis of primary *receiver roles* can be off, so you should have in mind the most likely initial-backup-desired contingency. And this, of course, leads to a revision of your *outline of ideas,* meaning that you'll need a backup plan to accompany your contingent receiver role handling. Backup for *equipment and aids* is also very important. What if you have a power shortage? Could you use a blackboard to sketch your flow chart? What if the projector lamp burns out in the middle of a film showing? Do you carry a spare, and do you know how to put it in? What if your planned handouts cannot be printed on time? Do you have some alternative devices (such as a mimeographed outline) which would suffice? What about last-minute *changes of schedule* (for instance, if you find that the preceding speaker went 30 minutes over time, forcing you to reduce your planned one-hour presentation to 30 minutes)? These program changes happen more often than you'd think, and you'd best be prepared to meet them by having an "abbreviated" or "elongated" presentation in mind.

There is no need to try to list all the many unpredictables. If you carefully prepare to handle those we've mentioned, and then deliberately assume that your presentation will probably never go completely according to plan, you'll be able to effectively handle almost anything that arises.

Know That You Know

This is a self-review process. Here you want to go over: (1) *Your ideas*. (Are they complete, clear, and cogent? Do you have a backup outline? Make all needed revisions.) (2) *Your receiver analysis*. (Is it right in the light of all you now know? Are there some techniques and devices you should eliminate, or some you should add? This may require another revision of your idea outline.) (3) *Your presentation aids*. (Do you have enough—or too many—audiovisuals? Do you have the right written media to supplement your oral presentation? Do you have backup means in the event vital equipment or materials are unavailable or not usable at presentation time? Carefully check these out and take the necessary precautions.) (4) *Your delivery*. (This means self-rehearsal—that is, your going through the presentation, first silently, then aloud.) Self-rehearsal does two things: It gets the presentation "into your nervous system" and it gives you some first-hand idea of how it sounds. After all, your listeners will respond to the "sound" of your ideas, not the silent ones locked in your brain.

One of the best ways to know how the presentation really sounds is to tape record (or, even better, videotape) yourself, then play it back, record again, and play it back again, until you get the polished product you need (from yourself). When you arrive at this point you rightly *know that you know* what you are about.

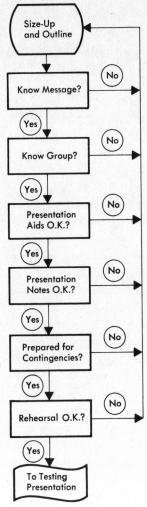

Figure 8-3.   Checklist: getting yourself ready.

Figure 8-3 is a "checklist" to help you prepare yourself for the presentation.

TESTING AND REVISING THE PRESENTATION

You are now ready to get further "pre-launch" assessment of your presentation. Sometimes only informal and perfunctory testing is needed; on the other hand, very important, survival-based presentations may require very careful, formal processing in order to assure that a vital communication mission is accomplished at the requisite level. Let's quickly look at several different testing methods, together with advantages and disadvantages.

Self-critique means that you use your own critical judgment to evaluate your own presentation. Essentially, this is what you do in self-rehearsal (discussed in the previous section). In other words, your "testing" begins and ends with self-rehearsal.

Self-critique does have advantages: it is relatively easy, fairly quick, generally inexpensive, and directly self-corrective. But there is a major disadvantage—it is difficult to be completely objective about your own presentation, which means that even with the best of intentions, you may fail to recognize weaknesses needing remedy.

Informal outside critique means a nonformal testing of the presentation using selected people who are willing and able to evaluate your product. Generally, you merely ask some people to audit a rehearsal and feed back their oral or written comments.

This testing method has all the advantages of self-critique, and it also overcomes the major pitfall of subjectivity built into self-evaluation. If you can get representative people who will "tell it like it is," rather than merely feeding back what you may want to hear, informal outside critiques are valuable pre-assessment means.

Formal company critique is where companywide systems and procedures are used to screen the most important presentations. Often this means that the company has its own presentations unit, which, essentially, controls the quantity and quality of important company oral or written communications.

Certainly this is the safest way to get the right presentations in the right numbers and at the right levels, but it is also costly. However, in firms where a great number of vital presentations are made, unit costs are relatively minimal, and if properly managed, this approach reaps rich returns.

A Critique Checklist for Testing and Revision

Let's now look at a simple but completely practical evaluation instrument that can be used for self-critiques, for informal outside critiques, and for many formal company systems (see Figure 8-4). If you use this sheet (or some modification) to get representative, plural

Figure 8-4. Critique checklist.

	Superior	Excellent	Good	Fair	Poor	Needed Improvement (Specify)
Message						
Did the *introduction* get attention?						
Were *basic* ideas clear and cogent?						
Were *ideas* adequately *developed*?						
Was the *conclusion* proper?						
Was the *essential message* clear?						
Receiver influence						
Did the presenter *address* himself to *you as a person*?						
Did he *address* himself at *your level of understanding*?						
Did he take *your viewpoint*?						
Did he appear to be *sincere, warm, open*?						
Were you *convinced* at the presentation's end?						
Language/voice/physical communication						
Were language, diction, grammar *correct*?						
Were language, diction, grammar *cogent*?						
Was there proper vocal *volume, tone, and variety*?						
Were *gestures* appropriate?						
Was *audience contact* sufficient?						
Presentation aids and facilities						
Were *audiovisuals* well prepared and handled?						
Were *written handouts* well prepared and handled?						
Was the *room* properly *set up* for the presentation?						
Was *equipment* well handled?						
Were *physical distractions* well handled?						

NOTE TO CRITIC: Complete this sheet as candidly and constructively as possible. Remember, the presenter will use your evaluations to improve his presentation, so he wants your realistic evaluation of his performance.

evaluations, you will have valuable indications as to where your presentation is strong and where it needs improvement. You should do whatever is necessary to overcome weaknesses, even to the point of retesting once you have made what you consider to be adequate revisions.

CARRYING OUT THE PRESENTATION

Everything you've done until now has been to assure that your actual presentation is successful. So it is to this payoff event that we now turn.

Although much could be said about it, a few essentials are all you need to remember and apply in carrying out the communication: controlling yourself; controlling your message; controlling your receivers; and controlling questions.

Controlling Yourself

If you've learned and applied all we've discussed to this point, you've made the best possible preparation for self-control. You will know your message and will be convinced of its worth; you will know your receivers and what must be done to get your message across; and you wil! have rehearsed, tested, and refined your presentation to ensure that it will do the job intended. Therefore, if you are realistic, you should have the fundamental self-control that comes from knowing that you are prepared as much as is humanly possible.

A few additional specific pointers will help you manifest self-control early in the presentation, which is often the most crucial time.

1. *Have the room and equipment ready.* This generally means arriving early to assure that the mike is working, that the lectern is right, that all equipment is in place and ready to go, that the room is adequately ventilated and lighted, and that seats are properly arranged.

2. *Get the right introduction.* If you are being introduced by someone, by all means be sure that the person is prepared to build you up rather than tear you down. Get a concise résumé to him in plenty of time for preparation of his remarks. And talk with him just before the presentation to furnish any other information he needs to set the stage for you.

3. *Have a starter.* Even if it means memorizing, have your initial

remarks ready. This is a very steadying influence in oral communication.

4. *Dress appropriately.* This means looking your best for the occasion. The presenter's proper attire helps him to command both himself and his audience.

5. *Assume a confident manner.* Walk confidently to the speaker's stand, pause and look at your group, start deliberately but forcefully, and proceed from there to the idea sequence you've spent so much time putting together.

Controlling Your Message

If you have outlined your ideas (written notes, graphic notes, or manuscript), and if you have planned for contingencies by preparing an alternative sequence, you will no doubt exercise fundamental control of your message. Here are a few additional suggestions to help.

1. Place your notes so that they are readily accessible, and so that you can move from idea to idea without losing your place.

2. Keep contact with your audience—not your notes. You should be able merely to look down to move yourself from idea to idea.

3. Make special marginal notations where you want to bring in audiovisuals, present handouts, or use audience participation.

4. Make sure that no equipment is blocking some auditor's view or hearing, thereby adversely affecting communication of your message to them.

Controlling Your Receivers

Again, if you've planned according to these directions, you will be more prepared for receiver control than 499 out of 500 speakers. These few tips will also help during the presentation.

1. Be sure that you follow your plan to handle the initial, backup, and desired roles.

2. Synchronize your presentation with the real shift of receiver roles. Although you've made your best predictions as to when a receiver may shift from, say, an apathetic to a credent role, you must watch your audience carefully to see when listeners actually come out of their lethargy and then adjust your communication concurrently.

3. Have your contingency plan handy in case you've missed in your analysis of primary receiver role. Knowing the most likely

alternative role syndrome can sometimes be the lifesaver for your presentation.

Controlling Questions

Many presentations will be followed by questions from listeners. And sometimes questions may be raised during the presentation. In either case you must be able to handle interrogations just as intelligently as your planned presentation. Indeed, it is wise to remember that each response to a question is a presentation in miniature, meaning that all the principles of hitting the target, communicating with receivers, getting the right impact, and using effective methods apply in each case. In any event, failure to handle a question-and-answer session adequately can wreck an otherwise excellent presentation.

Here are some basic suggestions in preparing for and answering questions:

1. Anticipate and plan for answering the questions your listeners are most likely to ask. When you can feasibly build answers into the presentation itself, this is even better.

2. Don't be afraid to admit your inability to answer tangential, complex, or involved questions. Don't bluff; your audience normally will recognize this. It is much better to say, "I don't know the answer to that one, but (if it is important enough) I'll try to find out." Make a written note, and get the answer to the person or persons asking the question.

3. Have notes with you on anticipated questions, especially where technical data, involved statistics, and specific names, dates, and places are called for. Your possession of these aids and their proper use can be powerfully persuasive with listeners.

4. With large audiences, use "buzz groups" (discussed in Chapter 4) to solicit questions in order to involve and give interrogative opportunities to all listeners.

5. Use a *plan for answering questions*. The following is a suggested sequence. First, *restate the question,* either in the listener's or your words in order to be sure that you have accurately heard and that other listeners may hear what was asked.

Second, *clarify the question* (for example, through definition, example, or illustration) in order to get proper understanding (the interrogator's and yours) of what is being asked and answered. Also remember receiver roles at this stage.

Third, *answer the question directly* (if possible within a minute or two) in order to give a quick but adequate response, then get to the next question.

Fourth, *ask if you've adequately answered* the question. If you have, go to another. If not, repeat the sequence, using your judgment as to how long you may feasibly spend on one question from one person. (If either the question or the interrogator is sufficiently important, you may need to allocate more time.)

EVALUATING THE PRESENTATION

This is the "postmortem" to determine (1) your presentation's effectiveness, and (2) where you may need follow-up.

In finding presentational *effectiveness,* several methods are possible:

1. Get *informal oral responses* after the presentation. Here you or others (such as department heads) talk with listeners to get reactions and comments. Frequently these responses are helpful in pointing out receiver information gaps, misunderstandings, and ill feelings. You can then take steps to remedy difficulties and to capitalize on assets.

2. Get *informal written responses* after the presentation. Here you get something down on paper, which frequently makes the listener think through his responses more carefully (thereby lending greater validity to his remarks). But at the same time, you may destroy the spontaneity and openness created by oral conversation, besides incurring the further disadvantage of being unable to read the visual cues of facial expressions or vocal intonations or pauses, which can signal important listener attitudes and feelings.

3. Get *formal responses.* These can be either written or oral—or both, in important cases. Here some standardized criteria, questions, procedures, and evaluational perspectives are used to get reliable and valid results. More costly and difficult to design and administer, these should be used only in vital presentations.

Your *follow-up* (guided by the above findings) can take one or more of several forms.

1. *Nothing* more may be needed. If your message and impact are all or more than you wanted, your presentation activity can terminate.

2. *Additional presentations* may be needed. Some facet of your original communication may need to be presented or discussed in

depth. Or some ideas may be so garbled in the listeners' minds that you may need to scrap the first presentation altogether and start anew. Or, happily, you may see the need to capitalize further on favorable outcomes.

3. *Additional communications* may be needed. That is, written media (such as memos, directives, brochures, and agreements) or other oral means (such as conferences, staff meetings, phone calls), whether singly or in combination, may be required to bridge gaps, create desired understandings, or exploit constructive situations. (These uses are discussed in depth in Chapter 4.)

SUMMARY: USING THE RIGHT METHODS

The last and payoff of TRIM components, methods, are the operational procedures for successfully carrying out the presentation. Built on all principles and concepts given in the preceding chapters, basic methods were discussed under five headings: (1) planning; (2) getting yourself ready; (3) testing and revising; (4) carrying out; and (5) evaluating. This chapter has set forth specific ways for doing each.

Concluding Remarks to the Text

In these eight chapters you have examined basic backgrounds, principles, techniques, and methods for effective communication. First, you studied important backgrounds: how to size up presentation needs, how to organize and develop ideas, and how to use presentation media. After this, you went successively through the four TRIM elements: the targets, receivers, impacts, and methods for achieving successful presentation results.

In all of the last four chapters, each principle was amply illustrated by references to specific parts of the twenty Specimens in Part III. This combination of principle and example is designed to permit you to see quickly and clearly how each concept is actively applied by prominent business, government, and professional speakers and writers. Furthermore, the examination of each item in the context of the total communication permits your seeing its contribution to the whole.

In conclusion, the purpose of this book is to give you constructive, practical guidance in presenting ideas correctly, clearly, and cogently. If you follow the TRIM approach intelligently and industriously, you can achieve this goal.

III

COMMUNICATION SPECIMENS

Specimen 1. Evaluation of Research and Development Proposals

CLARK E. BECK
Senior Project Engineer, Air Force Flight Dynamic Laboratory,
Wright-Patterson Air Force Base, Ohio

1. Because of the nature of my experience, this discussion of how proposals are evaluated is limited to solicited research and development technical proposals written by Industry and directed to the United States Air Force. The cost proposal is a separate document not treated here. I'm sure, however, that much of this discussion is applicable to proposals in general.

2. Any proposal may be considered an instrument of persuasion. That's really what it is. It is written to *convince* someone that they should agree with its contents—usually to the extent of financing the work it proposes. If it is to persuade, it must be aimed directly at the objectives and interests of the customer. Company interests, prejudices, and goals must be subordinated or eliminated. The writer must strive to achieve this customer-oriented tone in spite of his natural tendency to talk about his own viewpoint.

3. In technical circles, as in social circles, not all proposals are accepted. However, when one recalls that a number of proposals to conduct the same work may be written but that only one will be accepted, the low ratio of successful to unsuccessful proposals is understandable. But since every proposal represents an investment of time, money, and facilities, some degree of success must be achieved to justify continued expenditures. Unfortunately, as proposal writers know, it is difficult to maintain a very high average in this game. I hope that what I say here will be of some help in raising the reader's average.

Presented to the 13th International Society of Technical Writers and Publishers Convention, Fort Worth, Texas, 1966. Reprinted from *Technical Communications*, Second Quarter, 1968.

4. Research and development proposals are probably the most difficult to write and often the most difficult to evaluate. The nearer a proposal is to the research end of this realm, the greater the difficulties. The reason is the limited amount of knowledge available—for both the writer and the evaluator. In early research, too, there is often no predetermined "right way" or approach to take. Both the preparation and the evaluation of the proposal must be based on predictions and estimates, usually with a host of unknown factors involved. It is understandable that first the writer and then the evaluator feels that his task is the most difficult to perform.

5. *Request for Proposal.* Your solicited proposal is written in response to the statement of a technical problem which we feel that your company may be interested in and capable of attacking with some hope of success. The recipient of your proposal is already convinced that the work should be done, so convinced that he has expended his resources to prepare a complex document that asks you and several others to consider doing it for him. He is trying to convince you and others that you should want to do the work. In other words, you know in advance that someone is going to be given an opportunity to do the work. The only question is *who;* only the best one will be chosen.

6. The request for proposal (RFP) will contain a technical exhibit that outlines the work for which the proposal is solicited. Some of the difficulties encountered in the preparation of the proposal start with that technical exhibit. It may be less than perfect. Remember, after all, that it was written by an engineer, and as an engineer, I can say—without hesitation—that we are human and most of us could use the benefits of a good technical writing course.

7. Things are further complicated, especially in research and development work, because the engineer who writes the technical exhibit may be less than an expert in the field for which he solicits proposals. We must all realize that a frequent reason for the solicitation is that the necessary experts are not within the office sponsoring the work. The technical exhibit writer may not be sure of what he wants or what technical route will best lead him there.

8. This is the way it is in research, and this is one good reason why it is called research. What many research RFPs really say is, "You tell me what you feel can and should be done in this specific technical area, why you think it should be done, how much of it you can do, why

you think you can do it best, and how much time and money you want to do it." From the responding proposals a specific program will be formulated which one of the responders will be paid to complete.

9. *Proposal Contents.* Before a contract is awarded, there must be agreement on the approach to be taken and on which responder will do the work. These decisions are made by the technical proposal evaluation team. The technical proposal must be its own defender during the evaluation process. Technical proposals, as the most important consideration in contract awards, should be specific and complete. We understand that it is difficult to predict all engineering problems at the time a proposal is prepared, but we expect certain standard items in any well-prepared proposal.

10. *Proposed Line of Investigation.* Brief but specific; we are not interested in giving you a blank check for basic research. We have a specific problem and want a specific solution.

11. *Methods of Approach to Problem.* An obviously basic section.

12. *Recommended Changes.* Recommended changes to the technical exhibit are always welcomed. The technical exhibit may ask for work which your experts already know will contribute nothing to the solution or which has already been done elsewhere; or it may have omitted work which must be done. (After all, one of the evaluators is the writer of the RFP; the worth of the final program figures in his future as strongly as in yours.)

13. *Logical Work Units.* The logical phases, the order in which they will be completed, and the reasons for that order.

14. *Estimated Completion Time.* A timetable is important to indicate when results will be available and to define the proposed expenditure of funds.

15. The technical exhibit is not intended to be a statement of work. It is merely an indication of some of the possible approaches to the problem that we have recognized. You are not limited to these approaches but are actually encouraged to submit different ones for equal or even preferred consideration.

16. Your proposal should *not* merely offer to conduct an investigation "in accordance with the technical exhibit" of the RFP but should outline as specifically as possible the actual investigation proposed. We know that anyone can say, "yes, yes, yes" and still not be able to produce. Records show that this has happened. We want to

know what, why, how, and when. You must therefore propose a specific statement of work to be accomplished. This statement is vital in the evaluation process and in the later negotiation process as well.

17. *Evaluation Process.* You may be interested in just what happens to your proposal after you have packed it up and sent it on the journey to decide its fate. It arrives in the office of the contracting officer and is joined by several other contestants in the same main event. They are all held there until the deadline for proposals for this particular program effort.

18. In this office, which is legal in nature, each is studied to ensure that all required portions are included. The cost proposal, usually submitted as a separate document, is extracted and retained here for later reference. At the same time, any cost figures which may have been included in the technical portion of the proposal are carefully cut out and retained.

19. When the technical portion of the proposal includes only technical information, it and all others are sent to the project engineer. The project engineer is the man who has written the technical exhibit which caused you to write your proposal. He usually is the man who will monitor the contract which results from the proposals. It is at this point that the technical evaluation really begins. Although the number of proposals he receives depends on many things, there will probably be no less than two and no more than ten.

20. The team of evaluators is chosen from a list of men recommended by the project engineer and other top men knowledgeable and aware of the RFP, which was started some nine months earlier. The team will usually be three men, including the project engineer, who is the captain. The qualifications of each man chosen as an evaluator and the reasons for his being chosen are made a matter of record for this procurement. Each man on the team is given complete and detailed instructions by the project engineer. These instructions probably include background information on the program, why this contract is desired at this time, what is needed and/or expected from the resulting contract, instructions for the actual evaluating process, and a statement of the weight (value) of each of the several areas being evaluated. For some efforts the completion date may be more critical than for others; this information must also be known by the members of the evaluation team.

21. These items are discussed in a meeting of the evaluation team.

Questions from the evaluators are answered, and each is instructed to complete his evaluation by a certain date. During the evaluation process, the evaluators are forbidden to discuss the proposals with others. Each evaluator rates each proposal on the standard evaluation form which includes certain criteria to be covered later.

22. After the individual evaluators have completed their ratings, another general meeting of evaluators is called. Then the relative standing of each proposal is discussed and a final composite rating is given each.

23. The evaluation report includes each individual evaluator's form as well as the composite form. It is only at this point that the technical evaluator is permitted to have any information concerning cost. The buyer reviews the technical ratings, and if the top-rated proposal happens to be one for which the cost is considerably more than that estimated by the project engineer at the time he wrote the technical exhibit, the buyer makes this fact known to him. It then remains that either (a) additional funds will be found to buy the top-rated program or (b) a decision will be made to buy a lower-rated but still acceptable program within the available funds.

24. One very important point: If several proposals are rated technically acceptable, the one with the lowest cost will generally be the winner if its cost is considered to be realistic. There must be very good reasons for not buying the least expensive acceptable program. For example, it may be that a very low cost indicates that the company plans a lower level of effort than had been read into the technical proposal by the evaluators. Obviously, in these cases, restudy is in order.

25. *Evaluation Criteria.* Since the technical evaluation process is so very important, knowing the standards of evaluation that will be applied to your proposal should be of value to you as a writer. The most important of them may be divided into two general categories: qualifications of the bidder and the scientific/engineering approach.

26. *Qualifications of the Bidder.* Your company's qualifications, based entirely upon what the technical proposal says, are determined in five areas:

27. (1) *Specific experience.* The specific experience of both the company and the proposed investigators is of considerable importance, especially in research. Since it is so important, the proposal must include all previous related experience of the individuals to be

assigned to the program and any prior related company programs from which the proposed effort might benefit.

28. (2) *Technical organization.* Technical organization figures in the evaluation of a proposal in three ways: (a) as it relates to the arrangement or format of the proposal; (b) as it relates to the men and facilities to be used during the program; and (c) as it relates to the total organization of the company.

29. (a) The organization (arrangement or format) of every proposal is, quite naturally, noticed by evaluators just as the contestants for Miss Universe are looked over by the judges—official and unofficial. I do not wish to imply that there is a single "best" way to put all proposals together. Each situation is different and no true judge will insist that there are any three measurements which completely describe Miss Universe. There is much more to it than that.

30. Earlier, I listed some of the standard items which we expect to find in a well-prepared proposal. The way they should be arranged for program X may not be best for program Y. However, some proposals appear to have been thrown together at the last minute without the benefit of an editorial analysis. Such an omission can be costly to you and your company.

31. The better proposals will have information arranged in a logical easy-to-follow sequence—much as the phases of the effort should be. You should arrange the sections so that the evaluators can follow the development of the ideas easily, not so we are forced to hunt through page 25 for the answer to a reasonable question resulting from a statement made on page 10.

32. Briefly, you should review the information you have to present, place yourself in the position of the evaluator, and arrange the information and facts so that they tell the best possible story for your proposal. This is where you writers and editors can really earn your pay; this is your specialty.

33. (b) The organization of the men and facilities to be used during the program is important; this organization can include such factors as the lines of communication, the lead group for the program, who has control of facilities that must be used, and similar characteristics of the program organization. It is generally better if the equipment and machines required for the program are under the control of the group responsible for the program. Getting in line to have necessary work done in a facility under the control of others

(who may have priority work of their own) can be damaging to schedules. Likewise, there should be rapid and direct communication lines between the effort leader and other groups contributing to the program. We prefer an organization arrangement which facilitates "getting things done," unencumbered by excessive levels of administration, one that provides the contract monitor with direct access to responsible company personnel. This facet of technical organization is the most important from the technical evaluator's point of view.

34. (c) The over-all organization of some companies places research and development groups in more desirable situations than others do. Where the environment for research groups is good, where research groups enjoy status within the company organization, an evaluator can expect a better potential for success than in organizations where research is inhibited or suppressed.

35. (3) *Special technical equipment and facilities.* Certain research programs require special technical equipment and/or facilities. When these are required, it is important that their availability be made known in the proposal. I mentioned earlier that the proposal must be complete and must totally defend itself during the evaluation process. Just because we know that a special piece of equipment is needed, we cannot assume that you have or will get it. On the contrary, if you don't mention the need for and availability of special equipment, we must assume that you do not know that it is needed and have no access to it. Make your proposal complete!

36. (4) *Analytical capacity.* Research programs frequently require a considerable amount of analytical work. Today this usually means more than a desk calculator. If you will use special computing facilities, describe them and certify their availability for the program.

37. In addition to the mechanical and electronic analytical capacity, mental capacity is of prime importance. If a member of your company is a recognized authority in the field of interest or if your company had done advanced work in this same line, tell us in the proposal. In some highly specialized research programs, we would rather have one month of a certain individual's effort than a year of work from one who is not an authority. It is important to you that all specialized capability be stressed in the proposal.

38. (5) *Level of effort/support.* The proposed level of effort and support is evaluated in two ways. Of first concern is the level of effort proposed for the program. How many men working for how many

hours do you propose? What equipment and facilities are to be used and for how much time? What is the total time proposed for completion of the program? Just when can we expect to have the final report and data from the program? These answers are important because we must compare your estimates with those of your competitors and with our own best estimates of reasonable man-hours, equipment, facilities, and calendar time required to solve the problem. Differences shown by these comparisons are difficult to resolve when you have not adequately justified your proposed level of effort.

39. The second concern arises when your proposal indicates that a portion of the work will be done by another company that you will engage as a subcontractor. It is dangerous to have a large amount of the work done by others. We expect you, as the prime contractor, to do most of the work. If you cannot, perhaps another company should be the prime contractor and you should be a subcontractor for that company. We don't want to pay you just to oversee work that others do. This is one thing we can do for ourselves.

40. *Scientific/Engineering Approach.* The technical approach to the problem is very important in research work. The wrong approach can be costly with respect to both time and funds. In many research programs an answer must be obtained by a certain date so that it can be used to complete other work on schedule. A much larger and more important program can be endangered if we wander down the wrong path and do not have the right answer by a certain date. When this happens, both of us have lost.

41. Four specific areas are used as indicators in evaluating the scientific/engineering approach:

42. (1) *Understanding of the problem.* It is sometimes easy to misunderstand the real problem, especially if the technical exhibit is not well written. For this reason it is important that your proposal state, clearly, the problem to which it is addressed. It is usually wise to have several people in your company read the exhibit to ensure that the real problem has been recognized. If in doubt, the writer of the exhibit is a good source of clarification. He can be reached through the buyer, who is listed as the person to whom your proposal should be addressed.

43. Note: Only after going through this administrative contracting officer (buyer) may you talk to the exhibit writer, or he talk to you. This rule is not intended to make it difficult for you to talk to us but

rather to assure all proposers of the benefit of the same information while proposals are being written.

44. (2) *Soundness of approach*. Particularly in research work, as in real life, the manner in which a problem is approached frequently determines the degree of success one might expect. Your proposal must include enough information to substantiate the technical soundness of your approach. It must both demonstrate the feasibility of the approach and indicate the probability of successful results.

45. (3) *Compliance with requirements*. The technical exhibit will include a number of specific requirements, most of them technical, but also undoubtedly a number that are not. The latter may include submission deadlines, reporting schedules, reporting format, and proposal format. Someone, probably you, the technical writer, must assume the responsibility for seeing that these requirements are met.

46. Some of them are easily overlooked while the proposal is being prepared because everyone is fully occupied with the technical aspects of the proposal. However, there is a penalty during the evaluation process. If these nontechnical requirements are not met. Even though a technical person might see little need for some of them, they are still requirements and cannot be randomly omitted. It is small consolation to an unsuccessful proposer to know that the evaluators rated his total package high in most categories but that the loss was largely due to not complying with the nontechnical requirements.

47. (4) *Special technical factors*. This category may be considered a sort of "catch-all" area. We give consideration to simplicity of design, ease of maintenance, unique ideas, weight, size, configuration, reliability, and similar items that are applicable to the particular proposal. Several items in this list are applicable only when some piece of hardware or a working model is the end item; in research, unique ideas are especially desired.

48. *Summary*. Perhaps the best advice for technical writers should be:

Know exactly what your company wants to propose.

Describe it in a manner that is complete and impossible to misconstrue.

Leave nothing to the imagination of the evaluators (they are not permitted to imagine or assume). Make your proposal easy to read. Make your proposal logical and self-supporting.

49. I realize that you, as a technical writer, do not have the liberty

to change the technical content of a proposal. However, there are different ways to arrange and to say the same things. Technical people, whether they are writers or evaluators of proposals, appreciate well-written documents. It is very difficult for an evaluator to close his mind to the fact that the final report on a contract (often the only result he will have to use at the end of the contract) will be written no better than your proposal is. The proposal, itself, is a solid, practical indicator of what he will have to show for the money he invests in your company. With a time schedule to meet in the evaluation process, poorly arranged and/or incomplete proposals will be the first to suffer. There is a reasonable limit to the fancy dressing up that can be done to proposals. But there is also another lower limit.

50. Make your proposal easy to read, easy to understand, impossible to misunderstand, and truly indicative of the quality writing which we might expect from your company.

Specimen 2: Wanted: Effective Communicators
LAWRENCE A. DYSART
Richfield Oil Corporation

1. Will you do a bit of imagining with me? I'm told this is the place for it. Fantasyland is not far away. Will you travel back in time with me to the England of the 11th Century and imagine that you are living there? As a person of formal education, the language you speak is of Norman French, because this is the language of your country's conquerors. When you write, you write in Latin because this is the principal language of the scholars and the record keepers. You do not speak or write "English" as you think of it today.

2. But while you are speaking French and writing Latin, most of the other people in the country are using a completely different language. This other tongue is known as Kitchen English. It is called this because it is the language used by the scullions who work in the

Presented to a Regional Convention of The Desk and Derrick Clubs of North America, Los Angeles, California, June 1, 1963. Reprinted from *Vital Speeches of the Day*, August 15, 1963.

kitchens of the great houses—it is used by all other uneducated people as well.

3. Little by little the words of the kitchen begin to creep into your Norman French. This kitchen language is full of strange-sounding words—odd words with the sound of the ages upon them: ox, cow, calf, boar, deer, hunt, words that arise from a combination of ancient tribal dialects shaped and colored by the languages of the invading Angles, Saxons, and Scandinavians. As the years go on, more "kitchen words" enter your language. Ultimately, your heirs abandon Latin as a written language. Instead they use this new, impure mixture of Norman French—"kitchen" both to speak and to write.

4. This, then, is English—surprisingly like that of today—it was then and is now an unscholarly language not shaped so much by rules of deportment as by the experience of the streets. Shakespeare produced his great works without ever having studied English grammar. It didn't then exist.

5. This is English, termed by authorities as one of the most diversified and expressive of all the world's great languages. Yet flexible as it is, we sometimes get in trouble today when we try to stretch this wild pelt we call English over the complex framework of 20th century communication.

6. Communication consultants decry the use of jargon, yet we sometimes use a jargon of our own in trying to define it. We use confusing terms like "feedback" and "vertical and horizontal communication": Can't it be more simply defined?

7. Of course, communication is talking and listening and writing and reading, yet it's something more: it's talking and writing in a way that will get the message across to the person or persons for whom the message is intended.

8. For weeks, I tried to communicate to my 10-year-old son the fact that he was eating too much and, as a result, was getting too heavy for his height and age. I informed him somewhat patronizingly, I suppose, that I had had the same trouble when I was his age. I told him that my being too fat as a boy had made me the butt of many jokes. But all of this so-called communication on my part didn't produce the slightest result. I kept right on communicating and Jonathan kept right on eating. Then—one day at school a golden-haired little girl whom Jonathan adored chanced to make this comment within earshot of my son. "You know, Jonathan would be cute if

he were not so fat." That turned the trick. Within ten days, he had lost ten pounds.

Specimen 3. Changing Ground Rules for the CEO

T. MITCHELL FORD
Chairman and President, Emhart Corporation

1. The role and responsibilities of a CEO have been defined by every group that has been given a chance. Academicians have hypothesized them, M.B.A. curriculums have defined them, the SEC and other federal regulatory agencies have presented mandates, and the shareholders have vociferously made demands. But, I suggest, there is one dimension to the job that has not been tangibly drawn because it cannot be so drawn. It involves the changing sociology of business and the psychology of managing people who are better educated, independent, and more skeptical than obedient—people looking for more satisfaction from work than a paycheck. It means being comfortable and surefooted in the role of public advocate for the company and the free enterprise system. It means not resisting or resenting being thrust repeatedly into an open arena to explain, to defend, to report, or to persuade. Fundamentally, I believe, it means understanding historian Daniel Boorstin when he laments that America's problem is finding "a cure for success."

2. UNREALISTIC EXPECTATION

The obvious cure for failure is success. But, as Boorstin points out, our technology has made us all so well-off that success alone often leaves some of us unfulfilled because it has raised our expectations unrealistically. Thus business, in this context, is seen as single-handedly capable of—and responsible for—solving the energy crisis, eliminating pollution, eradicating unemployment, and providing total

Reprinted from *Advanced Management Journal*, Autumn 1979.

equal opportunity in all hemispheres. When it falls short of these unrealistic goals, it is criticized.

While the logic may be flawed, executives in tune with our present social environment will be at ease with the problem—not because they concur, but because they understand that, underneath it all, it is more positive than negative. This feeling reflects an almost naive optimism that the business system has the capability to accomplish *any* goal. In this sense the criticism is, fundamentally, a matter of impatience.

Executives in touch with reality will not be drawn into pointless debate on these issues, appreciating that the matter at hand is not so much what the public perceives as fact. It does not mean accepting a critic's point of view; it means accepting the reality of it to them—and reacting responsibly, not emotionally or even traditionally.

As I see it, this is the essence of the new and more subtle benchmarks that time and society are daily adding to the conventional measure of an executive's performance. The CEO is expected to be able to pierce the strident rhetoric and understand what is really being said and why—and know what to do about it without overreacting. He or she is expected to be comfortable with the public's insatiable demand for accountability on many fronts and is expected to be capable of handling touchy situations so that there is minimal disruption to the operational flow of the company's activities, and temporary matters do not fester into major confrontations.

These are some of the *qualitative* performance criteria being added daily to the traditional *quantitative* (or financial) measures of a chief executive.

3. A MATTER OF COMMUNICATIONS

Chief executives today must recognize that communication is not simply response to questions or allegations. Implicitly, it means regular initiatives taken by the company to keep its various constituencies—or publics—abreast of important developments (even those that are negative) before they are demanded.

C. Northcote Parkinson's latest law says, "The vacuum created by a failure to communicate will be quickly filled with rumor, misrepresentation, drivel, and poison." Contemporary executives need no such provocative reminders from Parkinson.

Executives today exercise extraordinary care over the integrity of financial data released to the public. Increasingly, they are recognizing that the company's credibility is delicately balanced on a host of factors other than the information they are obliged to report—sales and profit figures, EPA expenditures, minority employment, and so on.

So it returns full circle. The basic bottom line—what the public believes to be fact—is critical, almost more so than the facts as they actually exist. It's a complex amalgam of integrity, credibility, facts, nonfacts, and reputation.

Making the proper decisions in these instances may require some softening of rigid, overly cautious, legal, or technical prohibitions. There is a new personal judgment initiative being increasingly expected of CEOs by boards and shareholders.

The simplest case in point might be a product recall, an enormously expensive matter and one that is instinctively resisted until all legal or technical avenues are explored. However, it is a potential danger that may be best handled by decisive action in the earlier stages, before irrevocable public damage is done to a corporate reputation.

John D. DeButts, recently retired chairman of AT&T, put his finger precisely on these new standards when he commented, "Today, more and more of the time that used to be spent in running the business must now be devoted to representing it to the many constituencies on which its future depends."

This brings me to a final and no less pivotal aspect of the changing nature of our profession—the human relations part of it.

4. THE HUMAN FACTOR

In the 1990s, there will be some 78 million young workers in the "prime" 25- to 44-year age bracket. These are the ages generally perceived to be the years of ambition as well as of skill development. What will these people be like? What will motivate and move them?

Consider: A substantial portion of this prime age group is the generation that rolled through the public school system like a tidal wave, crumbling old concepts of discipline, revolutionizing the colleges, disrupting traditional values, and institutionalizing political protest.

Even the younger members of this group (the more recent college graduates) will be different, better educated, more conservative, but no less skeptical.

Collectively, they will place personal values before corporate goals. They're likely to turn down a promotion and refuse overtime or a transfer, even if it means economic gain.

Work for these young people will have as much economic meaning as it has for our generation, but they're going to demand more than economic reward. They'll demand of work the freedom to act as a whole, free person.

Thus, executives face the giant psychological problem of developing compatibility between the goals of the company and the individualism of this new kind of employee.

To make the right fit between the individual and the company is an art as much as a science; intuitive judgment is needed as well as computer analysis.

It may seem fundamental, but the best way I know to cope with these relentless humanistic pressures is for us to get out of our wood-paneled sanctuaries and practice old-fashioned people-to-people leadership.

This may seem to undercut the time-saving advantages and cold efficiency of the wide array of electronic aids to management and the decision-making process. But the ability to step back from technology, to recognize what can and cannot be delegated to a computer—when a word processor impedes communication rather than facilitates it—these are a few of the emerging new yardsticks I see entering the chief executive officer's job description.

Communications must never get so sophisticated as to exclude human relationships. Today's and tomorrow's executive is expected to be sensitive to the fact that people aren't loyal to an institution as defined by charts, statistics, and machinery. They're loyal to a living, breathing, and responsive organization—an entity that is nourished by their knowledge, intellect, experiences, attitudes, and opinions.

The ability to adapt to a changing environment was pivotal in the survival and success of species during the millions of years of earth history. The CEO must recognize and accept the changing environment in business and society and address these new circumstances through a responsive management style if he or she is to ensure the survival of the organization. As in competitive sports, although the ground rules might change, the game remains the same.

Specimen 4. Technology and Society

CORNELIUS E. GALLAGHER
Congressman from New Jersey

1. America has produced the richest and most complex society the world has ever known. The major impetus toward our unparalleled prosperity has been our ability to harness our resources and to use the gifts we have received as a nation for the benefit of our citizens. It is not an overstatement to say that technology has created America, at least in the sense that the applications of science have created the life led by most Americans. The fundamental premise of this speech is that technology should be morally neutral—it should have no values itself other than the manner in which society chooses to apply it.

2. Immediately, however, numerous objections can be seen to such a premise. For example, it has often been stated that technology opens doors for man, but does not compel him to enter. Yet it must be realized that in the real world of free enterprise, a logic is imposed which strips such technological advance of its ideal neutrality. The first application of a new technology—the first organization through the door—is likely to make the most money while the last is likely to find it slammed in its face. Risk taking by industry is motivated by the profit factor: thus, whatever neutrality a technology may have is already diluted by the financial facts of its development and the rush for its deployment.

3. When the decision is made to exploit a new technology, major social and institutional change follows. It is impossible to predict the range or the character of that change. A development and deployment decision is made solely upon the first-order effects, which are customarily profit, institutional advantage, or national policy in the case of federally inspired innovation. The evaluation of the second- or third-order effects, such as social costs and value dislocations, only takes place after a technology has been established.

4. What occurs then is a virtually dictated application of an innovation and the impact upon the rest of society only becomes visible after the technology has become operative. It is only by the time a sizable investment of money, resources, and commitment have

Presented to the Institute of Management Sciences, Chicago Chapter, March 26, 1969.

coalesced that society can know what it has really done. The innovation itself becomes a powerful reason for continuing in that direction and the difficulties and the dangers must be, in large measure, either ignored or rationalized. To put it bluntly, the problems have been transferred from ones of engineering to ones of public relations.

5. To illustrate the current status of technology in America, let us imagine that technology is a heathen idol and that Americans are primitives. What have we, as a society, offered this God in the way of sacrifice?

6. First, we have given him our air. Our cities form the bottom of an airborne cesspool. Our atmosphere is now so polluted that natural temperature inversions threaten every single person living in large metropolitan areas. For that simplest and freest of commodities—a breath of fresh air—we must depart from our homes and our jobs. The pilgrimage to Mecca for the infidels of America is the summer vacation to a place where man has not despoiled his heritage.

7. It is interesting to note in this connection that we have saved the whooping crane by creating wild-life sanctuaries and imposing the strictest rules and regulations for the preservation of this species. But man, who by his pollution-inspired cough emulates the cry that gives the whooping crane its name, has not been so fortunate. As columnist Arthur Hoppe has suggested, it may be necessary to establish human-life sanctuaries to assure the continuation of Homo sapiens.

8. The next sacrifice we have made to the God of technology is our water. All forms of pollution are dumped into our rivers and lakes, and a fresh, pure stream near an urban area is as rare today as a polluted one was earlier in our history. Raw sewage is dumped into rivers from which downstream communities take their drinking water. Lake Erie, according to many observers, can never be reclaimed from technology's abuse. Bodies of water which have existed practically since time began, are now being ruined in a few years. . . .

9. In addition to our air and our water, we have not hesitated to make human sacrifices to the idol of voracious technology. Our nation's highways are nourished by the blood of our children and the reports of the mangled victims of auto accidents make even the carnage of Vietnam seem insignificant. In sheer numbers, slaughter on the highways was approximately five times as great last year as were our losses in the tragic Vietnam conflict. In theory, we commit our youth to Vietnam in pursuit of a noble ideal; we destroy our

young men and young women on their way to the neighborhood drive-in.

10. Over all the world hangs the ultimate symbol of the God of technology—the mushroom cloud of atomic holocaust. Mankind genuflects to that God every time we say we coexist on our planet because of a "balance of terror." I have never felt that there is any true balance of terror; it is only the product of a universe that is out of balance.

11. How truly irrational we have become may be seen in the following hypothetical example. It is a basic assumption of the cold war, at least in some quarters, that should the American way of life be fatally threatened, we should incinerate those who oppose us. This would, of course, result in our own incineration and quite probably the fallout would make our globe uninhabitable. Yet those who advocate this course of future action are acclaimed as realists and patriots.

12. But any man who would propose that all industry stop and all autos be taken from the highways in order to make our atmosphere habitable would immediately be branded as insane.

13. So it is sane to destroy the whole world and yet it is crazy to take extreme action to make the world livable. The "balance of terror" has certainly unbalanced something.

14. The bomb, as terrifying as it is, merely promises the extinction of life. All men, be they free or enslaved, have come to some individual understanding with the fact of eventual death. But the latest visitation from the God of technology promises to make us less than human and threatens to make us slaves.

15. The computer demands that we poor dumb savages offer up our individuality, our dignity, and our privacy. It provides a new priesthood with a tool to drive us to our knees, to manipulate our actions, to petrify our past mistakes, and makes the sword of Damocles dangle, gleaming with its promise of eventual destruction, in every American's future. . . .

16. A viable democracy depends on an atmosphere in which people can go their own way for the vast majority of their daily experiences and satisfactions. Freedom from either subtle or overt coercion is the birthright of our citizens. In a nation as large and as complex as America, which contains so many different ethnic and cultural heritages, no one class of men—no matter how well-educated

or how nobly motivated—can impose the standards of their group on the remainder of American society.

17. . . . The argument over privacy is frequently confused by the belief that it is space alone that is the subject under discussion. This narrow emphasis permits the legitimate objection that man is a social creature and that he demands interaction with his fellows. If privacy merely refers to a physical area, this view is perfectly correct. Everyone knows that city life lacks many of the comforts and graces of rural life, and yet urbanization is perhaps the central fact of population movement throughout history. So it would be foolish indeed to ignore the absolute necessity for man to seek the company of neighbors. Yet most observers have found an equally powerful counterforce, and that is withdrawal from society for certain periods.

18. I would like to suggest to you that the personality needs a psychological living space just as the body insists upon an area of physical autonomy. I believe that the Territorial Imperative in lower animals has a counterpart in man which I call the Intellectual Imperative. The Intellectual Imperative is as essential to mental health as the Territorial Imperative is to a sense of physical security. In my view, psychological integrity is as important as bodily integrity. A stable society cannot be constructed or maintained if illegal searches and seizures are permitted through a man's ideas and beliefs while his papers and effects are protected by law.

19. Professor Charles Fried of the Harvard Law School puts the need for privacy in extreme terms. He says: "Privacy is the necessary context for relationships we would hardly be human if we had to do without—the relationships of love, friendship, and trust. Intimacy is the sharing of information about one's actions, beliefs, or emotions which one does not share with all and which one has the right not to share with anyone. Be conferring this right, privacy creates the moral capital which we spend in friendship and love."

20. In my concept of the Intellectual Imperative, man may choose those in whom he wishes to confide. He may discuss any issue in any terms he may desire and be assured that an indiscretion of phrase or even an indecency of thought will remain private. A space of psychological control permits ideas to be discussed freely and openly within his territory and with the guarantee that strict public accountability will not follow. It is just this blurring of the public and the private which makes invasion of privacy so obnoxious to personal

integrity and to civilized society. No idea springs, like Athena from the head of Zeus, fully formed. The tranʼslation of idea into insight, of knowledge into wisdom, follows as many different courses as there are individuals who think. It is impossible to produce a flow chart which can predict or channel the maturation of a thought.

21. This leads to the psychological truth that the betrayal of intimacy is, in essence, the greatest invasion of privacy. But it is equally harmful to society if the experiences of private life become shallow. If you cannot reside in an atmosphere of security, if you must remain guarded—suspicious of those in whom you confide—you diminish the commitments of private life. And without something to defend, without relationships to trust and love in your private life, you are going to have little reason to strongly defend the public welfare.

22. What I am saying is that the Intellectual Imperative permits man to strengthen his belief in abstractions like patriotism by creating personal realities like friendship and trust. I believe that my concept of the Intellectual Imperative leads to the point that you cannot love anything if you are afraid to reveal yourself to another.

23. The control of the flow of information about yourself, about your actions, about your beliefs, is then seen as a crucial aspect of a dynamic society. Urban mass culture has destroyed for most of us the opportunity to exercise freely the Territorial Imperative; the advance of computer and other technologies threatens the Intellectual Imperative. Physically, we are constantly in a crowd; intellectually, technology has provided devices to make our forgotten actions and our unacknowledged thoughts known to the crowd. This is, I believe, what is meant by depersonalization and dehumanization and, as I have tried to suggest earlier, may be a root cause for the violence in our nation.

24. The American use of technology has made man immense. . . . Yet technology has also diminished man and threatens to make him less than human. While every computer card received from a large organization as a bill, a financial statement, or a summation of personal history carries the warning, "Do not fold, mutilate, or spindle," individual man receives little assurance from the sender that he himself will not be folded, mutilated, and spindled.

25. There are those who say that anyone who criticizes the forms

taken by the new technology is somehow against technology and, therefore, progress. There is the implication that the expression of some of the views I have given you this evening would have caused me to oppose the use of indoor plumbing because it destroyed a society based around the village pump. This is simply not true. To paraphrase Shakespeare, I come to praise the new technology, not to bury it. But at the same time, we must praise man and see that he is not buried under the computer-generated data. Computer professionals by and large know the limitations of their machines and they know that the output of a computer depends on the quality of the data fed in. The standard acronym is GIGO: Garbage In, Garbage Out. My purpose is to disabuse nonprofessionals of the notion that it really means Garbage In, Gospel Out.

26. At the beginning of this speech, I constructed a slightly facetious example of technology as God and man as humble penitent. Some of the most vocal defenders of the unevaluated use of technology sound very much as if they truly believe they are theologians and they are justifying the operations' immutable laws, which are unchangeable because they are the dicta of divinity.

27. I take quite the opposite view. Tools are for the use of man and their valid use does not harm man; only their abuse does. Although I may be widely known as a computer critic, I firmly believe that the forceful assertion of privacy need not be contradictory to the fullest exploitation of the miracle of electronic data processing. The computer is as vital to efficient government as civil liberties are to the citizen's confidence in democratic government. This search for a balance, the attempt to isolate and control the toxic elements in the tonic of technology, is now a major challenge. For, basically, it challenges our faith in ourselves, it challenges our ability to use our skills in the service of man.

28. John Diebold has probably coined more money from the new technology than any other man; he even coined the word "automation." In 1964, he made the statement with which I would like to close my speech: "The problem of identifying and understanding goals to match the new means that technology provides us is the central problem of our time—one of the greatest problems in human history. Its solution can be one of the most exciting and one of the most important areas for human activity. And the time is now."

Specimen 5. How to Feather Your Nest When It's Time to Talk Turkey
ROBERT JAMESON GERBERG
President, Performance Dynamics International

1. Negotiating a salary when interviewing for a new job requires some careful planning if the prospective employee wants to get the best possible compensation package he can. This task entails acquiring an understanding of compensation alternatives and salary ranges, forming long-term goals, knowing when to discuss salary and how, and deciding if a contract should be negotiated. To help the candidate get the highest price for his services he can, the author offers some general guidelines to salary negotiation and bargaining.

2. Many job candidates do a highly effective job of obtaining and conducting interviews. They spend days, sometimes weeks, drafting and redrafting their résumés and covering letters. When they are rewarded with an interview, they visit their local library and thoroughly research the company they will be visiting. They then gather reams of personal documentation, and spend hours perfecting their interview techniques. Some even write down a list of expected questions (an excellent approach) and then rehearse their answers. This usually pays off with a good interview and definite interest on the part of the prospective employer.

3. But then it comes time to discuss salary, and these same meticulously prepared, indefatigable candidates are suddenly at the mercy of the interviewer. They seem to lose track of their objective, and the need for employment suddenly becomes their consuming passion. As a result, many end up accepting a job at less than they're worth, quickly become disenchanted, and are soon back in the job market.

GET THE FACTS ABOUT COMPENSATION

4. The fact is that salary negotiation is the "bottom line" of the job-hunting process and requires every bit as much diligence and

Reprinted from *Advanced Management Journal*, Winter 1979.

preparation as locating opportunities and getting ready for the interview. When you're finally offered that great position, and it's time to talk turkey, you must understand the host of alternatives that exist. You must be aware of the general guidelines of salary negotiation and keep many key bargaining tactics in reserve.

5. You should know, for example, when your present compensation constitutes an asset or a liability and when to use it as leverage or leave it out of the picture. You should also be knowledgeable about such special compensation alternatives as bonuses, commissions, expense accounts, matching investment programs, and stock-option plans. And you should be aware of some of the newer benefits, such as "up front" cash bonuses and termination agreements.

6. A key fundamental fact to keep in mind is that most companies are flexible in their salary policies. This means that a salary range is usually established for each position, and your salary objectives will be matched against this range. Even when a firm claims that the salary is open, you can be sure that the employer has an idea of what he is willing to pay. The most common range is one that differs by half the amount of the minimum salary. For example, a company may have a job that pays from $30,000 to $45,000, and while they would like to hire someone at the lowest possible salary, the usual procedure would be to allow the supervisor to offer any amount between the minimum ($30,000) and the midpoint ($37,500).

7. Generally, the lower the amount at which an individual is hired, the higher the annual percentage increase for which he is eligible. In some companies, too, the lower the salary range, the more frequent the salary review. There are, of course, instances where a salary is fixed or nonnegotiable, usually in smaller firms, and in top positions. Before you reach the salary-negotiation stage, you should do your best to find out what the employer hopes to pay and the range established. If it is too far away from your objectives, be prepared to skip the job opportunity entirely.

FORMULATING YOUR OBJECTIVES

8. When forming your objectives, take a look at the big picture and understand all of your opportunities. Concentrate on standard of living factors, and short-term take-home pay, rather than increases in

gross annual income. But also realize the long-term advantages of any benefit programs you may be awarded. Consideration of all of these will give you a better idea of all the possibilities.

9. If you are presently employed, keep your objectives firm. Discipline yourself against letting people discourage you, and aim for what you believe you are really worth. Obviously, if you are unemployed or under other immediate pressure to make a change, you will have to be more flexible. But under no circumstances should you undersell yourself. Set optimistic goals.

WHEN AND HOW TO DISCUSS SALARY

10. When asked by the prospective employer what salary you are looking for, don't state any numbers unless they are on the high side. Better yet, avoid the question until the company is completely sold on you. Also, once you have committed yourself, and the potential employer has met your requirements, remember he will be looking for immediate acceptance of the job.

11. Certainly, you should never attempt to negotiate salary unless you are sure that you are about to be made an offer. An employer who hasn't really made up his mind about you may be turned off very quickly by premature salary discussions. If you're offered the job, don't accept it immediately. Always ask for time to think it over. Then, if you want the job, you can try to negotiate a better financial package. No good organization will withdraw an offer just because you think you're worth more, and the worst that can happen is that it will hold firm on its original offer.

12. If you are looking for maximum salary, be enthuiastic about everything but your dollar offer. Show real excitement about the job, your future boss, the company, and the opportunity—everything but the money. Then make sure they know you would like to start immediately. At this point, you might say that after carefully reviewing your situation, the intangible costs of the job change, and other alternatives, you wish they could see their way to meeting your needs. If all of these approaches fail, try to get them to meet you halfway.

13. Candidates with low current salaries should obviously avoid stating them early in an interview, as such information in the hands of the interviewer will only put you at a disadvantage. There are some

people who have successfully negotiated offers without ever revealing their present income. But they are the exception. Most employers will not tolerate an individual's excuses for not revealing this information, and for good reason: they use present salary as an evaluation factor. For example, if you were earning $22,000, you might not be considered by some people for a $35,000 position. Someone else could have the same set of credentials but be earning $30,000, and he would be an eligible applicant. If you find yourself in this type of situation, it is essential that you sell your potential accomplishments—the benefits you can bring to the company.

14. One way to disclose salary and to exhibit ability at the same time is to show the earnings growth you have achieved. People associate salary progress with performance, and if you have something to say in this regard, it can frequently raise the offer.

15. Candidates with a high salary relative to their age and experience may want to hold disclosure of their salaries until later in the negotiations, in order to gain bargaining leverage. You'll have to play this by ear. If you don't want to waste time on interviews that will prove disappointing and if your hopes for a great increase start to dim during the interview, it may be wise to state your salary and get it over with. Remember, however, that when you discuss previous compensation, refer to salary, bonuses, commissions, profit sharing, and other benefits as a package.

16. If you are one of those people who tend to inflate their earnings in order to receive a larger dollar offer, be aware that it is very easy for an employer to check the accuracy of your information. He may ask to see your payroll stub, or he can request a copy of your latest W-2 income summary. He can even receive written or telephone verification or use an outside agency to investigate your background and earnings after you have been hired. In reality, this is infrequently done. But if you do state a higher earnings level than you are really at, you are taking a calculated risk of being discredited.

17. Apart from your base salary, there are many forms of compensation that you can receive and bargain for. They vary according to company, policy, level of position, experience, type of job, economic environment, and so forth. Corporate perquisites, commonly called "perks," frequently include a range of benefits from a company car, matching investment programs, and stock-option plans to executive dining-room privileges. Some of the more important

ones to consider are profit-sharing plans, stock options, pension plans, insurance and health programs, reimbursements of moving expenses, short-term loan privileges, mortgage funds, and deferred-compensation plans.

CONTRACTS

18. A growing trend in salary compensation dealings is the negotiation of employment contracts and termination agreements. These are always good for the applicant because they provide formal acknowledgement of the terms under which the candidate agrees to work for the company. Many organizations take forceful stands against contracts because the employer is guaranteed very little under such arrangements, and the employee can easily break them.

19. Contracts guarantee the employee certain compensation for a specific length of time, assuming the employee works to the best of his abilities during normal business hours. Corporations usually have to offer a financial settlement if they choose to dismiss a contracted executive, since the courts tend to rule in favor of the individual in cases where a contract is broken.

20. For senior executives, a contract is often more important than salary. This is especially true if the corporation has a large turnover in top management, or is frequently the subject of merger or acquisition discussions. As a general rule, we suggest that anyone above $40,000 a year in salary should ask for a contract. But be aware of the attempts that employers will make to dissuade you. The most common tactic is to hint that your contract request reflects a lack of confidence in the company, in management, and in your own ability. They may also ask if you are the kind of executive who values security more than opportunity. Here is an example of what the employer might say:

> Your contract request makes me wonder if you have the self-confidence and entrepreneurial qualities that you've indicated. We're also very concerned about your trust in us. If our relationship is going to be as successful as we all plan, I think it should begin on a note of mutual trust and integrity.

21. If you anticipate this kind of comment, it is easy to finesse it. However, your employer may insist on inserting a protective clause in the contract that limits your ability to take future employment with a

competitor. Such an insertion is often requested as a show of good faith and is difficult to refuse without creating serious doubts in your new employer's mind.

22. At the executive level, there are certain types of organizations with which you must be firm in requesting a contract. These include those in financial difficulties, merger or acquisition candidates, those that have recently merged or been acquired, family controlled and private companies, and those firms where one individual dominates the environment. If these unstable conditions exist, you might request a three-year contract that covers your minimum compensation and also has provisions for such things as bonuses, deferred compensation, moving expenses, annual renegotiations, and profit sharing. You should also negotiate life insurance, compensation in case of release by merger, outplacement fees in case of termination, and other such items. Don't ever treat contract terms lightly; be sure to review all the fine print with a competent lawyer.

23. Termination agreements are sometimes substituted for employment contracts, and they usually take the form of a short letter in which the employer agrees to an irrevocable severance compensation. Some industries have begun to regularly negotiate termination agreements at or above salary levels of $50,000. However, I know of a number of instances where people earning $30,000 have been successful in negotiating termination agreements. In most cases, they provide a minimum severance compensation of six months' salary, relocation expenses, professional outplacement assistance, and the extension of all insurance benefits for one year.

28. All of these contract comments pertain to employment in the United States. The European environment is completely different. Most European nations have enacted laws that are heavily weighted on the side of the employee. In addition, employment contracts are quite common at relatively low salary levels. It is not unusual for a European company to give an employee two years' notice prior to termination.

EVALUATING OFFERS

25. Your most difficult decision in salary negotiation may be evaluating two separate offers. If you're young or just starting out, the decision may be easy. My recommendation is always to put future

opportunity above starting salary. If you are an executive, there is little in the way of hard and fast rules. However, I have found that it helps to write down a "balance sheet" of the positives and negatives of each offer and to compare them. It's nice when the position with the most growth potential is also the highest offer, but it never seems to work out that way.

26. When you decide to accept a job, always accept it verbally and then confirm your acceptance in writing. The letter should restate the terms under which you have agreed to work. Hopefully, the company will do the same.

27. As you can see, salary negotiation requires much more than simply adding 10 to 15 percent onto your present income to determine a starting figure. There is a special psychology to understanding what to say and how to say it. If you prepare carefully, establish precise guidelines, and understand salary bargaining, you still might not be happy in your new job—but at least you won't be hungry.

Specimen 6. Patterns of Racial Exclusion in Top Management

PHILIP HARRIS
Professor, Baruch College of The City University of New York

1. In the recent past, front-page headlines announced that a leading metropolitan bank in New York had been charged by 14 employees with discriminating against Negroes. The bank had been pursuing a vigorous campaign of seeking job applicants in the ghettos and had been congratulating itself on its success in recruiting. One of the complainants, a computer operator, was quoted as follows: "No one ever said (the bank) doesn't hire Negroes. But what happens after they hire them? Is the Negro given the same chance to advance as the

Presented to the Academy of Management National Convention, Chicago, Illinois, December 1968. Reprinted by permission of author.

white man? No. Is he given the same job training to prepare him for a promotion? No."

2. Whatever the facts may be in the particular instance, it is clear that the equal opportunity struggle has now advanced from the level of hiring to the higher reaches of executive promotion. The new arena is portended by a statement made by Dr. Eugene Callender . . . who told a conference called by the Attorney General of New York State that jobs are not enough, and that entry of minority groups into the ranks of executives and business owners must now be implemented.

3. A starting point for action must inevitably be an assessment of the present composition of the executive force in American business. The evidence is clear the the failure of our society to integrate members of minority groups into the workforce is more than matched by their effective exclusion from the executive suite. This conclusion follows from a pilot study of the percentages of Negroes, Puerto Ricans, and Jews in executive ranks. While one might have deduced that discrimination against Negroes and Puerto Ricans in lower-level jobs would lead to a paucity of managerial personnel from these groups, it is startling to find that the discrimination in executive hiring extends to Jews who have otherwise been integrated into the nation's workforce for many years. Perhaps most significant is the fact that New York City, a major center of American Jewish population, has but a slightly higher percentage of Jews in executive ranks than other sections of the country.

4. As a group, corporate leaders have the reputation for giving generously of their time and money to worthy causes. Many have even played an important role in bringing members of minority groups to the factory floor, the clerical desk, and the sales counter. But bringing them into the executive suite is another matter.

5. Our Study . . . was sponsored by the United States Equal Employment Opportunity Commission and the New York City Commission on Human Rights. The methodology included an open-end questionnaire and interview at ten companies in the "Wall Street" and "Madison Avenue" complexes. In each case, the company selected for study was among the three largest in its field and had its principal office in New York City.

6. *Problem of Definition.* Data on the numbers of Negro and

Spanish American executives were readily obtained because each company was required by law to file Equal Employment Opportunity—Employer Information Report EEO-1. This form calls for the total number of employees in each of several job categories, and the number of Negroes, Orientals, American Indians, and Spanish Americans in each. The job category "officials and managers" was used in this study to identify the "executive."

7. Form EEO-1 defines "officials and managers" as "occupations requiring administrative personnel who set broad policies, exercise overall responsibility for execution of these policies, and direct individual departments or special phases of a firm's operations. Includes: officials, executives, middle management, plant managers, department managers and superintendents, salaried foremen who are members of management, purchasing agents and buyers, and kindred workers."

8. The number of Negroes classed as "officials and managers" on Form EEO-1 was therefore the figure sought from the interviewee. In only one of the ten companies was the request refused. Its representative stated that the data were already available to the interviewer from the forms submitted to Washington, and that so many researchers were calling on this company for various studies that a policy of refusing interviews was adopted to reduce the burden.

9. The definition of Spanish Americans in Form EEO-1 includes those of Latin-American, Mexican, Puerto Rican, or Spanish origin. One interviewee was cooperative to the point of checking the employee's application form for a clue. In this company, 90 percent of the Spanish Americans were not Puerto Rican. Most of the interviewees refused to examine the records, stating that such a check was too difficult. Consequently, it is probable that the number of Puerto Ricans offered by the companies is significantly overstated. Based on the 90 percent figure cited above and on inferences drawn from the interviews, and using the representation of Negroes in these same companies as an indicator, the best available estimate of the actual numbers of Puerto Ricans is presented in the table below.

10. The count of Jewish executives was even more difficult to arrive at. Company representatives stated that the information was unnecessary because the company did not discriminate, and that the very idea of such a count was wrong, undemocratic, and immoral;

even if the company wanted to know, it could not tell because of changes of name or religion, or non-observance of the religion. All the interviewees objected on one ground or another. When pressed, however, six of them complied by consulting a list of executives and indicating which were thought to be Jewish. A seeming contradiction then emerged with the cooperating companies. The official often made knowledgeable comments, such as "His mother (or father) is not Jewish" or "His wife is not Jewish," even though at the outset such personal data were said to be unavailable. Consequently, it is possible that the number of Jewish executives may be understated. However, it should be noted that other researchers in the field have validated the technique of scanning lists of names to determine Jewish representation.

11. *Job Titles.* For purposes of further analysis, interviewees were asked to provide the job titles of their executives who belong to the minority ethnic groups. The responses led to an additional reconsideration of the data given by the companies. For example, one company representative stated that he had included in the category of "officials and managers" all persons exempt from the overtime provisions of the Wage-Hour Law. Several companies included job titles not ordinarily considered as "executive," such as Typing Team Supervisor, Supervisor of Stencil Addressing, Assistant Index Captain, Senior Clerk, Senior Mail Station Clerk, Delivery Foreman, and Personnel Control Clerk.

12. One company alone accounted for more than 90 percent of the Negro and Puerto Rican executives found in this study. A careful reading of the organization's job titles leads to the conclusion that at least three out of the four are not truly appropriate for the category of manager or official. Also, very few reach top management positions, judging by titles. Another company had no Puerto Rican executives in New York but several Spanish Americans elsewhere in the United States. Discussions led to agreement that no more than 25 percent of the Spanish Americans could possibly be Puerto Rican. The percentages shown of Jewish executives would diminish by two-thirds if one particular company were excluded.

13. *The Basic Data.* A measure of employment opportunities is the number of each minority represented in executive ranks. The following table shows the resulting data.

14. *Minority Composition of the Executive Suite*

	New York City		Elsewhere	
	Number	*Percentage*	*Number*	*Percentage*
Executive population studied:				
Nine companies	4,359	100.0%	4,043	100.0%
Negro executives	41	0.9%	6	0.1%
Puerto Rican executives	6	0.1%	5	0.1%
Executive population studied:				
Six companies	2,216	100.0%	4,047	100.0%
Jewish executives	198	8.1%	305	7.5%

15. These data must be read in conjunction with the latest figures on the ethnic composition of New York's population. Negroes and Puerto Ricans in white collar jobs comprise 5.7 percent each, compared with 18.2 percent and 10 percent of their incidence in the population. The EEO-1 form does not yield data on Jews. But it is significant that Jews, though comprising approximately one-third of the population of New York City, hold only 8.1 percent of the executive jobs. This underutilization is further manifested at higher levels in the organization, judging from the job titles in this study.

16. *Company Explanations of Data.* Defending the conditions revealed by the data, company representatives offered a variety of interpretations:

• A smaller percentage of Negroes and Puerto Ricans attend college.

• Negro colleges provide inferior education.

• Experienced Negro and Puerto Rican executives are in short supply.

• When Negroes are finally hired, they are soon lured by higher salaries elsewhere.

• The absence of Jewish executives is not by design—it just happens that way.

• Jews tend to gravitate toward certain companies and industries, as do Masons, Catholics, and so on. This is a good thing, according to one interviewee. Another interviewee noted that "Jewish executives gravitated to the delivery end of the business."

• Negroes are not satisfied with lower positions. They are impatient for advancement.

• One company representative said, "We don't have any occasion to hire Puerto Ricans here."

• Negroes don't respond to the want ads as others do.

• One Negro was fired partially because he had the poor judgment to be seen in a night club with a white woman. (His job required his calling on, and entertaining, women clients during the day.)

• Companies hire less qualified Negroes in an effort to promote quality of employment, but these people have to be fired for incompetence, or are kept on as tokens.

• The spokesman for a company with one Jewish executive stated that Negroes are being sought to work their way up as did the Jew who is employed in the specialty of computers. Such people are hard to find.

• "Equal opportunity is dead. Preferential hiring is replacing it, this being discrimination in reverse. An unequal Negro is replacing a qualified white."

17. *Company Recommendations.* Several suggestions were made by the interviewees on how to overcome the racial barriers to executive employment:

• "Someone has to scare the hell out of the company president, such as by threatening to cancel a contract."

• Teach Negroes to be concerned with punctuality and appearance.

• Negroes must prepare themselves through education and training.

• "Barriers are in the minds of those thinking they are being discriminated against. Who educated other groups?"

• "How can a person be expected to stay on a job at $80.00 a week when he gets $65.00 weekly from welfare, nontaxable?"

• As to further government intervention: "This will cause the second Civil War."

18. *Conclusions.* "Business as usual" seems to be the rule in the executive suite. The underutilization of minorities remains a persistent characteristic of American blue-chip companies. Until the welcome mat is meaningfully displayed for all, employers will continue to be responsible for spreading the social poison of discrimination. Apparently, the hardened attitudes will not disappear on their own. The strong hand of government will have to provide the antidote if the picture is to start changing in the near future. All the companies

asserted that performance is the best test for promotion. But the elimination of discrimination cannot occur without equal opportunities at the point of both hiring and promotion.

The rationalizations offered for not hiring from minority groups—lack of education or competence—obviously cannot explain the small number of Jews in executive circles. Even if recruiting is confined to Ivy League colleges, the fact that Jewish students number about 25 percent should result in a larger Jewish executive population in the companies under study. Other conclusions suggested by the data follow:

• A company without Jewish executives probably will not have Negro or Puerto Rican executives. A company with Jewish executives does not necessarily have Negro and Puerto Rican executives.

• A company hiring a minority executive who is a specialist will probably do little more by way of meaningful integration. Such a specialist is likely to remain a token, whose presence and contribution will be "understood" as a token and will be accepted by his superiors and clients to be one.

• The validity of hiring standards must be continually questioned. If a company is successful and recruits only M.B.A.s who are at least six feet tall, an obvious cause-effect relationship explains the average education and height of the staff.

• Patterns of prejudicial behavior are strong and can be changed only by compelling motivations. Therefore profit through government contracts will have to be related to compliance with antidiscrimination laws.

• The oft-cited loss of Negroes to higher-paying jobs cannot be taken seriously: such movement would not alter the total figures. Since the companies studied here are themselves among the leaders in their fields, they should be the targets of such a Negro migration, not the victims.

"Piecemeal legislation in America was too little and too late." So reads a comment in a report recently prepared for the Race Relations Board of Great Britain. In the United States, we are not now free to consider the issue closed. The need to take meaningful steps toward unshackling the minorities persists. A major change in attitudes is still required. Dr. Martin Luther King, Nobel peace laureate, has said: " . . . our country must undergo a revolution in values." Henry Ford

2nd has said that equal opportunity is our first national priority and requires a massive commitment of all our resources. Helping to condition us for the change is the Negro's awareness that the power structure responds to the "hot summer." A riot gets antipoverty money, Bedford-Stuyvesant gets a community college division, Detroit gets Ford recruiting activity within poverty centers, and so on. Hopefully we will act before conflagrations occur, not afterward. Toward this end, our large corporations must take the lead.

Specimen 7. Interpol

JAMES P. HENDRICK
Special Assistant to the Secretary of the Treasury
and Vice President of Interpol

1. The other night I saw the beginning of a movie replayed on the TV scene: a mountain high up in the Alps. Down the steep slope speeds a skier, performing his traverses and parallel turns with unusual verve and grace. One heard in the distance a crack, as if a small branch of a tree had been broken. Then suddenly the skier fell. How could so expert a man be so clumsy? But no, it was not a fall—something had hit him. He was lying inert. Now the camera zooms back up the mountains. We see a heavy-jowled man in military uniform caressing his telescopic sight rifle. "One more Interpol agent dead!" he growls in a thick foreign accent. "Decadent capitalistic stooges! My country will get rid of them all!"

2. So begins the movie and so go the impressions of many people in regard to this extraordinary organization, the International Criminal Police Organization, familiarly known as Interpol (a name which, by the way, has been registered as a trademark by the organization in the United States and a number of other member countries).

3. Actually the movie gave a completely false impression of what Interpol is about. Interpol deals with law enforcement when it in-

Presented to the Graduating Class of the Treasury Law Enforcement School, November 22, 1968. Reprinted from *Vital Speeches of the Day,* March 1, 1969.

volves crossing international borders—a robber, a counterfeiter, a rapist, or what have you, who after committing his crime flees from one country to another. But Interpol never involves itself in political, military, religious, or racial matters. These activities are forbidden by its constitution.

4. Interpol concerns itself only with normal, everyday crime, and it is pledged to action always in conformity with the Universal Declaration of Human Rights. . . . It is concerned with apprehension of criminals, exchange of information, identification, arrest, and extradition. It also works in the field of crime prevention. It puts out literature on counterfeits, automobile thefts, and any number of other subjects designed to facilitate the law enforcement officer in his task of dissuading potential criminals from breaking the law before they actually do so. It also holds symposiums on these and other subjects.

5. There is such a symposium going on right now on technical methods of tracking down criminals. Treasury's Dr. Mayard Pro, from the Alcohol and Tobacco Tax Laboratory, is in Paris at this moment advising other member country experts of the extraordinary progress made by the United States in neutron activation. This technique makes possible conviction of a safecracker by proving that dust on the floor by the safe in question is the same as that on his trouser knees, gathered there when he knelt to do his work. And by proving further that such dust could not have come from any other place in the world.

6. A word about the Organization's history. The idea of Interpol arose in 1914 when a number of police officers, magistrates, and lawyers met in Monaco to lay the foundations for international police cooperation. Here was established an International Criminal Police Congress. A few months later World War I broke out and the plan was shelved.

7. In 1923 the International Criminal Police Congress met again, this time in Vienna. Delegates from some 20 countries approved creation of an International Criminal Police Commission. Its headquarters was established in Vienna, and a satisfactory start was made with operations limited to Europe. But again hostilities brought a stop to the activity with the advent of World War II.

8. In 1946 high-ranking enforcement officers met in Brussels to breathe new life into the temporarily discontinued Commission. At

this meeting the Organization's constitution was revised and head-quarters set up in Paris. This time there were only 19 member countries represented, but in contrast to the past they came from all parts of the world.

9. By 1956 the membership had increased to 55 countries. A meeting was held in Vienna; here significant regulatory changes were agreed to which have remained for the most part unchanged.

10. Since grown to more than 100 members, from Algeria to Zambia, Interpol is directed by a General Assembly, meeting once a year to discuss matters of crime and of organization. The 1968 Assembly . . . took up, among other substantive matters, recent developments in juvenile delinquency, disaster victim identification, international currency counterfeiting, forged bills of lading, police planning, international drug traffic, and protection of works of art. Among organizational subjects considered, in addition to budget, elections, and appointments, was a United States plan, which was unanimously approved, for better auditing procedures.

11. Held each year in a different country, . . . the Assembly provides an unrivaled opportunity for top-echelon enforcement officers throughout the world to exchange views and to become well acquainted so that when problems arise involving two countries the officer in each will know just whom he is dealing with.

12. General Assembly resolutions are passed which often carry great weight in the international enforcement community and with the public at large. The year before, for example, a strong resolution on the dangers of marijuana was drafted by then United States Commissioner of Narcotics Henry L. Giordano. Passed at a time when public debate raged over the question whether marijuana was not safer for one's daughter than drinking a cocktail, the resolution, which expressed law-enforcement men's unanimous opposition to this permissive idea, did much to bring sanity to popular understanding of the subject.

13. Handling problems which must be treated in greater detail or greater depth than may be possible in the General Assembly is an Executive Committee presently formed of three members each from Africa, the Americas, Asia, and Europe, together with a president. . . .

14. While the governing policies of Interpol are established by the General Assembly and the Executive Committee, the day-to-day operations are handled by an Executive Secretariat. This consists of a

Secretary General together with officers who exercise various functions, including the operation of a worldwide communications system dealing with international police work . . . , a central record of international criminals (1,000,000 cards, 40,000 criminals), a research center, a section dealing with reports to General Assemblies, major international organizations and scientific bodies, and one which produces an International Criminal Police Review. Many documents are published by the Secretariat dealing with criminals who have left their home base, recidivists, or those most sought after, and dealing with the subject of international crime. In addition, a publication on counterfeit currency is widely circulated to banks and financial institutions, surely the most helpful publication of its kind that exists today.

15. The headquarters of the Organization was recently moved from an ancient building in Paris to a relatively small American-style office building in the environs of Paris at St. Cloud. Any of you who have been to Paris will know how rare indeed are new buildings in that beautiful city. The Interpol building is an extraordinary exception—extraordinary not only because it is new but also because the architecture, completely modern, nonetheless fits in with the surrounding countryside in a manner entirely pleasing to the eye.

16. One feature of the new building which is of interest to visitors is the Crime Museum on the ground floor. Here are typical exhibits of smugglers' tricks—the false-bottomed suitcase, the hollow heel of a shoe—and of ordinary and extraordinary weapons, jimmys, and tools of all sorts used in robberies, holdups, and murders.

17. Most impressive of all from our standpoint is a beautifully carved Colt single-action revolver which was given to Interpol a year ago by Mr. Samuel Pror, one of our General Assembly delegates. The revolver had been owned by one of America's great criminals, "Carbine" Williams. The adjective "great" is used advisedly.

18. While serving a 20-year term in prison for—and this is ironic—the killing of one of our Treasury agents during the Prohibition era, Williams had the imagination, energy, and courage to draw up plans for an unusual rifle adopting the hitherto unknown principle of a floating chamber. Pardoned after his plans became known to a sympathetic warden, Williams explained the working of the weapon to the United States Army Chief of Ordnance, and this became the M-1 carbine used throughout World War II by our armed forces.

Though he would accept no compensation for this extremely significant invention, he later worked up for commercial firms many new developments in the art. Independently wealthy as a result, Williams today is a leading and respected citizen of North Carolina.

19. From the financial standpoint, Interpol represents something to which all international organizations, and indeed all domestic corporations and all householders, aspire, most of them in vain: it has a modest budget which it does not exceed. Moreover, its new building was completed on schedule and cost less than the amount budgeted. Due credit for these accomplishments must be given to the extremely efficient and effective Secretary General, Jean Nepoté.

20. We, together with other developed countries such as the United Kingdom, France, Germany, and Italy, pay a larger share than do the developing countries. Nonetheless the United States percentage for Interpol is almost the lowest percentage figure for its contribution to any international organization. We pay 30 percent or more of the dues for the United Nations, FAO, ICAO, UNESCO, and WHO. For many inter-American organizations our contribution is over 60 percent.

21. A considerable number of the employees of the Organization are borrowed from the French police force, with the Organization paying only a relatively small amount for the work they do. The overall annual expense for 102 employees, including those loaned from the French police, is 1,142,500 Swiss francs, which works out an average of some 11,000 Swiss francs or approximately $2,500 per employee. No one can say that this is not an economically run organization!

22. The recipients of the day-to-day inquiries and releases put out by the organization, and the transmitters of information back to the Organization or to other members, are the National Central Bureaus. Each country has one. They function in conjunction with the Executive Secretariat as a permanent and truly worldwide network of international cooperation. The United States National Central Bureau, established in 1958, when our Congress voted adherence to Interpol, is in the Office of the Secretary of the Treasury.

23. On a recent trip to London, I was able to talk with the Scotland Yard men who form the United Kingdom National Central Bureau. They were delighted that only a few days before my arrival they asked our office in Washington if arrangements could be made for a

particular United States citizen to come to London to testify as a witness in a case which was unexpectedly being called for trial within only two days' time. To their delight, our telegraphed reply advised that the potential witness would be on a plane going to London that very night, and the reply went out within two hours.

24. I would like to conclude by giving a few examples of what Interpol actually accomplishes in specific cases. Of necessity, names and certain details have been fictionalized, because certain aspects of the cases are still pending.

25. A hoodlum named "Mickey the Mite" Mannheimer had been observed on the scene of a killing in the Bronx, New York, with a smoking revolver in his hand. Before the police could arrest him he got away, but not before he had been identified by Joey Angulo, a known and trusted informant in narcotic cases.

26. Weeks had elapsed with no sign of Mickey the Mite. The only lead police could develop was a Bronx girl named Gretchen who lived in the apartment above Mickey. Mickey and Gretchen had been known to have been what is called "very good friends"—although this had not interfered with Gretchen's carrying on her profession, which was the world's oldest.

27. Gretchen was German and her parents lived in West Germany. Acting on a hunch, the Assistant District Attorney in charge of the investigation called our Treasury man. We sent a cable at once to Paul Dickopf, head of the Bundeskriminalamt (Federal Criminal Police Office) in Wiesbaden. Dickopf's men started asking questions in Hamburg where it was believed the parents could be found. It didn't take long: Mickey the Mite was found with the parents. . . .

28. Another case: . . . A rather thin man with aquiline nose and heavy eyeglasses walked into the main American office of Banco di Roma e Ferrara. He presented a draft drawn on its Rome office for $60,000, together with a letter from a senior officer of the Bank of America and a passport purporting to establish that his name was Giovanni Semplice of 4001 Deep Valley Avenue. On the basis of the letter and the passport, the draft was cashed. The next day the same man repeated the performance at the Farmers and Mechanics Bank—another $60,000. Later on the same day, he tried it out on the Citizens First National Union Bank, again with success. In due course the banks discovered that the Rome office had no funds on deposit to support the drafts and that the Bank of America officer's letter was a

forgery. Fingerprints were lifted from one of the papers presented, but FBI latent print files were negative on them. Once more our Treasury man was called on. Over to the Interpol Bureau in Rome went the prints and a description; back came the identification, and not long after Semplice (whose name turned out to be Durante, well known to the Caribinieri with a criminal record long as his arm) was apprehended in Ferrara. The man is now awaiting trial.

29. One more example: For eight years the police in Los Angeles had been on the lookout for a man known to them under the names of Johnson, Henderson, Smithson, Jackson, and Williamson. The name always varied, except for a "son" at the end. The reason the police wanted this man was always the same. In each case, a personalized form letter was widely circulated through the mails to persons in the retirement-age bracket offering each lucky recipient an exclusive franchise for the sale of Coty perfumes within a large and carefully designated territory for a mere $6,000, only $100 down. It was surprising how many innocents accepted and how Mr. _____son could never be found after the checks had been sent and cashed.

30. Notice of the fraud was sent to us by the Los Angeles police and we gave a description to Interpol in Paris which in turn circularized it to the member countries. Scotland Yard reported a Wrightson recently had hurriedly departed from Manchester after a franchise offer. This news also was circularized to the Interpol membership. Two months later, the New Zealand police noted an advertisement in a small local paper inviting inquiries on a franchise for Ivor Johnson bicycles. It was signed by a Mr. Bankson. The New Zealand police had read the Interpol notices. Mr. Bankson was traced. He is now safe behind bars in Wellington. He would rather be there than in Los Angeles, but who knows whether he'll always be able to stay away?

31. More and more, crime will become international. In seeking to control it, the enforcement officer must use every legal weapon in his arsenal. Among these weapons, few if any can be more useful than ICPO-Interpol.

Specimen 8. Eulogy to John F. Kennedy

LYNDON B. JOHNSON
President of the United States

This is a sad time for all people.

We have suffered a loss that cannot be weighed.

For me it is a deep personal tragedy.

I know the world shares the sorrow that Mrs. Kennedy and her family bear.

I will do my best.

That is all I can do.

I ask for your help—and God's.

Presented November 23, 1963. Reprinted from *Vital Speeches of the Day*, December 1, 1963.

Specimen 9. Why Motivational Theories Don't Work

KENNETH A. KOVACH
Associate Professor, George Mason University

1. Despite voluminous writing on the subject, today's manager is no closer to understanding employee "motivation" than was his counterpart of 50 years ago. If anything, employee motivation is *more* of a problem now than it was in the early 1900s. This is not to say that the work of behavioral scientists has been counterproductive, for in fact their efforts have given today's manager a better insight into motivation. Rather, it is to suggest that the advances made in understanding what motivates workers have not kept pace with the rapid changes in employee attitudes and hence changes in those things that do in fact motivate them.

Reprinted from *Advanced Management Journal*, Spring 1980.

Employee attitudes should provide insights into motivation, but by the time data on these are studied and the results disseminated, it is already too late. Rapidly changing technology, crumbling traditions, media influence, and so forth have all conspired against the manager by changing the workers' attitudes, desires, and motivations. These changes take place so rapidly that most theories of motivation are outdated by the time they are implemented.

2. RELIANCE ON SELF-REFERENCE

But that's not the full problem. Another difficulty encountered when dealing with employee motivation is that the theories for improving motivation are just that—theories—until implemented. Unlike physical science theories that can be tested before implemented, social science theories can only be tested through implementation with human subjects. Managers, like all humans, have the tendency to shy away from implementing theories that are not in accordance with their own preconceived notions. They are, like all of us, subject to what I call "self-reference criteria," practicing only those suggested behavioral patterns that are most closely aligned with their own thinking.

A manager will offer rewards or exhibit behavior toward workers that would motivate him or her, but this may not necessarily be what will motivate the employees. The individual forgets that by virtue of being a supervisor, he or she receives a different level of monetary and psychological rewards—often resulting in a different lifestyle— than those people below.

It has been my experience that while many practitioners feel that self-reference used to be a problem, they do not view it as a major obstacle to employee motivation today. This change in thinking is usually attributable to the fact that the earnings gap between non-supervisory employees and first-line supervision has been drastically narrowed by labor organizations, thus creating a wage-earning middle class that hold similar values and are motivated by the same things as their supervisors. The logical conclusion of this line of reasoning is that self-reference is not a problem, since those practicing it hold the same motivational values as those it is practiced on.

I could not disagree more with this. While this argument has surface validity, the evidence argues against it.

3. THE CASE AGAINST SELF-REFERENCE

Numerous surveys have been conducted since World War II to determine what employees want from their jobs—that is, what can be offered to motivate them. Representative of these was one done in 1946 by the Labor Relations Institute of New York and reported in *Foreman Facts*. Subjects were first-line supervisors and the employees who worked directly for them. After the employees had ranked ten items in order of importance to them, their supervisors were asked to rank the same items as they thought their employees would. The results are shown in this table:

Employee Ranking	*Supervisor Ranking*
1. Full appreciation of work done	8
2. Feeling of being in on things	9
3. Sympathetic help with personal problems	10
4. Job security	2
5. Good wages	1
6. Interesting work	5
7. Promotion and growth in the organization	3
8. Personal loyalty to employees	6
9. Good working conditions	4
10. Tactful discipline	7

The absolute ranking of the items is not the most important issue. Rather, the significance of the survey findings lies in the wide variance between what the employees considered to be important in their jobs and what their supervisors thought was important to these same employees. And, clearly, this variance is evidence of the use of self-reference by the supervisors. Since these results are representative of the many surveys during the immediate postwar era, the use of self-reference then would certainly have been a problem.

However, the more relevant question today is, does this gap still exist between workers' wants and their supervisors' perceptions of these wants? If it does, then self-reference is still a major stumbling block to improving employee motivation.

To answer this question, the 1946 questionnaire was administered to a group of over 200 employees and their immediate supervisors to see if the results bore any resemblance to those of 35 years ago. The findings are shown in this table:

Employee Ranking	Supervisor Ranking
1. Interesting work	5
2. Full appreciation of work done	8
3. Feeling of being in on things	10
4. Job security	2
5. Good wages	1
6. Promotion and growth in the organization	3
7. Good working conditions	4
8. Personal loyalty to employees	7
9. Sympathetic help with personal problems	9
10. Tactful discipline	6

While a comparison of the results shows an improvement in the sum of the differences between the two groups (from 42 in 1946 to 34 in the recent study), seven of the eight improvement points are attributable to the change in the ranking of "sympathetic help with personal problems." With the exception of this one factor, the gap between supervisors and their employees has not closed at all since 1946, as these tables show (the first is from 1946; the second, from the present).

Perhaps the most revealing comparisons come from two groups of the items—security/wages and appreciation/being in on things. In 1946 wages and security were ranked as having middle importance by employees and as having top importance to employees by supervisors, while appreciation of work and feeling in on things were of top importance for employees yet perceived by supervisors as being of least importance to employees. The same discrepancy was uncovered by the present survey. There has been no improvement since at least 1946! Hence any argument that self-reference is not still a major problem is not supported by the evidence.

4. GETTING THE INFORMATION NEEDED

One of the things for today's manager to do when trying to improve worker motivation is to find out what it is that his or her employees want from their work—in other words, what will motivate them. As shown by the second of the two tables, any reliance on his or her own judgment about what will motivate employees will likely only aggravate the motivation problem.

The use of attitude surveys is the cheapest, most direct approach to gathering the information needed. Such surveys can employ ranking, the Likert scale, or some other technique whereby the results are easily quantified, tabulated, and understood. For very little time and monetary investment, an organization and particularly its supervisors are likely to get very insightful results that can go a long way toward improving employee motivation.

A word of additional advice is necessary here. We must learn from our earlier mistakes and make sure that the results are transmitted to those supervisors who most directly interact with the employees involved. Many times the results are made available only to managers at levels above those having direct daily employee contact. As a result, the individuals who could best make use of the findings are never aware of what they are or at best get a biased verbal summation. (Remember, our human tendency is to emphasize that which we agree with during verbal transmission.)

Allowing for the cost and length of time needed to administer the instrument, a good rule of thumb is to conduct the attitude survey approximately once a year. Such frequency is necessary to avoid the problem discussed at the beginning of this article, that of attempting to improve employee motivation using outdated and often inaccurate information.

Additionally, it is important to analyze the responses not only collectively but in subsets based on organization and earning levels if there is a variance within the respondent group. According to Abraham Maslow's theory, man is motivated by his desire to fulfill certain hierarchical needs. Once one level of need is fulfilled, there is a desire to satisfy the next higher level. Individuals at different organization levels with different earning power may well be at different levels in Maslow's hierarchy. Hence, what motivates individuals at one level of the organization very likely will not be the same as what motivates those at another level, thus necessitating differentiating by level when analyzing attitudes for motivational purposes.

5. DIFFERENT STROKES FOR DIFFERENT FOLKS

The results in the second table indicate that nonsupervisory employees in this country have progressed beyond the basic needs that can be satisfied by economic rewards. Yet it is important to remember that the results presented there are averages for all the employees sampled and are intended only to show discrepancies between the two groups. They should not be interpreted to mean that all employees see money as having middle relative importance, or that all employees see interesting work and appreciation of work as what they want most from their jobs.

Within a given organization, and certainly among different individuals, results will vary. This is why it is so important that each organization conducts its own attitude survey. Reward structures can then be manipulated with an eye toward what kind of return in terms of motivational value the organization can expect to receive. If, for instance, interesting work is the major desire of the particular respondents, then perhaps job enlargement or enrichment can be tried on a limited basis. On the other hand, if higher wages are what motivate employees, then the introduction of an incentive pay system might be a wise move.

Robert Townsend, past president of Avis-Rent-a-Car, put it this way in his book *Up the Organization:*

> Get to know your people—what they do well, what they enjoy doing, what their weaknesses and strengths are, and what they want and need from their job. And then try to create an organization around your people, not jam your people into those organization-chart rectangles.

As a manager, you need to remember that you cannot motivate people. That door is locked from the inside. What you can do, however, is to create a climate in which most of your employees will find it personally rewarding to motivate themselves and in the process contribute to the company's attainment of its objectives. If you can achieve this state of mind among a reasonable number of your subordinates, many of your other problems as a supervisor will take care of themselves.

Specimen 10: A New Social Order
JOHN F. KENNEDY
President of the United States

1. I'm most honored, Mr. President, to be able to speak in this city before this audience, for in this hall I am able to address myself to those who lead and serve all segments of the democratic system— mayors, governors, members of Cabinet, civil servants, and concerned citizens.

2. As one who has known the satisfaction of the legislator's life, I am particularly pleased that so many members of your Bundesdag and Bundesrat are present today, for the vitality of your legislature has been a major factor in your demonstration of a working de- mocracy, a democracy worldwide in its influence. In your company also I see several of the authors of the Federal Constitution who have been able through their own political service to give a new and lasting validity to the aims of the Frankfurt Assembly.

3. [In 1848] . . . a most learned parliament was convened in this historic hall. Its goal was a united German federation. Its members were poets and professors, and lawyers, and philosophers, and doc- tors and clergymen, freely elected in all parts of the land. No nation applauded its endeavors as warmly as my own. No assembly ever strove more ardently to put perfection into practice. And though in the end it failed, no other building in Germany deserves more the title of "Cradle of German Democracy."

4. But can there be such a title? In my own home city of Boston, Faneuil Hall—once the meetingplace of the authors of the American Revolution—has long been known as the "Cradle of American Lib- erty." But when, in 1852, the Hungarian patriot Kossuth addressed an audience there, he criticized its name. "It is," he said, "a great name—but there is something in it which saddens my heart. You should not say American liberty. You should say liberty in America. Liberty should not be either American or European—it should just be liberty."

5. Kossuth was right. For unless liberty flourishes in all lands, it cannot flourish in one. Conceived in one hall, it must be carried out in

Presented in the Paulskircke, Frankfurt, Germany, June 25, 1963. Reprinted from *Vital Speeches of the Day*, July 15, 1963.

many. Thus the seeds of the American Revolution had been brought earlier from Europe, and they later took root around the world. And the German revolution of 1848 transmitted ideas and idealists to American and to other lands. . . . Democracy and liberty are [now] more international than ever before. And the spirit of the Frankfurt Assembly, like the spirit of Faneuil Hall, must live in many hearts and nations if it is to live at all.

6. For we live in an age of interdependence as well as independence—an age of internationalism as well as nationalism. In 1848 many countries were indifferent to the goals of the Frankfurt Assembly. It was, they said, a German problem. Today there are no exclusively German problems, or American problems. There are world problems—and our two countries and continents are inextricably bound together in the task of peace as well as war.

7. We are partners for peace, not in a narrow bilateral context, but in a framework of Atlantic partnership. The ocean divides us less than the Mediterranean divided Greece and Rome. Our constitution is old and yours is young—and our culture is young and yours is old—but in our commitment we can and must speak and act with one voice. Our roles are distinct but complementary—and our goals are the same. Peace and freedom for all men, for all time, in a world of abundance, in a world of justice.

8. That is why our nations are working together to strengthen NATO, to expand trade, to assist the developing countries, to align our monetary policies, and to build the Atlantic Community. I would not diminish the miracle of West Germany's economic achievements. But the true German miracle has been your rejection of the past for the future—your reconciliation with France, your participation in the building of Europe, your leading role in NATO, and your growing support for constructive undertakings throughout the world.

9. Your economic institutions, your constitutional guarantees, your confidence in civilian authority, are all harmonious with the ideals of older democracies. And they form a firm pillar of the democratic European community.

10. But Goethe tells us in his greatest poem that Faust lost the liberty of his soul when he said to the passing moment: "Stay, thou art so fair." And our liberty, too, is endangered if we pause for the passing moment, if we rest on our achievements, if we resist the pace of progress. For time and the world do not stand still. Change is the

law of life. And those who look only to the past or the present are certain to miss the future.

11. The future of the West lies in Atlantic partnership—a system of cooperation, interdependence, and harmony, whose people can jointly meet their burdens and opportunities throughout the world. Some say this is only a dream, but I do not agree. A generation of achievement—the Marshall Plan, NATO, the Schuman Plan, and the Common Market—urges us up the path to greater unity.

12. There will be difficulties and delays, and doubts and discouragement. There will be differences of approach and opinion. But we have the will and the means to serve three related goals—the heritage of our countries, the unity of our continents, and the interdependence of the Western alliance.

13. Some say that the United States will neither hold to these purposes nor abide by its pledges—that we will revert to a narrow nationalism. But such doubts fly in the face of history . . . the United States has stood its watch for freedom all around the globe. The firmness of American will, and the effectiveness of American strength, have been shown in support of free men and free governments; in Asia, in Africa, in the Americas, and above all, here in Europe, we have undertaken, and sustained in honor, relations of mutual trust and obligation with more than 40 allies. We are proud of this record, which more than answers doubts. But, in addition, these proven commitments to the common freedom and safety are assured, in the future as in the past, by one great fundamental fact—that they are deeply rooted in America's own self-interest. Our commitment to Europe is indispensable—in our interest as well as yours.

14. It is not in our interest to try to dominate the European councils of decision. If that were our objective, we would prefer to see Europe divided and weak, enabling the United States to deal with each fragment individually. Instead we have and now look forward to a Europe united and strong—speaking with a common voice—acting with a common will—a world power capable of meeting world problems as a full and equal partner.

15. This is in the interest of us all. For war in Europe, as we learned twice in 40 years, destroys peace in America. A threat to the freedom of Europe is a threat to the freedom of America. That is why no administration in Washington can fail to respond to such a threat—not merely from good will but from necessity. And that is why

we look forward to a united Europe in an Atlantic partnership—an entity of interdependent parts, sharing equally both burdens and decisions, and linked together in the task of defense as well as the arts of peace.

16. This is no fantasy. It will be achieved by concrete steps to solve the problems that face us all: military, economic, and political. Partnership is not a posture but a process—a continuous process that grows stronger each year as we devote ourselves to common tasks.

17. The first task of the Atlantic Community was to assure its common defense. That defense was and still is indivisible. The United States will risk its cities to defend yours because we need your freedom to protect ours. Hundreds of thousands of our soldiers serve with yours on this continent, as tangible evidence of this pledge. Those who would doubt our pledge or deny this indivisibility—those who would separate Europe from America or split one ally from another—would only give aid and comfort to the men who make themselves our adversaries and welcome any Western disarray.

18. The purpose of our common military effort is not war but peace—not the destruction of nations but the protection of freedom. The forces that West Germany contributes to this effort are second to none among the Western European nations. Your nation is in the first line of this defense—and your divisions, side by side with our own, are a source of strength to us all.

19. These conventional forces are essential, and they are backed by the sanction of thousands of the most modern weapons here on European soil and thousands more, only minutes away, in posts around the world. Together our nations have developed for the forward defense of free Europe a deterrent far surpassing the present or prospective force of any hostile power.

20. Nevertheless, it is natural that America's nuclear position has raised questions within the alliance. I believe we must confront these questions—not by turning the clock backward to separate nuclear deterrents, but by developing a more closely unified Atlantic deterrent, with genuine European participation.

21. How this can best be done—and it is not easy; in some ways it was more difficult to split the atom politically than it was physically—but how this can best be done is under discussion with those who may wish to join in this effort. The proposal before us now is for a new Atlantic force. Such a force would bring strength instead of weakness, cohe-

sion instead of division. It would belong to all members, not one, with all participating on a basis of full equality. And as Europe moves toward unity, its role and responsibility, here as elsewhere, would and must increase accordingly. Meanwhile, there is much to do. We must work more closely together on strategy, training, and planning. European officers from NATO are being assigned to Strategic Air Command headquarters in Omaha, Nebraska. Modern weapons are being deployed here in Western Europe. And America's strategic deterrent—the most powerful in history—will continue to be at the service of the whole alliance.

22. Second: Our partnership is not military alone. Economic unity is also imperative—not only among the nations of Europe, but across the wide Atlantic.

23. Indeed, economic cooperation is needed throughout the entire free world. By opening our markets to the developing countries of Africa, Asia, and Latin America, by contributing our capital and skills, by stabilizing basic prices, we can help assure them of a favorable climate for freedom and growth. This is an Atlantic responsibility. For the Atlantic nations themselves helped to awaken these peoples. Our merchants and our traders ploughed up their soils—and their societies as well—in search of minerals and oil and rubber and coffee. Now we must help them gain full membership in the twentieth century, closing the gap between the rich and the poor.

24. Another great economic challenge is in the coming round of trade negotiations. Those deliberations are much more important than a technical discussion of trade and commerce. They are an opportunity to build common industrial and agricultural policies across the Atlantic. They are an opportunity to recognize the trading needs and aspirations of other free countries, including Japan.

25. In short, these negotiations are a test of our unity. While each nation must naturally look out for its own interests, each nation must also look out for the common interest—the need to reduce the imbalance between developed and underdeveloped nations—and the need to stimulate the Atlantic economy to higher levels of production rather than stifle it by higher levels of protection.

26. We must not return to the 1930s when we exported to each other our own stagnation. We must not return to the discredited view that trade favors some nations at the expense of others. Let no one think that the United States, with only a fraction of its economy

dependent on trade and only a small part of that with Western Europe, is seeking trade expansion in order to dump its goods on this continent.

27. Trade expansion will help us all. The experience of the Common Market, like the experience of the German Zollverein, shows an increased rise in business activity and general prosperity resulting for all participants in such trade agreements, with no member profiting at the expense of another. As they say on my own Cape Cod, "a rising tide lifts all the boats." And a partnership, by definition, serves both partners, without domination or unfair advantage. Together we have been partners in adversity. Let us also be partners in prosperity.

28. Beyond development and trade is monetary policy. Here again our interests run together. Indeed there is no field in which the wider interests of all more clearly outweigh the narrow interest of one. We have lived by that principle, as bankers to freedom, for a generation. Now that other nations—including West Germany—have found new economic strength, it is time for common efforts here, too. The great free nations of the world must take control of our monetary problems if these problems are not to take control of us.

29. And third and finally, our partisanship depends on common political purpose. Against the hazards of division and lassitude, no lesser force will serve. History tells us that disunity and relaxation are the great internal dangers of an alliance. Thucydides reported that the Peloponnesians and their allies were mighty in battle but handicapped by their policymaking body—in which, he related, "each presses its own end . . . which generally results in no action at all . . . they devote more time to the prosecution of their own purposes than to the consideration of the general welfare—each supposes that no harm will come of his own neglect, that it is the business of another to do this and that—and so, as each separately entertains the same illusion, the common cause imperceptibly decays."

30. Is this also to be the story of the grand alliance? Welded in a moment of imminent danger, will it disintegrate into complacency with each member pressing its own ends to the neglect of the common cause? This must not be the case. Our old dangers are not gone beyond return, and any division among us would bring them back in doubled strength.

31. Our defenses are now strong, but they must be made stronger.

Our economic goals are now clear, but we must get on with that performance. And the greatest of our necessities, the most notable of our omissions, is progress toward unity of political purpose.

32. For we live in a world in which our own united strength will and must be our first reliance. As I have said before, and will say again, we work toward the day where there may be real peace between us and the Communists. And we will not be second in that effort. But that day is not yet here.

33. We in the United States and Canada see 200 million people, and here, on the European side of the Atlantic alliance, 300 million people. The strength and unity of these half-billion human beings are and will continue to be the anchor of all freedom, for all nations. Let us from time to time pledge ourselves again to our common purposes. But let us go on, from words to actions, to intensify our efforts for still greater unity among us, to build new associations and institutions on those already established. Lofty words cannot construct an alliance or maintain it; only concrete deeds can do that.

34. The great present task of construction is here on this continent where the effort for a unified free Europe is under way. It is not for Americans to prescribe to Europeans how this effort should be carried forward. Nor do I believe that there is any one right course or any single final pattern. It is Europeans who are building Europe.

35. Yet the reunion of Europe, as Europeans shape it, bringing a permanent end to the civil wars that have repeatedly wracked the world, will continue to have the determined support of the United States. For that reunion is a necessary step in strengthening the community of freedom. It would strengthen our alliance for defense. And it would be in our national interest as well as yours.

36. It is only a fully cohesive Europe that can protect us all against fragmentation of our alliance. Only such a Europe will permit full reciprocity of treatment across the ocean, in facing the Atlantic agenda. With only such a Europe can we have a full give and take between equals, an equal sharing of responsibilities, and an equal level of sacrifice. I repeat again—so that there may be no misunderstanding—the choice of paths to the unity of Europe is a choice which Europe must make. But as you continue this great effort, undeterred by either difficulty or delay, you should know that this new European greatness will be not an object of fear, but a source of strength for the United States of America.

37. There are other political tasks before us. We must all learn to practice more completely the art of consultation on matters stretching well beyond the immediate military and economic questions.

38. Together, for example, we must explore the possibilities of leashing the tensions of the cold war and reducing the dangers of the arms race. Together we must work to strengthen the spirit of those Europeans who are not now free, to reestablish their old ties to freedom in the West, so that their desire for liberty and their sense of nationhood and their sense of belonging to the Western community over hundreds of years will survive for future expression.

39. We ask those who would be our adversaries to understand that in our relations with them we will not bargain one nation's interest against another's, and that the commitment to the cause of freedom is common to us all.

40. All of us in the West must be faithful to our conviction that peace in Europe can never be complete until everywhere in Europe—and that includes Germany—men can choose, in peace and freedom, how their countries shall be governed, and choose, without threat to any neighbor, reunification with their countrymen.

41. I preach no easy liberation and I make no empty promises, but my countrymen, since our country was founded, believe strongly in the proposition that all men shall be free and all free men shall have this right of choice.

42. As we look steadily eastward in the hope and purpose of new freedom, we must look, and ever more closely, to our trans-Atlantic ties. The Atlantic Community will not soon become a single over-arching superstate. But practical steps toward stronger common purpose are well within our means. As we widen our common effort in defense, and our threefold cooperation in economics, we shall inevitably strengthen our political ties as well. Just as your current efforts for unity in Europe will produce a stronger voice in the dialogue between us, so in America our current battle for the liberty and prosperity of all our citizens can only deepen the meaning of our common historic purposes. In the far future there may be a great new union for us all. But for the present, there is plenty for all to do in building new and enduring connections.

43. In short, the words of Thucydides are a warning, not a prediction. We have it in us to build our defenses, to strengthen our economies, and to tighten our political bonds, both in good weather

and bad. We can move forward with the confidence that is born of success and the skill that is born of experience. And as we move, let us take heart from the certainty that we are united not only by danger and necessity, but by hope and purpose as well.

44. For we know now that freedom is more than the rejection of tyranny, that prosperity is more than an escape from want, that partnership is more than a sharing of power. These are, above all, great human adventures. They must have meaning and conviction and purpose—and because they do, in your country and in mine, in all the nations of the alliance, we are called to a great new mission.

45. It is not a mission of self-defense alone—for that is a means, not an end. It is not a mission of arbitrary power—for we reject the idea of one nation dominating another. The mission is to create a new social order, founded on liberty and justice, in which men are the masters of their fate, in which states are the servants of their citizens, and in which all men and women can share a better life for themselves and their children. That is the object of our common policy.

46. To realize this vision, we must seek a world of peace—a world in which peoples dwell together in mutual respect and work together in mutual regard, a world in which peace is not a mere interlude between wars, but an incentive to the creative energies of humanity. We will not find such a peace today or tomorrow. The obstacles to hope are large and menacing. Yet the goals of a peaceful world, today and tomorrow, must shape our decisions and inspire our purposes.

47. So we are all idealists. We are all visionaries. Let it not be said of this Atlantic generation that we left ideals and visions to the past, nor purpose and determination to our adversaries. We have come too far, we have sacrificed too much, to disdain the future now. And we shall ever remember what Goethe told us—that the "highest wisdom, the best that mankind ever knew" was the realization that "he only earns his freedom and existence who daily conquers them anew."

Specimen 11. Law Day

ROBERT F. KENNEDY
Attorney General of the United States

1. For the first time since becoming Attorney General, . . . I am making a formal speech, and I am proud that it is in Georgia.

2. Two months ago, I had the very great honor to present to the President Donald Eugene McGregor of Brunswick, Georgia. Donald McGregor came to Washington to receive the Young American Medal for bravery. In twelve bad hours, he led a family of four to safety from a yacht which broke up in high seas off the Georgia coast.

3. He impressed all of us who met him with his quiet courage. And, as the President said, Donald McGregor is a fine young American—one of a long line of Georgians who have, by their courage, set an outstanding example for their fellow Americans.

4. They have told me that when you speak in Georgia, you should try to tie yourself to Georgia and the South, and even better, claim some Georgia kinfolk. There are a lot of Kennedys in Georgia. But as far as I can tell, I have no relatives here and no direct ties to Georgia, except one. This state gave my brother the biggest percentage majority of any state in the Union, and in this last election, that was even better than kinfolk.

5. We meet at this great university, in this old state, the fourth of the original thirteen, to observe Law Day.

6. In his proclamation urging us to observe this day, the President emphasized two thoughts. He pointed out that to remain free, the people must "cherish their freedoms, understand the responsibilities they entail, and nurture the will to preserve them." He then went on to point out that "law is the strongest link between man and freedom."

7. I wonder in how many countries of the world people think of law as the "link between man and freedom." We know that in many, law is the instrument of tyranny, and people think of law as little more than the will of the state, or the party, not of the people.

8. And we know, too, that throughout the long history of mankind, man has had to struggle to create a system of law and of government in which fundamental freedoms would be linked with the

Presented to the Law Day Convention, University of Georgia Law School, May 1, 1961.

enforcement of justice. We know that we cannot live together without rules which tell us what is right and what is wrong, what is permitted and what is prohibited. We know that it is law which enables men to live together, that creates order out of chaos. We know that law is the glue that holds civilization together.

9. And we know that if one man's rights are denied, the rights of all are endangered. In our country the courts have a most important role in safeguarding these rights. The decisions of the courts. however much we might disagree with them, in the final analysis must be followed and respected. If we disagree with a court decision and, thereafter, irresponsibly assail the court and defy its rulings, we challenge the foundations of our society.

10. The Supreme Court of Georgia set forth this proposition quite clearly in 1949 in the case of Crumb v. the State (205 Ga. 547–552). The court, referring to United States Supreme Court decisions, said there, and I quote:

11. "And whatever may be the individual opinion of the members of this court as to the correctness, soundness, and wisdom of these decisions, it becomes our duty to yield thereto just as the other courts of this state must accept and be controlled by the decisions and mandates of this court. This being a government of law and not by men, the jury commissioners in their official conduct are bound by the foregoing ruling of the Supreme Court of the United States, notwithstanding any personal opinion, hereditary instinct, natural impulse, or geographical tradition to the contrary."

12. Respect for the law—in essence that is the meaning of Law Day—and every day must be Law Day, or else our society will collapse.

13. The challenge which international Communism hurls against the rule of law is very great. For the past two weeks I have been engaged, for a good part of my time, in working with General Taylor, Admiral Burke, and Mr. [Allen] Dulles to assess the recent events in Cuba and determine what lessons we can learn for the future.

14. It already has become crystal clear in our study, as the President has stated so graphically, we must reexamine and reorient our forces of every kind—not just our military forces, but all our techniques and outlook here in the United States.

15. We must come forward with the answer of how a nation, devoted to freedom and individual rights and respect for the law, can stand effectively against an implacable enemy who plays by different

rules and knows only the law of the jungle. With the answer to this rests our future—our destiny—as a nation and as a people.

16. The events of the last few weeks have demonstrated that the time has long since passed when the people of the United States can be apathetic about their belief and respect for the law and about the necessity of placing our own house in order. As we turn to meet our enemy, to look him full in the face, we cannot afford feet of clay or an arm of glass.

17. Let me speak to you about three major areas of difficulty within the purview of my responsibilities that sap our national strength, that weaken our people, that require our immediate attention.

18. In too many major communities of our country, organized crime has become big business. It knows no state lines. It drains off millions of dollars of our national wealth, infecting legitimate businesses, labor unions, and even sports. Tolerating organized crime promotes the cheap philosophy that everything is a racket. It promotes cynicism among adults. It contributes to the confusion of the young and to the increase of juvenile delinquency.

19. It is not the gangster himself who is of concern; it is what he is doing to our cities, our communities, our moral fiber. Ninety percent of the major racketeers would be out of business by the end of this year if the ordinary citizen, the businessman, the union official, and the public authority stood up to be counted and refused to be corrupted.

20. This is a problem for all America, not just the FBI or the Department of Justice. Unless the basic attitude changes here in this country, the rackets will prosper and grow. Of this I am convinced.

21. The racketeers, after all, are professional criminals. But there are the amateurs—men who have law-abiding backgrounds and respectable positions, who nevertheless break the law of the land. We have been particularly concerned lately in the Department of Justice about the spread of illegal price fixing. I would say to you, however, it is merely symptomatic of many other practices commonly accepted in business life.

22. Our investigations show that in an alarming number of areas of the country, businessmen have conspired in secret to fix prices, made collusive deals with union officials, defrauded their customers, and even in some instances cheated their own government.

23. Our enemies assert that capitalism enslaves the worker and will destroy itself. It is our national faith that the system of competitive enterprise offers the best hope for individual freedom, social development, and economic growth.

24. Thus, every businessman who cheats on his taxes, fixes prices, or underpays his labor, every union official who makes a collusive deal or misuses union funds, damages the free enterprise system in the eyes of the world and does a disservice to the millions of honest Americans in all walks of life.

25. Where we have evidence of violation of laws by these "respectables," we will take action against the individuals involved, as well as against their companies. But in the end, this is also not a situation which can be cured by the businesses and unions themselves.

26. The third area is the one that affects us all the most directly—civil rights.

27. The hardest problems of all in law enforcement are those involving a conflict of law and local customs. History has recorded many occasions when the moral sense of a nation produced judicial decisions, such as the 1954 decision in Brown v. Board of Education, which required difficult local adjustments.

28. I have many friends in the United States Senate who are Southerners. Many of these friendships stem from my work as counsel for the Senate rackets committee, headed by Senator John McClellan of Arkansas, for whom I have the greatest admiration and affection.

29. If these Southern friends of mine are representative Southerners—and I believe they are—I do not pretend that they believe with me on everything or that I agree with them on everything. But, knowing them as I do, I am convinced of this:

30. Southerners have a special respect for candor and plain talk. They don't like hypocrisy. So, in discussing this third major problem, I must tell you candidly what our policies are going to be in the field of civil rights and why I come to you in that spirit.

31. First let me say this: The time has long since arrived when loyal Americans must measure the impact of their actions beyond the limits of their own towns or states. For instance, we must be quite aware of the fact that 50 percent of the countries in the United Nations are not white; that around the world, in Africa, South America, and Asia,

people whose skins are a different color than ours are on the move to gain their measure of freedom and liberty.

32. From the Congo to Cuba, from South Vietnam to Algiers, in India, Brazil, and Iran, men and women and children are straightening their backs and listening—to the evil promises of Communist tyranny and the honorable promises of Anglo-American liberty. And those people will decide not only their own future but ours—how the cause of freedom fares in the world.

33. In the United Nations we are striving to establish a rule of law instead of a rule of force. In that forum and elsewhere around the world, our deeds will speak for us.

34. In the worldwide struggle, the graduation at this university of Charlayne Hunter and Hamilton Holmes will without question aid and assist the fight against Communist political infiltration and guerrilla warfare.

35. When parents send their children to school this fall in Atlanta, peaceably and in accordance with the rule of law, barefoot Burmese and Congolese will see before their eyes Americans living by the rule of law.

36. The conflict of views over the original decision in 1954 and our recent move in Prince Edward County (Virginia) is understandable. The decision in 1954 required action of the most difficult, delicate, and complex nature, going to the heart of Southern institutions.

37. I know a little of this. I live in Virginia. I studied law at the University of Virginia. I have been privileged to know many able Southern soldiers, scholars, lawyers, jurists, journalists, and political leaders who have enriched our national life. From them I have drawn some understanding of the South, but my knowledge is nothing to yours.

38. It is now being said, however, that the Department of Justice is attempting to close all public schools in Virginia because of the Prince Edward situation. This is simply not true, nor is the Prince Edward suit a threat against local control.

39. We are maintaining the orders of the courts. We are doing nothing more and nothing less. And if any one of you were in my position you would do likewise, for it would be required by your oath of office. You might not want to do it, but you would do it because it would be required.

40. For I cannot believe that anyone can support a principle which prevents more than a thousand of our children in one county from attending public school—especially when this step was taken to circumvent the orders of the court.

41. Our position is quite clear: we are upholding the law. Our action does not threaten local control. The Federal Government would not be running the schools in Prince Edward County any more than it is running the University of Georgia or the schools in my state of Massachusetts.

42. In this case, in all cases, I say to you today that if the orders of the court are circumvented, the Department of Justice will act.

43. We will not stand by and be aloof. We will move.

44. Here on this campus, not half a year ago, you endured a difficult ordeal. And when your moment of truth came, the voices crying "force" were overridden by the voices pledging for reason.

45. And for this, I pay my respects to your Governor, your Legislature, and most particularly to you, the students and faculty of the University of Georgia. And I say that you are the wave of the future—not those who cry panic. For the country's future you will and must prevail.

46. I happen to believe that the 1954 decision was right. But my belief does not matter—it is now the law. Some of you may believe the decision was wrong. That does not matter. It is the law. And we both respect the law. By facing this problem honorably, you have shown to all the world that we Americans are moving forward together, solving this problem under the rule of law.

47. An integral part of all this is that we make a total effort to guarantee the ballot to every American of voting age—in the North, as well as in the South. The right to vote is the easiest of all rights to grant. The spirit of our Constitution and our laws require that there be no further delay in the achievement of full freedom to vote for all. Our system depends upon the fullest participation of all its citizens.

48. The problem between the white and colored people is a problem for all sections of the United States. And, as I have said before, I believe there has been a great deal of hypocrisy in dealing with it. In fact, I found when I came to the Department of Justice that I need look no further to find evidence of this.

49. I found that very few Negroes were employed above a custodial level. There were 950 lawyers working in the Department of

Justice in Washington, and only ten of them were Negroes. At the same moment the lawyers of the Department of Justice were bringing legal action to end discrimination, the same discrimination was being practiced within the department itself.

50. At a recent review for the visiting leader of a new African state, there was only one Negro in the guard of honor. At the Bureau of the Budget, Negroes were used only for custodial work.

51. The Federal Government is taking steps to correct this.

52. Financial leaders from the East who deplore discrimination in the South belong to institutions where no Negroes or Jews are allowed, and their children attend private shcools where no Negro students are enrolled. Union officials criticize Southern leaders and yet practice discrimination within their unions. Government officials belong to private clubs in Washington where Negroes, including ambassadors, are not welcome, even at mealtime.

53. My firm belief is that if we are to make progress in this area, if we are to be truly great as a nation, then we must make sure that nobody is denied an opportunity because of race, creed, or color. We pledge, by example, to take action in our own backyard—the Department of Justice—we pledge to move to protect the integrity of the courts in the administration of justice. In all this, we ask your help, and we need your assistance.

54. I come to you today and I shall come to you in the years ahead to advocate reason and the rule of law.

55. It is in this spirit that since taking office I have conferred many times with responsible public officials and civic leaders in the South on specific situations. I shall continue to do so. I don't expect them always to agree with my view of what the law requires, but I believe they share my respect for the law. We are trying to achieve amicable, voluntary solutions without going to court. These discussions have ranged from voting and school cases to incidents of arrest which might lead to violence.

56. We have sought to be helpful to avert violence and to get voluntary compliance. When our investigations indicate there has been a violation of law, we have asked responsible officials to take steps themselves to correct the situation. In some instances this has happened. When it has not, we have had to take legal action.

57. These conversations have been devoid of bitterness or hate. They have been carried on with mutual respect, understanding, and

goodwill. National unity is essential, and before taking any legal action, we will where appropriate invite the Southern leaders to make their views known in these cases.

58. We, the American people, must avoid another Little Rock or another New Orleans. We cannot afford them. It is not only that such incidents do incalculable harm to the children involved and to the relations among people. It is not only that such convulsions seriously undermine respect for law and order and cause serious economic and moral damage. Such incidents hurt our country in the eyes of the world. We just can't afford another Little Rock or another New Orleans.

59. For on this generation of Americans falls the full burden of proving to the world that we really mean it when we say all men are created free and are equal before the law. All of us might wish at times that we lived in a more tranquil world, but we don't. And if our times are difficult and perplexing, so are they challenging and filled with opportunity.

60. To the South, perhaps more than any other section of the country, has been given the opportunity and the challenge and the responsibility of demonstrating America at its greatest—at its full potential of liberty under law.

61. You may ask: Will we enforce the civil rights statutes?

62. The answer is: Yes, we will.

63. We also will enforce the antitrust laws; the antiracketeering laws; and the laws against kidnapping, robbing Federal banks, transporting stolen automobiles across state lines, illicit traffic in narcotics, and all the rest.

64. We can and will do no less.

65. I hold a Constitutional office of the United States Government, and I shall perform the duty I have sworn to undertake—to enforce the law, in every field of law and every region.

66. We will not threaten, we will try to help. We will not persecute, we will prosecute.

67. We will not make or interpret the laws. We shall enforce them vigorously, without regional bias or political slant.

68. All this we intend to do. But all the high rhetoric on Law Day about the noble mansions of the law, all the high-sounding speeches about liberty and justice, are meaningless, unless people—you and

I—breathe meaning and force into it. For our liberties depend upon our respect for the law.

69. On December 13, 1889, Henry W. Grady of Georgia said these words to an audience in my home state of Massachusetts:

70. "This hour little needs the loyalty that is loyal to one section and yet holds the other in enduring suspicion and estrangement. Give us the broad and perfect loyalty that loves and trusts Georgia alike with Massachusetts—that knows no South, no North, no East, no West, but endears with equal and patriotic love every foot of our soil, every state of our Union.

71. "A mighty duty, sir, and a mighty inspiration. . . . We, sir, are Americans—and we stand for human liberty!"

72. Ten days later Mr. Grady was dead, but his words live today. We stand for human liberty.

73. The road ahead is full of difficulties and discomforts. But as for me, I welcome the challenge, I welcome the opportunity, and I pledge my best effort—all I have in material things and physical strength and spirit to see that freedom shall advance and that our children will grow old under the rule of law.

Specimen 12. How Women Can Get Out of Dead-End Jobs

EDITH M. LYNCH
President, American Employers for Free Enterprise

1. Getting out of dead-end jobs is not a task peculiar to women alone. Men also get stuck in jobs from which there seems no escape. But it's a well-known fact that women make up the bigger proportion of those in low-paying, low-prestige jobs. If you have been to a management conference lately, or if you have ridden the executive flight from Chicago to New York, you will see relatively few women. Read the roster of the officers of a company in its annual report and see how many women you find! Look at your company, your church, or your

Reprinted from *Advanced Management Journal*, Spring 1980.

club and see how many women there are in management positions. Companies brag about having *a* woman on the board, or point with pride to the female vice-president. But let's not kid ourselves—it's still a man's world when it comes to influential jobs.

It's a long, slow process, but upward mobility remains the rallying cry of today's women workers, and the laws are with them. You can find a number of court cases and agency decisions from the Wage-Hour Division of the U.S. Department of Labor and from the Equal Employment Opportunity Commission that have granted women thousands of dollars in back pay because they were not promoted as fast as men were. Furthermore, the companies involved have promised to go straight from now on and have scheduled faster promotions for women.

2. THE DEAD-END JOB

Although the climate is right for movement, there is still an enormous number of women in dull, no-advancement jobs who do not believe they can break loose and get into the upward-mobility stream. Why do they feel stuck? Here are some of the reasons given:

"My boss gives me a scroungy raise every time I talk about a promotion. He says that I'm the best secretary he's ever had, and he'll be damned if he's going to lose me just for a few bucks. Trouble is he's right—the money has looked good all these years, and now I think I'm too old to move."

"I never got my degree, so I find I'm blocked from the next step of every job I try for."

"I've been assistant production manager for three years, but my boss is only two years older than I. I just don't think I have a chance here."

"I was promised a fast track when I took this job right out of college two years ago. Since then, all the men hired with me have been promoted. So where's the fast track I was promised?"

"You think you have trouble. I'm black and I'm smart. In spite of all the talk, there's still a lot of prejudice against me."

Do these lamentations sound familiar? They probably do. If they're not true of you, they may be true of your women subordinates. There are many working women who are capable of holding managerial positions but who too often get little support or who lack the knowledge of how to get ahead. If this is also your situation, the first step for you is to determine whether or not your job is really dead end, and then to decide how to move onward.

3. IS YOUR JOB REALLY DEAD END?

Fortunately, there are many ways of looking at a job. Take, for example, the secretary whose boss keeps giving her raises to keep her there. Secretaries as a group are probably one of the most restless. They sit close to the decision-making job, but they do not make the decisions.

If you are a secretary and want to move up, it's up to you not to be satisfied with the outward show of a few dollars. There is, instead, a recognized path from typist to stenographer to secretary to manager to executive. Moving up entails building your reputation, being watchful, and convincing your boss or someone else that you want to break from your current status. And that process holds true whatever your current "dead-end" job may be. Needless to say, if you are beset with family problems and financial burdens (such as a sick mother or child or putting your children through college), you may feel pressured to stay in a dead-end job for a while. But be ready to move when your problems ease.

4. WHAT YOU CAN DO

If you are ready to move on, you should decide on the job you want. Then ask yourself the following questions:

1. What are the qualifications for that job? What interpersonal and technical skills are involved? Do I have these skills? If not, how can I obtain them?

2. What about my education? The job requirement says four years of college, and I have three. Can I allocate time and money and make arrangements to get the extra year if that is indeed the requirement? Also, have I checked the education policy at the company to see if it will pick up the whole tab or at least part of it?

3. Have I revised my résumé? A résumé should emphasize the functions that you do well rather than be a straight historical document.

4. Have there ever been any women in the job before? Am I willing to break new ground and take the guff that goes with it?

5. What about my age? If everyone else in that department is young, do I have a chance of getting the job? What qualifications do I have to offset my age handicap?

6. Even though I know it's the law not to discriminate against women with children, do I really have the situation under control at home, or should I wait until the children are a bit older?

7. What is the overall picture of the company for which I want to work? Is it a dying organization? Find out about the company and the future of your place in it. If there is no opportunity to move after a year, it may pay to wait for a growing company.

8. What is the attitude toward women at the company for which I want to work? Does top management give lip service to advancing women but in fact block their promotion to meaningful jobs?

9. Have I remembered to ask for help from my boss (if this is wise), from my peers, from my friends, and from agencies? Have I talked to other people who do the kind of work that interests me?

10. Have I planned on getting a mentor? A mentor is perhaps your most important asset to moving up. A person who has clout at a company can help you explore a job, learn what you need to know to do it well, and get promoted to the next job. Some companies make a special effort to assign newcomers to executives who are particularly good at helping others reach full potential. Other companies allow you to choose your mentor. In such a situation, pick a supervisor who can make things move for both of you.

Once you have thoroughly answered these questions, plan your course of action, for good jobs and promotions don't just happen. And if the going gets rough—don't give up. The process of changing may seem to take forever; but if you are persistent, you will find the job you want.

Specimen 13. Abraham Lincoln: The Writer
CLIFFORD D. OWSLEY
The U.S. Forest Service

1. When Lincoln was in the White House, a well-known literary man objected to Lincoln's calling a certain Greek history "tedious." The man said to Lincoln: "Mr. President, the author of that history is one of the profoundest scholars of the age. Indeed, it may be doubted whether any man of our generation has plunged more deeply in the sacred fount of learning." "Yes," said Lincoln, "or come up dryer."

2. All too many people seem to plunge deeply into the sacred fount of learning and still manage to come up quite dry. I don't understand this, for learning, scholarship, ought to be exciting, and when anyone makes it dull and dry, he has gotten off the track somewhere.

3. We in America are off the track in some way when we relegate the study of Abraham Lincoln and the occasional newspaper mention to a once-a-year bow on his birthday. That may be better than nothing, but it falls short of what we should do. Every university in this country ought to have at least a semester course on Abraham Lincoln.

4. Why do I say this? Because there is much anyone can learn from this strange, most unusual genius. While most Americans know that Lincoln was a great man, a great President, and those who have done much reading know that he was a great writer, I say that most Americans have not yet come to realize the true stature of this fantastic man. They will someday, but not yet.

5. I maintain that Lincoln was a genius with words. He was not—and here is the great difference—a born genius; he made himself one. Where we would say that John Keats was largely a born genius, since he lived to be only 26 years old, Lincoln accomplished it the hard, slow, plodding way—the ancient Greek way of the artist or genius—the slow and patient development of talent.

6. Lincoln, as we know, was many things as every man is, but he was first and foremost a writer. He did not pursue writing as a career, but he employed his great writing skill to get where he was going.

Presented to the Lincoln Group of the District of Columbia, Washington, D.C., May 21, 1968. Reprinted from *Vital Speeches of the Day*, July 1, 1968.

7. This interest, almost preoccupation with words, began early in his life, at age 13 or 14, at about the same time that he learned handwriting—and it never left him. Even earlier, he had been annoyed by big words, such as "independence" and "predestination," which he heard his father use in talking with friends. And the young boy would go to his attic room and puzzle over these big words and try to express the same thing in words that any of his young friends could understand.

8. In the little schooling that he had, at about 14, he began to write out his thoughts. One of the first little essays was in defense of a lowly turtle. The other boys were playing a cruel schoolboy game of putting live coals on the back of a mud turtle to make it run. And this feeling for animals never left him. Somewhere around this time, he wrote a little political essay which he showed to a lawyer. The lawyer sent it to a newspaper in Ohio and it was printed, although I think it does not now exist.

9. At New Salem where he began his adult life, he took some part in a literary society that met in the Rutledge Tavern. It was there that he met Jack Kelso, a kind of vagabond, but one who knew and loved Shakespeare and Robert Burns, and was fond of quoting them. With his characteristic taste for odd characters, Lincoln liked Kelso and through him found two more literary favorites. Why would Lincoln take to these two writers? We can only speculate. But, apart from their being two of the greats in English literature, neither had a college education. The young Lincoln, who saw no chance of going to college, might have mused, "If they could do it, maybe I have a chance to do something in writing."

10. Lincoln referred to himself as a learner, and the evidence is that he was one of the most determined students who ever lived. Mentor Graham, a school teacher, said he had taught more than 5,000 students, but that Lincoln was the "most studious, diligent, straightforward young man in the pursuit of knowledge and literature" he had ever met. "I have known him," said Graham, "to study for hours the best way of three to express an idea."

11. When he was young, a man and his wife and two daughters stopped at the Lincoln home for a few days. Years later, Lincoln told a friend, "I took a great fancy to one of the girls. And when they were gone, I thought of her a great deal, and one day sitting out in the sun

by the house I wrote out a story in my mind." Here is the writer thinking out his stories. He tried his hand at several poems.

12. Later, as lawyer and politician, he wrote (ghosted) an occasional editorial for a Springfield newspaper. While there is no record of his having written speeches for others, he may have; he nearly always wrote his own speeches out, indicating the writer was dominant over the speaker. He said, "I am never easy, when handling a thought, till I have bounded it north and bounded it south, and bounded it east and bounded it west." This is the instinct of a writer, and a superior one.

13. Now, let us turn to a masterpiece of this master craftsman, the Gettysburg Address. This, my own discovery, serves as another illustration of the writer at work, and shows where the seeds of this great speech came from.

14. The starting point of the speech is the letter of invitation, written by the lawyer David Wills, agent for Pennsylvania Governor A. G. Curtin. The fact that the letter and the speech are the same length, 272 words, is an interesting curiosity. Of more interest is the fact that most of the words and ideas in the letter are in the speech, but truly transformed by the magic of Lincoln's touch. Each idea is either changed, compressed into fewer and simpler words, or broadened and elevated intellectually and emotionally. Wills's long first sentence referred to the soldiers killed at Gettysburg, using 33 words. These in the speech became six simple words, "those who here gave their lives."

15. Lincoln accepted Wills's word consecrate, used it twice, but gave it a new and larger meaning. After saying it was "fitting and proper" to dedicate the cemetery, Lincoln turned the idea around and said "in a larger sense," it could not be done because those who had fought there had "already consecrated it far above our poor power to add or detract." This phrase in the letter, "the comrades of these brave dead, who are now in the tented field, or nobly meeting the foe at the front" came out in the speech as "The brave men, living and dead, who struggled here." Nine words doing the work of 21.

16. In his fifth paragraph, Wills used 97 words to tell the President what his appearance there would mean. Lincoln rejected this idea, but reshaped it. While characteristically dismissing his own role as unimportant, he greatly enlarged the scope of the dedication to say that it

had meaning not merely for widows, orphans, and veterans of the battle, but to the whole world: "The world will little note nor long remember what we say here, but it can never forget what they did here."

17. Finally, to the most interesting and important part of the analysis, the theme of the speech, *dedicate*. Wills said only that "These grounds will be consecrated and set apart." But observe how in Lincoln's hands the theme became a much larger and nobler concept. No longer is it limited to setting apart a cemetery, but it embraces a whole nation and its living, "dedicated to the proposition that *all men* are created equal."

18. Lincoln not only dedicated a cemetery; he dedicated a nation to the eternal cause of freedom throughout the earth. Thus, a theme that had its genesis in the prosaic setting apart of a burial ground ended magnificently embracing the earth and man's ageless struggle for freedom. How much further could an idea be enlarged? Who else has taken such ordinary clay and molded a masterpiece that will survive the centuries?

19. It is interesting to note three phases of Lincoln's literary development. The first phase ended in 1854, when he came out of a five-year intense legal preoccupation, and reentered the public arena. Up to this time, age 45, his speeches had a certain immaturity, both in style and thought. They are the stump speeches of a young politician—slashing attacks on opponents, broad humor and satire, and strong defense of his own party. They are the products of a man who had not found himself. But even in this period he was mainly concerned with expressing thoughts clearly. He had his moments of windy bombast, or "ornamental language," but he soon abandoned this. His taste, influenced by his reading of Blackstone, Euclid, Shakespeare, and the Bible, was good and growing, just as he was.

20. The second phase, 1854–1860, was a time of growth and improvement. He was constantly speaking against the expansion of slavery. In this phase were the debates with Douglas, the famous "Lost Speech," and near the end, "Cooper Union." Now, Abraham Lincoln has changed. The humor is gone, and in its place there is an all-pervading seriousness, a tone of moderation, fairness, and humility. The man had found himself by finding a cause. These speeches are excellent examples of political argument, but they are not the writings of the Lincoln who has become part of the American heritage. His

style had clarity, simplicity, and the ordered march of ideas, but it did not have beauty or poetry.

21. Now comes 1860 and the third and final phase. His First Inaugural in 1861 shows an exquisite poetic imagery. The last paragraph, drafted by William H. Seward, marks the first great beautiful production. Now come the masterpieces—the not-so-well-known message to Congress July 1, 1861, the Gettysburg Address, and the Second Inaugural. A hard personal life and the breakup of the country had changed Lincoln. The ordeal of secession and war touched hidden springs in his nature and brought out all the mystic poetry he had earlier restrained.

22. It would surprise some people to know the total production of this greater writer. The Basler edition of his collected works—known to be the product of his own hands—fill eight volumes, or total about a million words, approximately equal to Shakespeare's production. With such a volume of writing and unknown quality, few will argue that this man was not one of the world's great writers.

23. H. G. Wells called Lincoln one of the six immortals of civilization. Who the other five were I don't know; but it is likely that Abraham Lincoln towers over them as he did most men in real life and most historical figures in the perspective of world history. It is little short of amazing that he excelled in so many ways, and then, with such bare beginnings, ended up an undisputed master of language.

24. What was this man's secret? Probably many things, but the nearest I have come to an answer is found in a poem by William Butler Yeats: "God guard me from those thoughts men think in the mind alone. He that sings a lasting song thinks in the marrow bone." His thoughts were not only in his mind; they went deeper, to be part of his bones.

25. Abraham Lincoln was a man so different from the ordinary run of humanity that we can find no equal in a thousand years. To find equals we must hark back to antiquity—to the Gods and heroes of mythology, the legendary days of Greece and Rome. The record of his life presents us with a picture that will live through all the mists of time. From his own words he can be judged by each generation. In unexampled perfection, he embodied the natural goodness and valor of the human race. Infinite compassion, unconquerable courage, singular humility, the virtue of the simple, the wisdom of the just—all shone forth in him. He glorifies the soil and nation from which he

sprang. All Americans would do well to ponder the words and deeds of this true statesman of liberty. Though untaught by schools, he revealed in every situation the key to sublimity. The freedom he loved and defended will endure. As it covers the earth, Abraham Lincoln's name will go with it, to reign in the hearts and minds of people, forever enthroned in the hallowed temples of democracy.

Specimen 14. Communicating for Improved Motivation and Performance

LARRY E. PENLEY and BRIAN L. HAWKINS
Assistant Professors, College of Business, The University of Texas at San Antonio

1. The problem with so many of today's motivational theories is that they place too much emphasis on describing the motivational process. Such descriptions are important for the development of knowledge, but they do not address the problems of the practicing manager. These theories, on the whole, do not identify strategies for modifying and changing individual behavior, and these are what managers want. They want concrete, effective strategies for dealing with motivation.

2. Theorists often describe motivation as a process that occurs between the work environment and the individual's performance. Based on this concept of motivation, Douglas McGregor in *The Human Side of Enterprise* suggests that a manager cannot motivate another person. His contention is that a manager cannot *directly* affect the motives going on inside the employee's head. The manager can only indirectly affect these motives by manipulating the environment in which the employee exists.

3. What can a manager do to affect the environment of the employee? The answer lies in the communication that occurs between manager and employee.

4. To understand clearly the relationship between communication

Reprinted from *Advanced Management Journal*, Spring 1980.

and motivation, let us briefly look at one well-received motivational model, that of Victor Vroom, and see how communication strategies can be integrated with it.

5. In his book *Work and Motivation,* Vroom suggests that three factors are important: (1) the "valence," or importance, of various outcomes in meeting an individual's needs; (2) the extent to which an individual perceives that his or her effort will result in the desired performance, and (3) the extent to which an individual believes that desirable performance will be rewarded.

6. From what has been observed, the manager cannot directly affect what another person values; thus, valence falls outside the realm of managerial strategy. A manager can, however, affect both the extent to which an employee believes he or she can perform a task and whether or not that performance will result in desired rewards.

7. Vroom refers to an employee's belief that he or she can perform the task as "expectancy." This belief that one can accomplish a task is affected by self-confidence, learned skills, and native abilities. The manager can increase an employee's confidence by coaching, encouraging, and being supportive of the employee who has low expectancy for a particular task. This may be the case for an employee who is new on the job or for one who has recently changed jobs. Further, the managers can train employees who have not learned the necessary skills, thus increasing expectancy.

8. The second variable from the model that can be modified by a manager's communication is called "instrumentality." Instrumentality is the employee's perception of the results of personal performance. In other words, it is the degree to which the employee believes that rewards are commensurate with successful performance. Does good performance result in merit pay? Does bad performance result in termination? The answers to both of these questions reflect the extent to which employees perceive that rewards or punishments are tied to performance.

9. What things can a manager do to affect these perceptions of expectancy and instrumentality? Are there contingency strategies that a manager can adopt to heighten these perceptions, thus encouraging better employee performance?

10. These questions were addressed in a survey of employee attitudes in a Southwestern financial institution. The balance of this article offers conclusions based on the findings of this study. (For

details on study methodology, see the accompanying section, "The Nature of the Study.")

11. *Receptivity and Responsiveness Are Key.* Study results show that a supervisor's receptiveness or willingness to listen to subordinates' ideas, problems, and concerns will improve the motivation of subordinates. Through such receptiveness, supervisors develop knowledge of areas in which they need to provide additional training or explanation in order to build expectancy that the worker can perform tasks. A supervisor, however, must not only be receptive to the messages subordinates communicate; they must also respond to questions and problems. The study indicates that listening to the employee is not enough. If high levels of motivation are to be obtained, follow-up and communication of that follow-up are essential.

12. *Praise Is More Than a Reward.* Praise is a reward that many employees seek in organizations, both for its own sake and as a guidepost in directing their organizational behavior. More than that, however, praise also builds confidence in an employee that he or she can perform the task. This means that expectancy can be modified for an employee if a manager communicates praise, reducing employee anxiety as he or she moves toward success in task performance.

13. *Effective Media Use Is Needed.* Management can improve its communication of benefits and goals through more frequent communication and the use of varied media, including meetings, memoranda, bulletin boards, and orientation sessions. Management can also raise motivation through improving the clarity of written reports and instructions. Adapting written messages to the reader by writing at the reader's level and in terms of the needs or viewpoint of the reader means that employees will have greater understanding of what is expected of them as well as of what behavior will be rewarded by the organization.

14. Supervisors and management can also sharpen motivation by increasing the information that workers have on the reasons for doing a task, job procedures, specific goals of the job, how to do a job, the relationship of one job to another job, and organizational goals. The data from this study indicate that motivation and performance are higher for employees who can place their job in a "bigger picture."

15. *Feedback Is Motivational.* Adequate information concerning performance will improve the perception of the instrumental relationship between performance and rewards. By providing em-

ployees with information on performance and what is necessary to get a pay increase, management can help employees relate performance to reward. The net result should be higher motivation and performance.

16. *Awareness of Career Options Helps.* Employees who possess high expectancy describe themselves as having good information on career development. The communication of performance, followed up with information on the career "ladders" to positions in top management, may be an important key to employee motivation and performance.

17. *Summing Up: The Big Five.* Overall, this study suggests that managers need to examine closely their conduct in five areas: (1) their receptiveness and responsiveness to employees, (2) the clarity of their communication, (3) the adequacy of the performance-related information they give, (4) the adequacy of the task-related information they provide, and (5) the adequacy of information concerning career development they give. Based on the study, there is a clear justification for increasing management's emphasis on communication planning and on communication training for supervisors and managers.

THE NATURE OF THE STUDY

18. The conclusions drawn in this article are based on the findings of an employee survey conducted at a financial organization in the Southwest. Soliciting views on job communication, motivation, and performance, questionnaires were submitted to the firm's 354 employees, of whom some 75 percent responded. Supplementing this source of information, supervisors were surveyed and asked to evaluate employees' performance.

19. A number of areas were investigated:

20. The quality of *supervisory communication* was measured with a scale formed of 11 items. The scale included items concerned with the responsiveness of the supervisor to subordinates' questions and problems, the degree to which the supervisor is receptive to the ideas of subordinates or listens to subordinates, and the degree to which the supervisor praises subordinates when they succeed.

21. The quality of *managerial communication* included items concerned with the degree to which upper management communicates information on benefits and goals, is sincere in its communication, is

perceived to understand the employees, and clearly writes instructions and reports.

22. Three scales were developed to measure the degree of information adequacy that employees face concerning their performance, their career development, and their tasks. These scales were formed by asking respondents to rate how much information they *now* receive and how much information they *need* to receive in the three categories: The *adequacy of performance-related information* was determined by gauging responses to questions regarding the information employees now get on their job performance, and what they believe they must do to get a pay increase; the *adequacy of task-related information* was determined by evaluating the information employees reported receiving on task objectives, job procedures, task interrelationships, and organizational goals; the *adequacy of career-development information* was determined by assessing employees' knowledge about how to get promoted and how to get additional training.

23. The measure of *expectancy* was formed by asking employees about their perceptions of the relationship between their effort and resultant performance. The measure of *instrumentality* was formed by asking employees about their perceptions of the extent to which they are rewarded for performance by their supervisors.

24. As an additional element in assessing the effectiveness of communications, supervisors evaluated job performance of subordinates in terms of dependability, organizational ability, application of job knowledge, adaptability, initiative, interpersonal skills, leadership ability, and overall work performance.

25. The data for this study were analyzed using multiple regression techniques. These techniques allowed the researcher to determine whether motivation and performance were affected by communication, and they revealed that measures of communication affect motivation and performance.

Specimen 15. Today's Challenge in Education
MAX RAFFERTY
Superintendent of Public Instruction, State of California

1. That introduction was undoubtedly better than this talk is going to be. One gets all kinds of introductions in this business. Especially is this true in the hustle and bustle of a campaign such as I was engaged in recently. Once I was introduced by a rather flustered lady as "Roctor Dax Mafferty!" . . .

2. I thought you might, before we get started into this little seminar today, be interested in some of the things that happen to an educator when he runs for office. I know that most of you are profoundly interested in education and in California. This is not true in some other states incidentally. Here, however, we have a situation in which once every four years an educator runs for elective office. It's a fascinating experience—a rather traumatic one, but a fascinating one nonetheless, if you can retain your sense of humor. There is one thing that is fatal, though: if you have an overly developed bump of ego at the start, I guarantee you won't have it after you're through, because the citizens and voters in the State of California will take that sort of thing out of you in a hurry. They have absolutely no qualms about what they say to you or how they say it. Bless their hearts!

3. I'm reminded of the time I was in a motorcade in San Francisco at the midpoint of the campaign. I don't know whether any of you have every been in a motorcade or not, but it's sort of the closest thing politics have to a football serpentine, homecoming night. Everybody gets in cars, decorates them with banners, sends balloons out the windows; boys proceed down the street trying to attract votes. And on this particular motorcade, they stuck me in the lead car and I felt pretty foolish, as you can imagine.

4. There we were tooting horns down through the middle of San Francisco. And to make things worse, on the side of the car, they had a larger-than-life-size picture of me (I take the world's worst picture) look like Dracula coming out of the swamp somewhere! This particular one was the one used throughout my campaign, and it had to be

Presented to Pepperdine College Forum, Los Angeles, California, February 28, 1963. Reprinted from *Vital Speeches of the Day*, May 15, 1963.

posed for 22 times before they could finally get one that even looked faintly human. Finally, they caught me absentmindedly looking at the progress of a fly across the lens of the camera, and they shot it quickly as my eyes were raised rather soulfully toward heaven with a pious look, you know, and that's the one they used for lack of anything better.

5. Well, anyway, this was on the side of the car and the motorcade stopped at a San Francisco intersection, and there on the corner was a little old lady waiting for the red light to turn green so she could cross. Well, I'd always thought that all little old ladies lived in Pasadena, you know, but this one lived in San Francisco and she was a typical one. She had her hair in a bun behind her ears, and she had steel-rimmed glasses. She carried this little beaded string bag, and she was standing there waiting for the light to change. She saw the motorcade draw up. She looked at the picture on the side of the car; she took a step down from the curb, and she rapped with her handbag upon the glass window where I was sitting.

6. I carefully put down the window as quickly as possible (hoping to corral the elusive vote) and the lady said very primly and precisely, "I do not know your candidate, but my, he is goodlooking!" Well, I reacted just like Jack Benny. I said, "Well! thank you, madam." She took a step back up the curb, looked at me very severely over her steel-rimmed spectacles and she said, "Are you the candidate?" I said very proudly, "Yes ma'am." She said, "Oh, no!"

7. You meet some very interesting people. You also get some very interesting telephone calls—usually at 1:30 in the morning. There is a sort of singular tendency for candidates to be awakened from a sound sleep by people wanting to talk to them in the wee, small hours of the morning. After this happened many times, I finally evolved a theory that there is a certain irreducible percentage of the population which suffers from insomnia. As these people toss and turn, sleepless, they decide they are going to try to get someone to talk to them who has the maximum chance of putting them to sleep in the minimum amount of time, and they think immediately of a political candidate. If that candidate happens to be an educator, so much the better, for obvious reasons.

8. So I got this call. I had just gotten to sleep. I was dead tired and I had been campaigning all day. The room was dark; the phone rang; I leaped out of bed half asleep, barked my shins painfully on a stool

that happened to be in the middle of the floor, hopped across the room, picked up the telephone, and in no very good mood, I answered this anonymous phone call. (Now, you ladies must not listen to this because this is not meant for you, but you gentlemen may listen.) On the other end of that telephone, there was a voice which was the absolute epitome of all the voices of all the mothers-in-law who ever lived. It was a harsh, rasping, hectoring sort of a voice—you know the type. She did not identify herself. She just started out like a machine gun. She said, "Doctor, are you familiar with this school (and she named it) in Baja, California?" I said, "Wh-a-t?" She repeated the question. I said, "Madam, I never heard of it." She said, "What! You never heard of it!" I said, "No, ma'am." She said, "Well!" and hung up the phone. 1:30 in the morning!

9. Well now, you see she had succeeded doubly in her original goal of getting to sleep because I'm sure she went back to her downy couch and went promptly to sleep, satisfied by the thought that she had discovered in a candidate a Grade A fraud, one who didn't know the first thing about his profession. Obviously, I didn't, since I didn't know about this school. So, she was satisfied and happy and went off to sleep, and of course she had succeeded doubly because she had traded her insomnia with mine; now I couldn't get to sleep wondering what it was that I had been missing—and I never did find out, incidentally. So, you have to get used to all sorts of strange things in a campaign, and I (if anyone is harboring a secret itch to be a candidate) would recommend that you follow Jack Dempsey's advice. Back in the 1920s, whenever Jack was getting ready to fight, he spent several hours each day before the fight soaking both fists in buckets of brine to get a consistency on the skin of his hands which would resemble the skin of a rhinoceros. I recommend it to any would-be political candidate among the ranks of educators—only, gentlemen or ladies, do this in a bath tub. You'll need it.

Specimen 16. The Environment

DR. GLENN T. SEABORG
Chairman, U.S. Atomic Energy Commission

1. Everyone talks about the environment, but nobody does anything about it. This is one way we might update that popular old complaint about the weather. But while such an expression might become timely and popular, it would hardly be true. More is being done today than at any time in human history to understand our natural and man-made environments and bring man and nature into a more harmonious relationship. Surely we are experiencing more "confrontations" with nature than ever before. But it is also true, as I hope to show later, that we are also conducting many more promising "dialogues" with her.

2. Before I go into detail on some of our environmental problems and some of the ways we are trying to solve them, let me spend a few minutes calmly attempting to put the environment in perspective. This may be difficult, as "environment" has become an emotionally charged word these days—almost on a par with words like "crime in the street," "student revolts," or "Raquel Welch," depending on which emotion you want charged. Perhaps I risk some criticism if I speak at all lightly about this subject, but sometimes I feel that a good portion of the public has been so saturated by our excellent pollution press coverage that they are now what we might call "environmentally uptight." Granted that the facts and projections on many of our environmental prospects are frightening and that we do have to meet this challenge, we also suffer in this area from what Daniel P. (Pat) Moynihan has termed in urban programs "maximum feasible misunderstanding." There is a great deal that needs to be clarified and spelled out about the environment—about what it is, about man's relationship to it, about the effects of our modern technologies on it (not only detrimentally but in terms of what can be done to improve our environmental situation), and about the economic and social implications involved in dealing with it.

3. Today one can detect a growing hysteria among a large segment

Presented to the National Academy of Sciences, National Research Council Solid State Sciences Panel, Argonne National Laboratory, Argonne, Illinois, May 5, 1969. Reprinted from *Vital Speeches of the Day,* June 15, 1969.

of the concerned public that should be tempered to a more rational outlook toward environmental problems—while of course retaining the necessary sense of urgency about solving them. Working along these lines, let me point out some of the current thinking and misconceptions and try to put some of these matters in a different light.

4. To begin with, many of us in this country are entering what might seem like a new era of nature worship. As an ardent hiker and nature-lover myself, I can appreciate this attitude. In our increasingly urban and technological society, a return to the "great outdoors," enjoyment of the natural surroundings, and a new respect and fondness for wildlife are, understandably, growing. Of course, what is usually overlooked is the extent to which technology has made nature accessible to us as a friend to be understood and enjoyed rather than a foe to be overcome. Time, money, good transportation—not to mention modern agriculture and industry—make this possible. The new conservationist often reaches the wilderness in his camper trailer via a new interstate highway. He "toughs it" on his own terms with a good supply of "store bought" items at hand. But he invariably forgets a great deal of this in his attacks on his technological society.

5. It is also understandable that from the scientific point of view, our environmental backlash (the reasons for which I will dwell on later) has fostered a new outlook on nature and a rise in emphasis on ecology. Therefore, it is quite fashionable today among some scientists and laymen alike to talk of the "balance of nature" but to consider it as economists used to consider the policy of laissez-faire—to imply that this balance is the only one and that it is a totally benign process. The implication also is that if man would only effect a completely "hands off" policy concerning natural processes, nature would somehow adjust all to everyone's benefit. This simply is not true. And it does not take much examination to show it.

6. Objectively studied, the "balance of nature" is indeed remarkable, even awe-inspiring. But modern man cannot be totally objective about it when it comes to his own survival and evolution. He must to some extent "tamper" with that "balance of nature"—at least to the point of working with it to favor himself occasionally.

7. We tend to forget that nature plays no favorites. Though it creates magnificently, it often destroys whimsically and sometimes totally. . . .

8. We also tend to forget the extent to which nature destroys—and pollutes—segments of itself, sporadically and violently—with man often a major victim in these upheavals. Witness the great earthquakes, volcanic eruptions, tidal waves, floods, and epidemics that have been recorded. Among the greatest of these were the earthquake in Shensi Province of China in 1556, killing an estimated 800,000 people, and the one in Japan in 1923 which took close to 150,000 lives and destroyed more than half a million homes; the volcanic eruption of 1470 B.C. that destroyed much of the Minoan civilization; the 1883 explosion of Krakatoa, an island in Indonesia, which, in addition to wiping out 163 villages and killing 36,000 people, sent rock and dust falling for ten days as far as 3,000 miles away; the great flood of the Hwang-ho River in China in 1887 that swept 900,000 people to their death; the famine in India in 1770 that claimed the lives of a third of the country's population—tens of millions of people—and the 1877–1878 famine in Northern China that killed 9,500,000. And centuries before man seriously tampered with nature through modern medicine, between 1347 and 1351, the Black Death (bubonic plague) wiped out 75,000,000 people in Europe. History records numerous other types of plagues and natural disasters that have periodically destroyed various forms of life and changed the face of the earth—and most of this, I remind you, long before man and his new technology interfered with the balance of nature.

9. I state all this not to offend nature lovers, or to decry the beauty and mystery of Mother Nature, but only to point out that she is not always goodness and light and can be fickle and tempetuous. What we must realize, though, is that it is not a matter of "you can't live with her and you can't live without her". We are a part of nature. We have no choice but to coexist with her, and in view of our own creative evolution that does produce some rapid and extreme change, this is going to take a lot more understanding and effort than we have put forth in the past.

10. Part of this understanding can be gained from a brief look at man and his technology, and their effect on the natural environment. To read some material popular today, you would get the feeling that man-made pollution is a brand new phenomenon. What is new is the extent to which we are contaminating our environment and our current reaction to it. The rest is almost as old as recorded history.

Man has caused and been affected by pollution throughout the ages. In the Holy Bible, passages in Revelation tell us "and from the shaft rose smoke, like the smoke of a great furnace, and the sun and the air were darkened with the smoke from the shaft. . . . By these three plagues a third of mankind was killed, by the fire and smoke and sulphur issuing from their mouths" (Revelation 9:2 and 18). To offer us such dire warnings of this kind of air pollution, our forebears of biblical times must have experienced some of its effects themselves.

11. Water pollution became a great problem in the cities of medieval Europe when there was no longer a central authority to collect public funds for and regulate sanitary and water services, as had been done during the Roman Empire. Here was a perfect example, not of too much technology, but of a neglect of the use of known sanitary engineering methods. According to Singer's *History of Technology:* "As the efficient superintendence of sewers and street cleaning declined, hygienic conditions fell far below the standard of Imperial Rome, where pure water had been available even far beyond the confines of the city. Wells, being also used for storage of rainwater, were often in low-lying ground and close to cesspools and latrines. Thus epidemics spread quickly. Open gutters in the middle of the street carried refuse, while rainwater pouring from the roofs was not properly drained. The streets, seldom paved, were often mud-pools from which the excreta of pigs and other animals leaked into wells and private plots."

12. It was this sort of neglect that precipitated the Black Death of 1348, which I mentioned before, and which led to the first British urban sanitary act, in 1388, forbidding the throwing of refuse into ditches, rivers, and waters.

13. One of the first laws against air pollution was recorded earlier than 1300, when King Edward I (1239–1307) issued an edict against the burning of coal. The penalty was death—and history records at least one execution for this offense. But some years later, after the reign of Elizabeth, economics triumphed over health considerations, and air pollution became an appalling problem in England—so much so that the English writer John Evelyn (1620–1706) compared "dark London" to "the picture of Troy sacked by the Greeks or the approaches of Mount Hecla." In fact, Evelyn was so disturbed by what he saw and breathed that he wrote a pamphlet called "Fumifuguim; or the inconvenience of the aer and smoak of London dissipated.

Together with some remedies humbly proposed." One of his proposals was that sweet-smelling trees should be planted throughout
London to purify the air.

14. But to those anti-technologists and conservationists who are
about to say, "I told you so," let me remind them that if coal had not
taken over as the chief fuel of that time, the forests of Europe would
have been stripped bare because of the need for wood for charcoal
and shipbuilding.

15. As a final historical example of man's effect on his environment through his technology, or lack of it, let me sketch for you a
brief picture of one aspect of life in a large American city as we
entered the 1900s. It was a bright weekend day and everyone was out
shopping and admiring each other's finery, for this too was a period
of affluence in America. But this affluence presented a problem.
Everyone who was anyone—and many who were not—could now
afford a horse and carriage, and so the streets were jammed with
them. It was not just the traffic that presented a problem, however.
The technology of the horse, like all other energy converters, produces waste. And the proliferation of the horse on the city streets had
reached the point where it had become difficult to walk—and sometimes unpleasant to breathe. Other than employing every able-bodied
man as a streetcleaner, could nothing be done to alleviate this impossible situation? Of course. A new technology was waiting in the
wings—enter the "horseless carriage."

16. I will let you draw your own conclusions and moral directly
from this last scene, but let me comment generally on what I am
driving at in looking back in history on our man-made environmental
problems. Associated with the causes of such problems have always
been some of the following: general population growth and the
concentration of population; excessive and unplanned use of
technology, not technology per se; neglect and lack of self-imposed
standards; and, until recently, the inability to anticipate the detrimental effects of a technology or its applications.

17. Today we suffer from a combination of all of these. As our
population grows, so does the influx to our urban area. We seem
more concerned about our immediate comforts and conveniences,
with the possession of products than the waste associated with their
production, and, generally, with short-term benefits rather than
long-term costs when it comes to serious considerations of matters

that could better environmental conditions. At least all this was true before some of the recent feedback we have been getting from nature, and some of the forecasts we have been getting from science, began to worry us. Now, while there are still many people who are more interested in the size, options, and horsepower of their "horseless carriages" than the building of a local rapid transit system, or in the amount of their local taxes than in the improvement of their municipal waste and water systems, there are some who have gone to the other extreme. In their eagerness to stop all pollution—instantly— they simply believe the solution lies in something like turning off a single faucet marked "Technology."

18. As an example of such thinking, I recently received a letter from a prominent national organization advising me of a resolution their membership had passed. This resolution, I was informed, put them on record as opposing further industrial development on any "wild, natural, native, pristine, scenic, or pastoral portion of coasts or shores of the United States, including the shores of the Pacific, Atlantic, and Arctic oceans or the Gulf of Mexico, and their bays and estuaries and inland waters." Needless to say, that is a pretty all-inclusive and definitive statement. If it were also a "non-negotiable demand," I'm afraid we would have to declare an immediate moratorium on any and all further growth in the U.S.—including that of the offspring of the members of the organization that drafted the resolution.

19. While it is usually against my nature to be at all facetious on such matters, I cannot help imagine what the reaction might be if it were possible to carry out such an edict or even to spell out all the changes in our society that would have to take place as a result— changes that I am sure this organization, with all its good intentions, had not considered would be the consequences of carrying out its demands.

20. There is something further I should point out related to this matter of looking at this either/or approach to our environmental problems that tends to polarize the conservationist and the technologist. Granted the well-meaning concern and dedication of the conservationist and nature enthusiast of today, must the attitude prevail that any and all intrusions of man and technology must be detrimental to nature? Because some technologies of the past have been destructive or have been used destructively, does it follow that

this must be the case today? If some technologies of the past have been ugly or offensive, does it mean we cannot make them attractive or aesthetic or even blend them into natural surroundings, so that they almost dissolve the interface between nature and modern man?

21. All this is possible—and desirable—but only if we can balance indignation with information and concern with understanding and compromise. I recall one heated controversy in which this was done, and all parties today are still pleased with the results. This involved strong objections to the running of power lines for an accelerator laboratory across a scenic wooded hillside adjacent to a local community. The problem was solved by using specially designed utility poles, setting them up, and running their lines without cutting a swath through the trees.

22. Of course, we need to be able to solve more difficult problems than this. Better still, we have to be able to anticipate them and work around them before issues and people become polarized and harder to deal with. To do this we will need better communications—a more effective dialogue—not only between scientist and citizen, but among the ranks of the scientists and engineers. The challenge of today's environmental problems should be the greatest impetus to interdisciplinary activity among scientists—and among public organizations and the government.

23. There is no doubt that this challenge is having an impact. I am encouraged when I note the growing references to, and use of, such words and phrases as Spaceship Earth, Ecology, Symbiotic, Synergistic, Biosphere, and the extension of systems analysis and systems engineering thinking to our overall environmental problems. While we cannot sacrifice the rigorous demands of our own specialties, whatever they may be, we can—scientists and laymen alike—take a broader, more encompassing view toward today's environmental concerns. We must realize that these concerns delicately relate physical sciences (including your specialty of solid state physics), life sciences, engineering considerations, economics, law, manpower training, and employment—all these as well as possible conflicts of human rights and values.

24. Few people appreciate the complexities and subtleties involved in our dealing with today's major environmental problems. It is even difficult in some respects to define pollution—to set standards for clean air and clean water. For example, as Dr. Abel Wolman, one of

America's leading authorities on sanitary engineering, has often asked in hearings or interviews on our environmental problems, "How clean do we want our waterways? Clean enough to drink from? To swim in? To sustain its fish and wildlife?" These are choices, Dr. Wolman cogently points out, that involve various degrees of effort—in applying known technologies and in carrying out new research and development, in resource expenditure, and in setting goals and establishing priorities. They involve far more than simply the demands of one particularly vocal interest group. More often the question is not just "how clean do we want our air and water?" but "what are we willing to pay for what kind of air and water?" And this payment may be other than merely money; it may involve many radical changes in our lives, including some control of what we produce, the way we produce it, how we use it, where we use it, and how we dispose of it or recycle it.

25. I am not stating these things to make excuses for our not setting goals and priorities now, and for not acting vigorously to achieve them, but only to point out that we do have a complex, difficult task ahead of us that is going to take a great deal of new thinking and a great amount of cooperative effort on the part of many people. . . .

26. We know today how much we live in a world of our own making. More than anything else, our new environmental relationships—both with nature and our man-made environments—tell us this. They thrust on us awesome new responsibilities. They ask many probing and sometimes painful questions. They ask us to choose between new alternatives and to accept new risks. They also fill many people with many doubts about the human race—about its powers, its limitations, its role on this earth, and now even its destiny in this universe. It is natural then that many of us are apprehensive, that some yearn for simpler times, that many warn "go slow" and others cry "retreat."

27. But there is no turning back. We are experiencing the birth shock of being born into a brave new world—and the bravery must be ours. It cannot be a false bravery, an empty bravado of mankind flaunting his knowledge and technology. It must be a courage tempered with compassion, a quest for more knowledge and understanding and the humility that comes when one reaches a peak only to gaze out on new and unexplored horizons, and then moves on. Our

new "discovery" of our environment—the demands it makes—must bring us this kind of courage. It must make us a new and better breed of man. I think it will.

Specimen 17. The Ten Marks of the Conservative
GERALD J. SKIBBINS
Research Executive, Opinion Research Corporation,
Princeton, N.J.

The biggest problem with the conservative movement in America is that few people can describe it, including many of its proponents or popular figures. We have a tremendous educational task on our hands.

Like any dynamic, modern movement, conservative belief draws upon many strands of thought that have been important to the history of civilization:

The Christian ethic

The ideas of Aristotle

American political philosophy

Pragmatism

Humanism

Free market economics

The social sciences

and all those varicolored skeins of thought which seek individual freedom under an equitable system of law and regulation.

The major objectives of the movement can be set down fairly clearly. We see similar objectives in the credos of college conservative clubs, conservative groups in both political parties, and in the thinking of conservative individuals. These general objectives are:

Limit the power of the Federal government

Combat Communism worldwide

Preserve and extend the ideas of individual freedom and liberty

Halt the trend toward the welfare state

Presented to The Central New Jersey Conference of Conservatives, Princeton, New Jersey, September 15, 1962. Reprinted from *Vital Speeches of the Day*, November 15, 1962.

Introduce rational, modern thinking into politics and international affairs.

Strengthen the free enterprise system

There are some others which might be added, but these are matters for future debate.

To recapitulate, I have set forth the sources of ideas which give strength to the conservative movement and just now, I have listed its modern *objectives*. Unfortunately, these lists of sources and objectives do not yet clearly separate the conservative from the reactionary or the modern liberal. The latter movements borrow from the same traditions and often claim kinship, in varying degrees, with the same goals.

Can we set down the particular way in which believers in conservatism fit into the overall group which espouses the free society? I will not try here to catalog the various rights, laws, institutions, and concepts which make up the fabric of a person's belief in the free society. That would take too long. I will try, however, to spotlight those characteristics which set off the conservative from his fellows.

These, then, are the ten marks of the conservative:

1. SELF-RESPONSIBILITY

The conservative believes that the individual possesses total responsibility for his life, his obligations, and the consequences of his actions and beliefs. We do not believe that anyone else should commandeer this responsibility (such as the representatives of the state itself) unless the facts demonstrate that the individual has exhausted normal channels of assistance and is clearly incapacitated by factors beyond his control. Conservatives are charitable to those who need help; in fact, you'll find them gathering most of the funds for voluntary welfare in this country. They carry on this activity of conscience with the view that those who need help are those who have fallen short. However, they do not believe in reinforcing delinquency, as does much of our state-administered aid.

2. BELIEF IN THE MORALITY OF PROFIT AS THE FREE MARKET'S REWARD FOR RESPONSIBLE BEHAVIOR

The founder of Opinion Research Corporation, the late Claude Robinson (a strong conservative, incidentally), wrote in *Understanding Profits* that aside from the profits of gangsters and those who use force, earned profits are the surest long-term sign of responsible behavior by all who make up an enterprise.

Conservatives believe that any enterprise which does not clearly demonstrate profits, either in human values or in dollars, is probably superfluous, incompetent, or irrelevant, as is much of our government bureaucracy, some business enterprises and associations.

3. VOLUNTARISM

The conservative believes that no one can choose for a man as well as he can choose for himself—in the marketplace and on his right to join organizations, such as clubs, churches, or unions, in choosing careers and establishing his goals. Thus, a conservative would disagree with the attempts of our present and past administrations to set spurious "public sector" goals for this nation, using the people's money to seek them. Conservatives believe a country is strongest when men and women set their own goals in life.

The goal of this nation is the sum of its individual goals and not the directive program of any politician. This right to set our own goals has been the greatest incentive to American progress. Thus, conservatives oppose all existing forms of legal compulsion, such as our government's threatening farmers or telling them how they shall farm; such as laws that force company workers into unions whether they want to join or not; or laws to grant a single company a monopoly in the marketplace, and so on. Conservatives believe people have enough wisdom to choose constructive goals. They know that social goals set by force, such as Prohibition, are doomed to failure in a free society. They also recognize that "liberals" who use government to force their goals upon the people, demonstrate by this action that they do *not* believe in the wisdom of the public to choose its own goals.

Conservatives believe that if individual rights and the choosing of goals are kept in the people's hands, this nation has its best guarantee of progress, peace, economic growth, and justice for the individual.

4. EQUALITY UNDER LAW

Conservative thought demands a legal fabric which insures fair play, free competition, redress for injury, and fair trial, and allows a man to protect his home and his property under law, as we have developed law within the English-American tradition. It opposes law which grants privilege or penalty to the few, discriminates against

minorities, or in any way fails to embody both protection for responsible productive behavior and penalty for irresponsible or antisocial
actions which use force against others.

5. RESPONSIBILITY FOR SOCIETY

Look around you at the men or women of conservative belief. You
will find a high proportion are actively involved in society, its problems, its work, and its achievements. These are not rebels or reactionaries who sit on the sidelines and carp at their fellows. Conservatives are usually people who bear the biggest real burdens of our time.
They are running the constructive and profit-earning activities in our
communities, states, and nation. They are doing important invention
or research, leading our military services, ennobling the arts, keeping
sanity in government activities, practicing the vital professions. They
lead and staff the community chest drives, the charities, the hospitals,
the job-creating business. These are not headline-winners, but the
tough-minded stalwarts who keep the machinery of civilization in
operation; creating new growth and building new careers for others;
helping those who need help, managing institutions which produce
valuable services or goods, and creating the sensible and life-giving
core of this industrial society. Conservatives are aware of their responsibilities to family, community, and society, and *they discharge
them*. The pay the bills of our society.

6. BELIEF THAT RIGHTS ARE WEDDED TO RESPONSIBILITIES

Conservatives believe that you can get very little for nothing. Most
things that are worthwhile in our lives, the most valuable personal
achievements or traits of character, have a high price in effort, mental
anguish, and responsible behavior. Individual freedom, the greatest
right of all, they believe, is tied to its twin—the responsibility we each
have to preserve and extend freedom within our borders and outside
of it.

7. BELIEF IN THE DISPERSION OF POWER FOR THE PUBLIC INTEREST

The checks and balances of our republic have proved to be a
remarkable deterrent to wild or temporarily irresponsible lawmakers

or administrations. Conservatives believe that any concentration of power is dangerous to the public. Thus, the conservative would:

Cut up monolithic cartels or industrial monopolies too great for the free market to control.

Disperse giant union monopolies seeking strangleholds on the economy.

Cut down bureaucratic goals to have government run everything.

And all for the same reason—to disperse excessive power into the hands of individuals, because power tends to be abused.

8. A BELIEF THAT MAN'S LOT ON EARTH CAN BE IMPROVED

True conservatives do not have slogans such as:

"Don't rock the boat"

"Let's do things as we did before"

"You can't change the rules of life"

"Anything new is suspicious"

These are the cries of the reactionaries. They would fit the British Tories . . . of the American Revolution, a revolution in which conservatives profoundly believe and would support with their lives and their resources. A modern conservative wants to get on with the job of figuring out how to deal with today, not by limiting and chaining man with government red tape nor by walking backward, but by working out new forms and institutions that can *advance* the ideas of freedom. Conservatives welcome change. They know that each change in our world is a new opportunity for the conservative to exert his constructive influence upon the direction our civilization might take.

9. BALANCING THE BOOKS

In modern history, economic and political fads, such as socialized medical care or payment for not farming, continually stumble over the vital necessity to balance the books or go bankrupt. No wild, political giveaway or social scheme can long endure if the people insist that their government shall balance its books each year, pay off its debts, and behave in the manner which any responsible person knows is necessary to survive.

10. THE IDEA THAT ACTIONS REFLECT BELIEFS

The conservative has learned that if a man goes bankrupt, repudiates his debts, deserts his family, steals from his neighbor, and kills those who annoy him, he cannot be dealt with as a responsible member of society. He must be put away or contained from further injury to other men's rights.

Yet our "liberals" today insist that men or governments, like Russia, who behave this way, deserve to sit among us as equals. They say we should ignore their continued immoral actions, such as shooting boys who try to escape to freedom over the Berlin Wall. For another example of the antithesis to these ten marks of a conservative, I suggest a neighbor who was once welcomed by this Princeton community, some of its institutions, and some of its homes. Consider Fidel Castro. On his visit to America, Fidel earned the plaudits of much of our "liberal" press, and the tolerance of our government. He has since rewarded our public and private foolishness by:

Confiscating American business in Cuba
Destroying the economic machinery of his country
Stealing the money in Cuba's banks
Chopping down dissenters with machine guns
Creating poverty, unrest, and slave labor
Setting himself up as a dictator
Inflaming Latin America against the United States
Bringing Soviet missiles within easy range of this community
  and installing Communist terror in Cuba.

It's hard to make a conservative believe, as do some in our government, that neighbors who act this way deserve our forbearance.

In Summary. To me, conservatism comes down to the common sense a man or woman acquires when he or she attempts to lead a worthwhile, constructive life in a free society. Karl Marx could never imagine it, nor Hitler or Mussolini; yet this is the natural condition of man to which the peoples of this world aspire.

Once people understand it, they crawl over the wall in Berlin, they sail in the Mayflower, they fight the American Revolutionary War, as they did here in the Battle of Princeton. They flee from despotism and desert the slaveries of today for the free lands of personal liberty. This is what we conservatives would defend and expand until no more Berlin Walls or barbed wire enclosures exist on this planet, except for criminals and animals.

In this task there is a great need for scholarship from thoughtful people in our universities and in the ranks of authors, playwrights, historians, and authorities in the social sciences. I am pleased to note that the conservative tide is rising among these intellectuals, as at long last it should. Once the task of definition is achieved to some degree, then with patience, with love for our fellow man who may at first disagree, with understanding and tact, we can begin the long job of educating the people around us to conservative beliefs. The winning of this educational contest against superior forces in our society is this nation's sole guarantee of dynamic economic growth, international peace, and personal happiness in a free society.

Specimen 18. Some Things That Worry Me About Public Relations

ROBERT VAN RIPER
Vice President and Director of Public Relations, N.Y. Ayer & Son, Inc.

1. It seems to me that *two elements* are *essential* to successful public relations. *First* is mastery of the techniques of communication. At the P.R.S.A. convention in Boston, we heard Professor Allen Nevins's fascinating account of the great public relations campaign waged by Alexander Hamilton and James Madison to secure ratification of the federal Constitution.

2. Their message was right and their strategy was brilliant. I do not mean to take anything away from them at all. But as I listened to Professor Nevins, I could not help but think of how fantastically complex our communications network is today compared with the handful of journals that existed in 1788. Mastery of today's communication techniques is a high achievement in itself—even if it is not accompanied by the logic and eloquence of the Federalists.

3. The *second* essential element, I think, is a talent which is associated primarily with playwrights and novelists. It is the ability to see things as others see them—not just by reading an opinion survey, but by projecting oneself inside the minds of other individuals whose

Presented to the Chicago Chapter, Public Relations Society of America, Chicago, Illinois, January 15, 1963. Reprinted from *Vital Speeches of the Day*, April 1, 1963.

backgrounds and points of view may be quite different from one's own. This requires a high order of both understanding and imagination. I don't care what aspect of public relations you're engaged in—whether it's product publicity or full-time consideration of the most sophisticated policy matters—this talent for imagining accurately the attitudes and emotions of other people is the difference between successful communication and wheelspinning. Fortunately, it is a talent that can be developed, but only by intelligent, imaginative analysis.

4. I believe that if we give thoughtful attention to developing this talent both in ourselves and in those whom it is our responsibility to train, then in another generation or so it won't matter whether public relations is recognized as a profession or not. More of the people who practice it will be recognized as professionals—and that is what really counts.

Specimen 19. Controlling Written Communications

GEORGE T. VARDAMAN
Associate Dean and Professor of Administration, College of Business Administration, University of Denver

1. One of the most important—and some may say, most difficult—problems facing any manager is controlling the quantity, quality, and effectiveness of his firm's written communications. The purposes of this paper are twofold: (1) to present some differing general methods currently used by American organizations in diagnosis and redesign of their communications; and (2) to set forth a new diagnostic model which puts together the several discrete methods into a coherent, useful system.

Presented to the First International Symposium on Technical Communication, Tel Aviv, Israel, December 9, 1968. It is an adaptation of Chapter 1, "Diagnosing Communications," from *Cutting Communications Costs and Increasing Impacts* (John Wiley & Sons, New York, 1970), subsequently published, co-authored by George T. Vardaman, Carroll C. Halterman, and Patricia B. Vardaman.

2. I need not remind this group that controlling the firm's communications is no easy task, and that there are no simple answers. This means that all of us need a clear understanding of current attempts to solve this very complex and costly organizational problem. For this reason, I start by presenting concise overviews of four different current approaches to assessment of the firm's written documents: (1) the systems and procedures orientation; (2) the media orientation; (3) the human relations orientation; and (4) the organizational orientation.

The Systems and Procedures Orientation

3. The analyst, in examining communications by this method, will determine who starts, who handles, and who receives the items in question. For example, through a series of interviews, surveys, discussions, and meetings, he will be able to tell just how many copies are generated, where they are filed, how many are transmitted, and for what purposes the copies are used. He will draw a flow chart, develop frequency counts, make estimates of costs and returns from the activity, and will eventually come up with recommendations for "improvement."

The Media Orientation

4. Here the analyst focuses on the different technological means, both hardware and software, by which communications are exchanged. For example, the use of computers to accumulate and formulate direct printouts of reports; the use of copiers in lieu of carbons to effect multiple distributions; the use of combined written-video displays to demonstrate more than one or two processes. Audiovisual aids and charts and graphs come under consideration. The formats and production methods for letters and proposals are examined. In essence, the analyst seeks the most efficient and effective use of the media he has to work with, and insures that any procedures (such as were discussed above) are compatible with his technology.

The Human Relations Orientation

5. The center of attention here is directed to the human factors involved in communication. For example, such questions as, "How will the reader interpret this?" or "What did the writer really mean to

say?" are raised. Psychology and sociology, as well as psychiatry, provide much of the ammunition used by the analyst. Concern for human values and societal norms is evoked. The basic focus of the analyst, when looking at communications from the human relations approach, is *not* the format of the letter, nor even how or where it was generated; he is concerned with the "under the skin" impact on the receiver.

6. Methods used by the analyst include attitudinal analyses, "wants and needs" surveys, and interviews with recipients. Recommendations coming out of such analyses are usually heavily laden with suggestions about style (based on the presumed reader stereotype); with lists of tabooed words and phrases (based on the particular ethnic and cultural backgrounds of readers); and with warnings to avoid, say, polysyllabic words and phrases.

The Organizational Orientation

7. Here the analyst attempts to determine what relationships do and should exist among members and parts of the organization (for example, between members of their sub-departments, their salesmen and customers), from which he will develop proposals for changing the organization's communications. Starting from the nature and purpose of the organization, which are hopefully reflected in its guiding policies and directives, he sets out the best ways to do the firm's total job. In the process he will generate recommendations for written communications to complement this total scheme. This is the method least often used by communications analysts, because only recently has it appeared in management and communication literature.

How These Approaches Normally Relate

8. As I stated above, the four most common approaches taken to evaluate an organization's written communications are (1) to examine the *procedures* for getting letters and other documents written and distributed; (2) to look at the *media* and the technology available, in order to assure that those procedures which are employed are compatible; (3) to look at the *people* involved, in order to improve the "human interface" between senders and receivers; and last (4) to work from the basic policies and objectives of the *organization*—in order to

insure that all necessary communications are provided (and that no unnecessary communications go out).

9. Unfortunately, only one or two of these approaches are used by most communications analysts. As I said, the "procedures" approach is the most common. "Attention to media" is perhaps the next most frequently used. "Human relations" is employed to a lesser extent; but rarely is the total organizational orientation applied.

How the Approaches Should Relate

10. One of the reasons why the average communications expert is tempted to look first at procedures is that this is where the greatest number of "errors" can most readily be seen. In addition, he feels most secure with his criteria. What he is looking at, however, are mainly mechanical and typographical mistakes which he can fairly easily rectify. And all too often he assumes without question that the communications under scrutiny are indeed legitimate. Much the same rationale is used when one approaches a letter or memorandum from the "human impact" standpoint. Disregarding the *organization's* need for the communication, most of the analyst's attention is directed to determining how well the written ideas are set forth and understood. Each of the above approaches, used separate from the rest, can be likened to a tail wagging a dog.

11. Rationally and logically the examination of communications in any organization should proceed by using the same approaches outlined above, but in proper conjunction. First, all of these approaches are contributory, and all should be used, not just one or two. Second, all must properly relate to each other as in the following sequence: (1) An *organizational* orientation must be first assumed, in order to determine the need and direction for communications; (2) *media should be selected* which will accomplish the communications job in the most expeditious fashion; (3) the personal *characteristics* of writers and readers should be kept in mind, so that what is written and read is what should be communicated; finally (4) a *systematic* approach to communications handling, storage, and distribution must be established. In this way, the organization's needs—in light of the people involved and the media employed—can be economically met. Relationships between these approaches, now placed in context, are shown as follows:

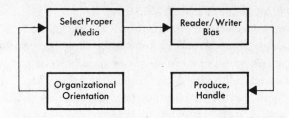

A Model for Auditing Communications

12. I now want to translate the rather simple framework developed above into one a bit more complete and useful, although just as easy to understand. For this purpose I relate the four approaches in a general model, although in somewhat different terms. Additionally, I shall treat each of them in quite a bit more detail.

13. Our new model, applicable to any communications situation, contains four parts, and is based on how organizational communications should be designed, which is:

Determine organizational requirements

Select communications media as appropriate

Determine reader perspectives

Systematize communications production

14. In other words, a rationally designed organizational communications activity uses the sequence above in order to insure that the communications it produces are connected to what the organization wants done. This can be related to how we audit communications in the following way:

• First, analyze the organization's requirements to determine its actual communications need.

• Next, evaluate the communications media to see that they are compatible with the organization's need.

• Then look at the organization's communications from the perspectives of the people receiving them to determine how they will be accepted, understood, and acted upon.

• Finally, *and in light of the above,* perform an analysis of the production system to determine how to improve the origination, processing, output, and distribution of communications.

Explanation of the General Model

15. The elements of organizational requirements, communications media, reader perspective, and communications production will now be more fully explained (so that each can be better understood).

16. *Organizational Requirements.* Essentially this phase answers the question, "What is the communication mission in relation to the company's goals?" It includes examining communication need, communication purpose, intended effect, and communication task. It can be seen that only when the unit's requirements are known can the analyst judge the real worth of any communication.

17. *Communications Media.* Growing out of the assessment of requirements, this stage answers the basic question, "In what basic way should the communication be presented?" It covers the inspection of communication form, structure, support of ideas, and symbolic means. In essence, it is concerned with the basic shape and mode of the communication.

18. *Reader Perspective.* To what receivers is the communication addressed? What is the *willingness* of the reader to understand and respond? And what is the *capacity* of the reader to understand and respond? What *reader roles* are built into the situation? What *communication barriers* must be overcome? And what *techniques* must be used to overcome the barriers? These questions are answered at this point. Clearly, proper sizing up and handling of the reader is an absolute for adequacy of any company communications.

19. *Communications Production.* The basic question is "By what procedures are the communications launched?" Subordinate questions are: "How are preliminary preparations and drafts made?" "How is the tentative product tested? How are revisions made? And what is the real-world impact of the actual communication?" Since the communication product is the only thing to which the reader will react, it is the payoff of all preceding steps, the phase that spells success or failure.

20. *A General Algorithm.* The four steps comprise a hierarchy which can be quantified for practical application. This is done in the figure on the opposite page (Algorithm of General Method).

A study of this drawing reveals three things: First, the factors of organizational requirements, communications media, reader perspective, and communications production are set forth in an ascending order of importance. Second, a total of ten points is

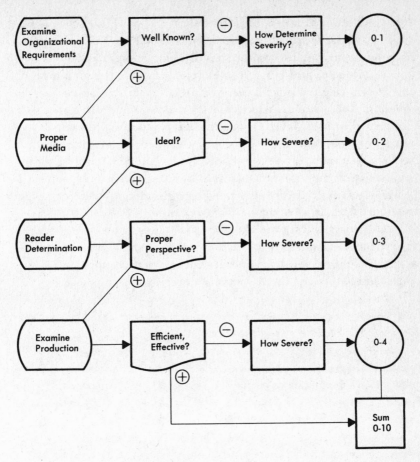

assumed, the ten points relating to severity (or weakness) of the communications. That is, "0" represents "optimum" in the communications; "10" represents the severest weakness (or departure from optimum). Third, out of the total of ten points, priorities are weighted as follows:

Organizational requirements	1
Communications media	2
Reader perspective	3
Communications production	4
Total	10

21. These rankings are rationalized in this way: organizational requirements (1) exist or not; and they are realistic and clear to

greater or lesser degrees. This dimension is basic, but easy to determine; communication media (2) can be good or bad apart from adequate or inadequate requirements. It is a more complex dimension to evaluate, and since it is closer to the final communication output, it is rated 2; since it is concerned with the "consumer" of the communication, reader perspective (3) is a more important step than either of the latter. It is obvious that even though otherwise highly rated, the communication fails if the reader is not influenced as desired; communication production (4) is given the highest weighting because it is the "payoff." Unless the communication output is efficiently and effectively generated, processed, and launched to get the desired result, all other steps are futile.

22. *Summating Values in the Algorithm.* This is a process of adding the "departure values" from each of the four steps. Since ten points are possible, the result is some proportion of that number. This is illustrated in the hypothetical example in the following table:

	Possible Value	Assigned Value
Organization requirements	1	1
Communications media	2	2
Reader perspective	3	1
Communications production	4	2
Total Value		6/10

23. *Summary.* This paper has presented four diverse methods currently used in analyzing organizational written documents. I have put these into a conceptually sound but completely practical diagnostic model. It is my thesis that the system given here will permit organizational managers to allocate more wisely precious company resources—money, people, and material; at the same time, the organization's real communications problems can be more precisely pinpointed and corrected.

Specimen 20. Supervisory Relations: Minding the Bag Bearers

WILLIAM E. ZIERDEN
Associate Professor, University of Virginia

Everyone has a bad day now and then, but when an employee sees every day as bad, and for the *same* reasons, a chronic emotional problem has developed. Some call this problem an "obsession"; I prefer calling it the "stinking bag" syndrome. Either way, it causes difficulties not just for the person so afflicted but for everyone around. That's why supervisors should learn how to deal with it.

THE BAG

What happens when a person encounters something that he or she doesn't like and the person neither changes his or her thoughts nor attempts to correct the thing at fault? As long as the person continues to encounter the offending situation, he or she will continue to experience bad feelings, and those feelings will accumulate. I call that putting feelings in a bag.

To understand the bag, I think of it as being similar to a sack used to ship five pounds of oranges: cotton mesh, about two feet long and one foot wide, with a length of rope tied to the top. A person may have several or even many bags, and each is labeled with the name of the person, the thing, or the event to which the person responds with bad feelings. Bags have labels like "my boss," "my in-laws," "the company," and "taxes."

The feelings go into the bag and fall to the bottom where they sit. With each new encounter, more feelings go into the bag. It begins to fill up and become heavy. Also, the feelings start to decompose as they remain in the bag. In fact, over time the feelings become soft, mushy, and liquid; they begin to take on an unpleasant odor. Before long the bag is filled with something that is heavy and runny and stinks.

What happens to bags? Frequently, they are dumped, and more often than not a bag is dumped on someone or something *not* associated with the label on the bag. For example, members of an

Reprinted from *Supervisory Management*, April 1980.

employee's family may receive the bag with the name of the boss on it, or an innocent store clerk may receive the contents of the bag labeled with the name of a product purchased in the store. Sometimes bags *are* dumped on the person whose name is on the bag, and often when that happens, the contents of the bag come out in an explosive rush, overwhelming the recipient.

Even more frequently than dumping, a person will take hold of the rope attached to the top of the bag and swing it around at a high rate of speed, usually in the presence of one or more people. Try to picture this in your mind's eye: a mesh bag on the end of a long rope, filled with a mushy, foul-smelling substance, being whipped around at a high rate of speed. What happens? The stuff ends up all over everybody.

It is my observation that swinging bags with varying degrees of intensity is a common pastime of many people. I could list hundreds of examples—the neighbor who over morning coffee swings the bag with her husband's name on it; the manager who swings the bag with the name of an associate on it; the supervisor who in the bar after work swings the bag with the company name on it.

IN THE SWING

In many organizations there are regular bag-swinging sessions. For example, consider the coffee break conversation of three supervisors in a large customer billing department:

Supervisor #1: "Did you see that stupid memo from personnel yesterday. Those people have to be idiots to think that I . . . *(swish, swish, swish).* . . ."

Supervisor #2: "Yes, well if there is anything that gets to me, it's people who don't put tops on their trash cans. My neighbor across the street hasn't put any tops on for five years, and . . . *(swish, swish, swish).* . . ."

Supervisor #3: "I'm glad I don't have to worry about my neighbor's trash cans. It's my daughter's room. What a mess! She never . . . *(swish, swish, swish).* . . ."

The statements by the supervisors in this example sound like familiar, human ways of dealing with frustrations, disappointments, and unrealized expectations. They are. So the question is, what, if anything, is wrong with bags?

First, it takes a certain amount of energy to carry the bags around. Since a person might have any number of bags, the more bags, the more energy the person devotes to maintaining them.

Second, as the bags fill up and become burdensome, a person will tend to dump or swing a bag even when the immediate situation bears no direct relationship to the label on a particular bag. Thus one or more partially filled bags get in the way of a person's ability to be in the present and deal in a straightforward way with immediate situations.

Third, bag dumping and swinging by a person affect other people. For example, one bag swinger tends to provoke other people to bring out *their* bags. Often, bag swinging is like an infectious disease.

Fourth, a person could use the time and energy devoted to bags in many other ways, ways that could be more effective both for the person and for the people around them.

Fifth, a person who channels bad feelings into a bag rarely has to take responsibility for those feelings. The person does not have to face the fact that a subjective reaction to an event and the event itself are *separate*, and that while the event may not be of a person's making, his or her reaction to it is his or her responsibility.

Sixth, the process of filling, carrying, swinging, and dumping bags is habit-forming. It inhibits a person's ability to try other ways of dealing with situations that the person finds disagreeable. Like any habit, the bag habit is difficult to change.

BY THE RULES

This brings us to two simple, straightforward rules that can break the bag habit and bring about a dramatic, positive change in the communication processes of an organization.

Rule #1: Complain about something that is bothering you only to someone who can do something about it.

Frequently, when I first suggest this rule to a group of supervisors and ask them how things might change if they attempted to implement the rule at work, the first response is nervous laughter. The laughter seems to be linked to two immediate reactions. The first is that complaining only to people who could do something about what was bothering them could endanger their jobs. In some companies, it seems, supervisors are not only reluctant to discuss what is bothering them with their managers, but fearful of the consequences of doing so.

The second reaction is tied to the idea that if a supervisor were to stop sharing complaints with co-workers, the supervisor would be viewed as odd or above it all, and would lose acceptance by other supervisors. As a corollary to this, many supervisors recognize griping as a "normal" mode of organizational conversation, and they often wonder what people would find to talk about if they didn't spend all of their time swapping ineffectual complaints!

To begin to behave according to Rule #1 would mean big changes for some supervisors in some organizations, while, for others, little or no change in behavior would be required. The degree of change would depend both on the nature of the individual supervisors and on the kind of organizational climate in which they work.

A great deal of change is probably *not* required for a supervisor who is assertive or confrontive, and who has his or her own feelings about situations. Also, implementation of the rule would probably not drastically alter relationships in an organization where free and open discussion within and between managerial, supervisory, and worker levels was the norm. Interestingly, a quick test of the climate in an organization is to ask what the effect would be if one or more individuals, or one or more levels of employees, suddenly began to operate by Rule #1. The conclusion that such an effort would result in change and possible conflict would indicate that the nature of the organizational climate might be improved.

Rule #2: Don't permit people to complain to you about things you can't do anything about.

Supervisors tend to react even more vigorously to this rule than they do to Rule #1. Some argue that a person who might try to live by this rule would soon have no friends, while others say that in order to put the rule into play a person would have to become very "impolite" to others. A supervisor will inevitably ask, "Does this mean I should not listen to complaints from my workers? That is part of my job."

To respond to this question, it is necessary to make a careful and important distinction between listening to someone complain and listening to someone with a view toward helping him or her do some *problem solving*. By listening to someone complain, I mean listening repeatedly to the same person talk about something that is bothering him or her when you, the listener, really don't want to listen. In one sense this means permitting another person to swing some of the contents of his or her bag all over you. To do this seems unproductive for the listener for many of the same reasons that I feel putting bad feelings into bags is not effective for the carrier.

By listening to a person with a view toward helping the person do some problem solving, I mean being willing to listen with an empathetic ear, *but* at some point asking, "How would you like me to help you figure out a way to do something about what is bothering you?"

What I am suggesting is that good supervisors should be open to listening to employee complaints, but if it develops that the subject of a complaint is something the supervisor can't possibly influence, the supervisor should ask the employee to accept responsibility for doing something on his or her own.

QUESTIONING IS THE ANSWER

Although supervisors and people in general find it difficult to say to another person, "I really don't care to listen to what you are talking about," there are two questions that can often be used effectively to change the course of such a conversation.

The first question is, "What would you like me to do about that [that is, the subject of the complaint]?" This question is often sufficient to cause the person to pause and consider his or her aims.

The second question is, "What do you propose to do about it [that is, the subject of the complaint]?" Frequently, in responding to this question the person will begin the problem-solving process.

One effect of both questions is to push the people doing the complaining toward taking responsibility for their "problem," or at least pushing them toward a confrontation with that idea. If nothing else, a person engaged in habitual complaining may cease complaining to a supervisor who counters the complaints with these two questions. The complainer instinctively comes to know that complaining to this supervisor will result in a disquieting encounter with the issue of the person's *own* unwillingness to act.

On the positive side, the process of having to respond to these questions repeatedly may stimulate a useful process of self-examination for the person.

Many supervisors seem to believe that part of their job is to listen to all complaints—however chronic, and however irrelevant to the work situation. Today, however, there are people whose profession is not only to listen to non-work-related complaints but to encourage and help a person to do something about the difficulty. When all else fails, a supervisor can suggest that an employee talk to (or, in many companies, can actually refer an employee to) an employee counselor, a counseling psychologist, a social worker, or a member of the clergy.

Effecting changes in communication patterns in organizations is difficult, particularly when existing patterns include much bag filling, swinging, and dumping. If the object of an effort to change communication habits is to encourage more direct, assertive problem solving within and between levels of managers, supervisors, and workers, such an effort can be aided by asking people to attempt to live by the two rules suggested here. If all members of an organization were to adopt these rules, much of the time and energy previously devoted to filling and hauling bags would be available for productive work.

Index

AMACOM Paperbacks

Author	Title	Price	Code
William A. Delaney	How To Run A Growing Company	$ 6.95	07590
J. Douglas Brown	The Human Nature Of Organizations	$ 3.95	07514
G.G. Alpander	Human Resources Management Planning	$ 9.95	07578
George J. Lumsden	Impact Management	$ 6.95	07575
Dean B. Peskin	A Job Loss Survival Manual	$ 5.95	07543
H. Lee Rust	Jobsearch	$ 7.95	07557
Marc J. Lane	Legal Handbook For Small Business	$ 7.95	07612
George T. Vardaman	Making Successful Presentations	$10.95	07616
Norman L. Enger	Management Standards For Developing Information Systems	$ 5.95	07527
Ray A. Killian	Managing Human Resources	$ 6.95	07556
Elam & Paley	Marketing For The Non-Marketing Executive	$ 5.95	07562
Edward S. McKay	The Marketing Mystique	$ 6.95	07522
Donald E. Miller	The Meaningful Interpretation Of Financial Statements	$ 6.95	07513
Robert L. Montgomery	Memory Made Easy	$ 5.95	07548
Summer & Levy	Microcomputers For Business	$ 7.95	07539
Donald P. Kenney	Minicomputers	$ 7.95	07560
Frederick D. Buggie	New Product Development Strategies	$ 8.95	07602
Dale D. McConkey	No-Nonsense Delegation	$ 4.95	07517
Hilton & Knoblauch	On Television	$ 6.95	07581
William C. Waddell	Overcoming Murphy's Law	$ 5.95	07561
Michael Hayes	Pay Yourself First	$ 6.95	07538
Ellis & Pekar	Planning Basics For Managers	$ 6.95	07591
Alfred R. Oxenfeldt	Pricing Strategies	$10.95	07572
Blake & Mouton	Productivity: The Human Side	$ 5.95	07583
Daniels & Barron	The Professional Secretary	$ 7.95	07576
Herman R. Holtz	Profit From Your Money-Making Ideas	$ 8.95	07553
William E. Rothschild	Putting It All Together	$ 7.95	07555
Don Sheehan	Shut Up And Sell!	$ 7.95	07615
Roger W. Seng	The Skills Of Selling	$ 7.95	07547
Hanan & Berrian & Cribbin & Donis	Success Strategies For The New Sales Manager	$ 8.95	07566
Paula I. Robbins	Successful Midlife Career Change	$ 7.95	07536
Leon Wortman	Successful Small Business Management	$ 5.95	07503
D. Bennett	TA And The Manager	$ 4.95	07511
George A. Brakeley, Jr.	Tested Ways To Successful Fund-Raising	$ 8.95	07568
William A. Delaney	Tricks Of The Manager's Trade	$ 6.95	07603
Alec Benn	The 27 Most Common Mistakes In Advertising	$ 5.95	07554
James. Gray, Jr.	The Winning Image	$ 6.95	07611
John Applegath	Working Free	$ 6.95	07582
Allen Weiss	Write What You Mean	$ 5.95	07544
Richard J. Dunsing	You And I Have Simply Got To Stop Meeting This Way	$ 5.95	07558